Tribal and Sustainable Development

TRIBAL AND SUSTAINABLE DEVELOPMENT

Pradip K. Bhowmick

Publications

KALPAZ PUBLICATIONS

DELHI - 110 052

Tribal and Sustainable Development

Rs. 790

ISBN : 81-7835-319-9

Published in 2005 in India by
Kalpaz Publication,
C-30, Satyawati Nagar,
Delhi-110 052
Email : kalpaz@hotmail.com

Lasertype Setting by: Tact Computer Graphics, Delhi
Printed at: Mehra Offset Press, Delhi

This book is dedicated to my father,
Late Prof. P.K. Bhowmick

Contents

	Preface	11
1.	Introduction	13
2.	Study Area	29
3.	The People	65
4.	Socio-Economic Profile of Sample Households	73
5.	Concept of Sustainable Development	181
6.	Facets of Bio-Diversity and Its Utilization	187
7.	Approaches to Biodiversity Conservation : Lessons from Field	221
8.	Scope of Sustainable Development	259
9.	Brief Recommendation and Policy Prescriptions	269
	Bibliography	277
	Index	285

List of Tables

Sl No.	*Contents*	*Table No.*	*Page No.*
1.	District Profile of Bankura	2.1.1-2.1.25	29
2.	District Profile of Jalpaiguri	2.2.1-2.2.27	37
3.	District Profile of South 24-Parganas	2.3.1-2.3.25	45
4.	Block Profile of Ranibandh	2.1a	58
5.	Block Profile of Dhupguri	2.2a	61
6.	Block Profile of Gosaba	2.3a	63
7.	Socio-Economic Profile of Bankura	4.1.1-4.1.11	74
8.	Socio-Economic Profile of Jalpaiguri	4.2.1-4.2.11	102
9.	Socio-Economic Profile of South 24-Parganas	4.3.1-4.3.11	129
10.	Socio-Economic Profile of West Bengal	4.4.1-4.4.11	156
11.	List of Floras and Faunas Exist in Ranibandha Block	6.1.1-6.1.2	193
12.	List of Floras and Faunas Exist in Dhupguri Block	6.2.1-6.2.2	201
13.	List of Floras and Faunas Exist in Gosaba Block	6.3.1-6.3.2	207
14.	Comparative Assessment of Forest of West Bengal	6.4.1	212
15.	Forest Types and other Land Use Categories	6.4.2-6.4.4	215
16.	Average Cost of Production and Net Income per Decimal from the Cultivation of Different Crops	8.1-8.5	261

Preface

Since utilisation of natural renewable resources is often linked with sustenance of man, strong arguments raised that utilisation of such resources should be allowed for the "people in and around" the protected areas, where the conservation of biodiversity is contemplated. The people living in and around the protected areas are still extremely poor and mostly belong to various tribal communities who had all along been living almost entirely on the forest and the renewable resources obtained there. These people had been "Eco-system peoples" and their living was more or less compatible to the ecological processes underway. But the situation at present is no longer so simple. The population of such direct users of the usufructs is also being siphoned out by urban users through indirect linkage, which often remain unnoticed. But the combined effect is devastating on the natural eco-systems.

In view of the above the project entitled "Sustainable Development for Tribal Community through Bio–diversity Conservation : A Micro – level Study in the State of West Bengal" was carried out by the Rural Development Centre, Indian Institute of Technology, Kharagpur. This book is the outcome of this project.

I thankfully acknowledge to the Ministry of Tribal Affairs (R. U), Govt. of India for sponsoring the project. We are also thankful to Dr. P.K. Mohanty, Jt. Director (R.U) and Shri R.C. Mahapatra, Research Officer of the Ministry. Thanks are also due to all the Senior and Middle level officials attached to the Department of Forest, Govt. of West Bengal for their whole-hearted co-operation.

I deeply acknowledge the services of our Project Staff namely, Sri Shyamal Kr. Jana, Sri Gokul Ch. Maity and Sri Debabrata Manna who made an extensive field tour in the studied Blocks and colleted the field level information.

Finally, my thanks to Kalpaz Publications who is kind enough to get it publish the manuscript in the form of book.

Pradip K. Bhowmick

1
Introduction

I
Problem and Issues

With gradual depletion of our global resources over the last century in particular, it has been clearly realised that we have been left-with very little room for further manoeuvring in our attempt to make more compromises between the demands of interest of conservation on one hand and utilisation of such resources for various human interests on the other. Unfortunately, these two aspects are directly opposed and naturally immediate human interest has almost always had the last say. Besides, the extremely foolish and dangerous human ego of winning over or improving nature, propelled most likely by stupendous scientific achievements during the last quarter of a country, which had admittedly been mind-boggling, has caused us to commit mistakes, often in the garb of unfounded scientific reasoning and also in the false plea of guarding human interest for the so-called "development". Obviously in doing so the all-important quality of life and the cobweb of lifeline on the earth has been simply overlooked. This has naturally resulted in living a poor quality of life, though we might have achieved the tantalising and debatable easy and comfortable life style in the name of "Development" in civilisation.

However, due to the global natural resource crunch, it has become crystal clear that we have no other option but to conserve whatever Biodiversity we are left at present, mostly in the form of wildlife resources. The main aim of this conservation is to ensure perpetual propagation of these resources and may also include rational utilisation, as may be found possible. This will certainly call for *in situ* conservation and ensuring the natural process of evolution to continue without any hindrance. Because it is the process that ensures the viability and the capability of any species to adjust with natural ecological chain of events and to evolve new species.

II

Sustainable Utilisation

Since utilisation of natural renewable resources is often linked with sustenance of man, strong arguments raised that utilisation of such resources should be allowed for the "people in and around" the protected areas, where the conservation of biodiversity is contemplated. The people living in and around the protected areas are still extremely poor and mostly belong to various tribal communities who had all along been living almost entirely on the forest and the renewable resources obtained there. These people had been "Eco-system peoples" and their living was more or less compatible to the ecological processes underway. But the situation at present is no longer so simple. Firstly, the population of such direct users of the *usufructs* is also being siphoned out by urban users through indirect linkage, which often remain unnoticed. But the combined effect is devastating on the natural eco-systems.

III

Conservation of Forest

Forests provide energy (half the world's population depends on fuel wood), industrial wood products (20% of which come from developing countries), food, fodder, pharmaceutical products, and other non-wood products such as fibres, rubbers, gums and resins. Forests are also priceless ecological resources, protecting land and water resources, controlling floods, checking wind erosion, storing and cycling nutrients and providing habitats for wildlife denizens. Finally, constitute a rich stock of valuable genetic resources, a common heritage of mankind.

IV

Indigenous People and Biodiversity Conservation

It is widely known throughout the world that people's participation is very helpful for successful forest management. But what is interesting to note that years before the forest department realised this truth, human societies have since their inception been developing mechanism of managing the natural resources to meet their needs and greeds according to the values and norms that have grown among the members of society through time. These norms and values get crystallised in the form of institution, which have been defined by anthropologists or sociologists as established procedures of doing things or getting things done with legitimacy behind them. Institutions are human devises designed to channel society's resources into stable patterns of interaction that are intended to meet one or more social needs. One essential function of institutions is to stabilise different people's activities into more or less predictable patterns of roles.

Initially, it was the tribal or village community (ies) living in or vicinity of forest which was (were) responsible for using and managing natural resources like forest produce of various kinds according to their needs, and, to get the situation worse confounded, for the satisfaction of their greeds. Their institutions grew and took shape accordingly. Any such community has got prescribed and established procedure determining how each member will use different species of herbs, shrubs and trees and in which measures (MacIver, 1974). Not only that, even the pattern of seasonal utilisation of the resources was prescribed by the complex of values, norms and procedures, i.e., institutions, of the community and more or less accepted by its members. The village and community economy depends on the natural resources, say non-timber forest produce (NTFP), available and the pattern of seasonal utilisation (Malhotra, et. al., 1992).

Indeed, these norms, values and procedures became embedded in the social structure of each such community and helped its members to manage the natural resources on a sustainable basis. The threat to this milieu however, came from denudation of forest mainly because of pressures of grazing by an increasing number of cattle, goats, sheep and other graminivorous animals, collection of ever – mounting volumes of wood and timber as well as other forest produce dictated by needs and greeds of the forest communities and the people with whom they came to interact through time. This becomes a part of culture. The members of a community inherit this experience to next generation. The shared experiences from the society's primary institutions give rise to the aspects of the culture (Ember and Ember, 1990).

V

Linkages Between Forest Management and Anti-Poverty and Eco-Conservation Schemes

Everyone accepts the importance of environmental protection, which results in ecological equilibrium in nature. It is also generally agreed that the only path towards a sustainable development of the economy is to devise environment - friendly socio – economic activities at the levels of industry, agriculture, forestry, handicrafts, etc. i.e., the policies and programmes of action for realisation of the objectives of a sustainable development.

The poor people living in and around the forests destroy the natural resources in their desperate bid for food and shelter. They have to ensure two square meals a day, so that they cannot bother about the degradation of soil, forest, water and other components of the environment. If one decides to shield the natural resources of the forests, for example, by keeping off the people of the localities away from its produce, then one takes away the food from their mouth. Though when the people plunder the natural resources for immediate livelihood, they do not understand that they are also making the future generation poorer because the latter will find very little resource on which to sustain, not to speak of a hostile environment. They take not only the bounties of nature but also from the well – being of future land – dependent generations. The short – term trade – off between immediate hunger and environment is stark. However, the interaction of poverty and environmental destruction sets off a downward spiral of ecological deterioration that threatens the life and well – being of the posterity. Hence, there must be appropriate policy instruments to reduce the conflicts with effects on degradation of limited natural resources and pollution of the environment caused by the short – term survival strategies. This point appears to have been ignored by our policy – makers for a long time. Only very recently, there seems to have arisen the awareness to reconcile anti–poverty and environmental improvement strategies (Chatterjee, T.K., 1995). We must perceive that poverty alleviation efforts should enhance, not thwart environmental protection programmes. The reverse also must be equally true.

Subsequent development in Participatory Forest Management (PFM) shows that there must be a shift of policy perceptions regarding afforestation. The main objective should be to strengthen the economy of the people in question by proper linkages with other social forestry and rural development programmes. The intrusion of rich farmers and contractors into the forests can also be prevented if this approach is followed.

VI
Review of Literature

Conservation and sustainable use of biodiversity to the benefit of both present and future generations has now a global political and legal sanction. Yet, irreversible loss of biological diversity and inequitable distribution of resource base remain the serious problems. While deficiencies of State driven conservation approaches have been brought out, proven examples of perfect conservation approaches are lacking.

A review of existing literature shows that most of the works done in the field of sustainable development and biodiversity conservation may be grouped into the following way:

I. Sacred Groves and Biodiversity Conservation;

II. Biodiversity Conservation – New Directions :

   a) Incentives and Conservation,
   b) Land Tenure and Conservation,
   c) Conservation through Community-based Enterprise,
   d) Gender and Equity concerns in Biodiversity Conservation, and
   e) Diversity and Sustainability in Community-based Conservation,

I. Sacred Groves and Biodiversity Conservation :

Sacred species, groves, forests and other ecosystems, which have been conserved for religious and cultural reasons, offer an opportunity to build on an age-old traditional ethos of conservation. Descriptive accounts of origin, religious and cultural practices and related to sacred groves/forests/eco-systems/landscapes have been extensively published in recent years in the works of Gadgil and Vartak (1976), Frazer (1980), Khiewtem and Ramakrishan (1989), Ramakrishan (1996), Nair et. al. (1997), Singh (1997) and others.

Though a number of descriptive accounts/qualitative information on Sacred groves have been published in recent years but the works of Chandrakanth and Romm (1991), Ingles (1994) and Roy Burman (1995) show that much more limited is the quantitative information regarding biodiversity status of these traditionally protected areas as a component of landscape, people's perceptions, intangible and intangible benefits from the biodiversity and, opportunities and constraints in improving the biodiversity resource base and its sustainable utilisation in the present scenario.

Since the late 1980s, a number of studies have focussed on the extent of extraction and use of wild biota (chiefly plants) by indigenous societies. Mention may be made of Malhotra and Deb (1992), Panayotou and Ashton, (1992), Plotkin and Famolare (1992) for their outstanding work in this regard. The estimation of their economic value has been illustrated in the illuminated works of Malhotra et. al. (1991, 1992), Appasamy (1993), Chopra (1993) and Gunatilake et. al. (1993). Malhotra et. al. (1991), however, demonstrate that the use of biodiversity for socio-religious purposes has seldom been mentioned in these studies mentioned above. Again Malhotra and Deb (1997) have shown that no detailed study of the use of wildlife in relation to the tribal socio-religious customs in India is available till date.

II

Gadgil et.al. (1993) state that due to failure of pure legal protection in guaranteeing biodiversity conservation, it became necessary to search for the solutions in the traditional conservation and resource management systems based on indigenous knowledge of the local communities. After such realisation, serious efforts have been started all over India. In the initial stages these studies were focussed on inventories of sacred groves and their floristic composition, but according to scholars like, Gadgil and Vartak (1976) and Nipunage et. al.(1988), very little has been thought about their present status and their possible role in resource conservation.

According to Roy Burman (1995), the sacred groves play a very important role though they may not feature very distinctively in the day-to-day activities of the local people. Folke and Berkes (1995) consider traditional ecological knowledge as differing from scientific knowledge in being moral, ethically based spiritual, intuitive and holistic and having a large social context. But Gadgil and Berkes (1991) and McNeely (1991) state that in contrast to the traditional ecological perception of nature found in indigenous societies, modern scientific management, with its roots in the utilitarian and exploitative world view, assumes humans have dominion over nature. Johnson (1995) demonstrates that ecologists are beginning to form more holistic view of biology, together with the realisation that humans are everywhere a vital part of the ecological landscape.

Poffenberger et. al. (1995) highlight that though there is increasing pressure for enhancement of people's participation in forest regeneration/ conservation and protected area management, emphasis is more on raising the authority of local communities than on scientific upgradation of traditional and transitional resource use practices. Saxena et. al. (1998) opine that there is a need of scientific evaluation of traditional conservation practices as all traditional practices may not be the best options in the present day world. Sustainable economies certainly cannot survive in the new circumstances. Monetary economy is increasingly becoming an attraction to the traditional people too. Dobriyal et. al. (1997) have demonstrated in their respective research papers how traditional knowledge and conservation practices have served as the source of clews for many pharmaceutical innovations but local communities have not been able to benefit from such indigenous potential. Saxena et. al (1998) have pointed out that cultural causes cannot rejuvenate conservation ethos in the present situations unless conservation is promoted as a means of sustainable economic development.

Cairns and Pratt (1995) stressed on the need of creation of mass awareness about the intangible benefits and ecosystem services provided by these forests patches and their biodiversity value would be an essential component of any sacred rove conservation plan. Like Cairns and Pratt, Tiwari et. al. (1998) also emphasised immensely on the development of ways and means for limited extraction of produce in order to sustain the interest of the people in preservation of the groves.

There is a lot of concern about the erosion of local knowledge. Gadgil (1998) attributes this to the loss of community control over resources. Gupta (1997) blames it on insensitive state systems, which have taken over resources. He brings in a new dimension by his argument that all knowledge is not necessarily in the communal domain, but individuals do exist who is bearers of such knowledge. Malhotra et. al. (1992) points to a JFM area where local people has taken measure to control diversity of species. The study also intensifies that if local community is allowed the management of resources the biodiversity increases.

II. Biodiversity Conservation - New Directions :

Since it has been acknowledged the world over that the conventional approach to conservation involving 'fences and fines' may not always work, several different approaches are being tried. One such is an attempt to motivate local communities to conserve instead of an approach, which alienates them and often leads to a situation of antipathy and distrust.

a) Incentives and Conservation :

Outstanding work over the years in this line is the classic work of McNeely (1988), where he had tried to establish the relationship between incentives and conservation. There could be direct incentives like cash, in terms of fees, rewards, compensations, grants, subsidies, loan, etc. There could also be indirect incentives such as tax incentives and community development activities. Other incentives could be land tenure and even employment.

Wells et. al. (1992) state that an innovative programme that attempts to use this 'incentive and conservation' approach is the Integrated Conservation Development Project (ICDP). ICDPs were designed to integrate conservation with the social and economic needs of local communities. They cite a project of this nature, which has been implemented in the Annapurna Conservation Area of Nepal. Brown and Wyckoff – Baird (1992) describe that development activities are provided in ICDPs as incentives for sustainable management of natural resources. The project in Annapurna Conservation Area of Nepal has attempted to focus particularly on increasing local benefits through tourism, and conserving the fragile ecosystem at the same time. Several activities such as introduction of fuelwood – saving technology, basic health services to the local community and training of local entreprenuers in tourism have been carried out.

Gadgil (1998) suggests value addition to biodiversity by building capacity of local communities. He further adds that financial inputs should be organised as a national biodiversity conservation fund, which should be rationally allocated to local communities. Shrestha (1998) points to the creation of autonomous committees in Nepal in the Protected Areas (PAs), which are now collecting tourism revenues for allocation to community development. Gupta (1997) suggests the need for a tailored approach to different contexts in which conservation takes place and raises the challenge of devising an incentive system, which fulfils four conditions of sustainable development that he has raised.

Rathore (1996) reports that in the Harda forests of Central India where JFM is relatively successful, the revenue generated by the village-level forest protection committee (FPCs) from the sale of grass was calculated to be Rs. 1,00,000 (US$ 3,000) in one year. Murty (1996) estimated that the Keoladeo (Bharatpur) National Park in Rajasthan, almost all the substantial tourism revenue generated goes to private tourist agencies or the government, while the local communities suffers a loss of about Rs. 20 million (US $ 60,000) per year on account of agricultural losses due to water logging related to the wetland management in the Park, restrictions on fuel and fodder, etc. Posey (1990) estimates that less than 0.001 per cent of the market value of plant-based medicines have been returned to indigenous peoples from whom much of the original knowledge came.

Shrestha (1998) states that community forestry in Nepal is aiming at alleviating rural poverty, mobilising rural people to make themselves self-reliant for basic needs and simultaneously conserving forest resources. Implementation of such management schemes in totality has resulted in improvement in biodiversity conservation, and has helped many communities to achieve self-reliance.

b) Land Tenure and Conservation :

DeCosse and Jayawickrama (1998) point out that in Sri Lanka, a form of traditional service tenure was prevalent, which had two basic aspect : *first*, community-based tenurial rights were legally recognised, and *second*, strong system for joint management of natural resources existed. According to Lynch and Alcorn (1994) community-based tenure systems are a set of institutional systems that include processes for establishing and allocating property rights to groups and individuals including tenurial rights to specific agricultural lands, trees or other resources within the community's territory. Choudhury (1998) reports that traditional tenure system often embodies conflict-resolution mechanisms and strategies for defending the local resource base against incursions by outsiders and resolving intra-community disputes. He furthers cites the example of North – east India, where communities have rules of tradition governing the system of cultivation, landholding, village administration, foraging and extraction of resources, many of which continue to exist.

Erosion of community-based tenure has been linked to loss of biodiversity. For instance, according to Lynch and Alcorn (1994), some Bangladeshi communities use community property regimes to regulate access to highly biodiverse fisheries in flood plain and wetland waterways, which are also the habitats for many migratory birds. This is however being threatened by loss of tenurial security, as waterways based upon community-based tenure and management are being appropriated by private enterprises. Chandrasekhara and Sankar (1998) explain a similar situation in Chinnar Wildlife Sanctuary in South India.

Poffenberger and Singh (1996) report in the context of joint community forestry programmes in South India, local villagers in the absence of clear tenure live in the fear of government agencies revoking the agreement under any pretext, just before harvesting the forest produce which they have been protecting for years.

c) Conservation through Community Enterprise :

Bhatt (1998) describes several experiments where value-enhancement through enterprise is being used as a means of ensuring a better livelihood and also creating a stake in conservation. Lele et. al. (1998) also discussed the preliminary results of an ongoing 'enterprise-based conservation' effort (Biligiri Rangaswamy Temple Sanctuary) taken up by them in south India. The project is an *integrated* plan for CBC that tries to mesh increases in *incentives* with increases in *responsibilities* and in *capabilities.* It increases the economic stake of the Soligas through better NTPF prices, increased employment, and profits.

WWF–India (1995) observes that revenue generation through conservation project does happen occasionally, but generally the focus of these projects is not to raise the income of local communities. A case in point is Community Biodiversity Conservation Movement (CBCM) whose central focus has been on practical field projects that demonstrates community–based conservation of biodiversity. Of these projects, there have been a few where conservation has successfully taken place and the community also benefits economically through the projects. One such was implemented by the Swa–Sahyog Sanstha in Rajasthan, which under the project established a seed bank to store seeds of about 205 local and traditional crop varieties, which may have gone extinct with the advent of modern agriculture. The seed bank has been set up with the active participation of the local farmers. Local people have stared procuring these seeds now, and the project is earning a marginal income, which is being reinvested into the running of the seed bank.

Agarwal and Saigal (1996) says that another example of biodiversity–based enterprises being created as a 'spin–off' from a major community conservation programme is that of Joint Forest Management (JFM). Over the years, JFM has progressed beyond simply meeting subsistence needs of local communities, to contributing to income generation and improvement of livelihoods. Campbell et. al. (1995) examined the ongoing Participatory Forest Management (PFM) Project of the Rural Development Centre, I.I.T., Kharagpur at Nayagram Block, located in the southwestern part of Midnapore, West Bengal. However, there is no value – addition in either of the products and the income generated as meagre.

Bhatt (1998) states that now the PFM Project of the I.I.T., Kharagpur is looking at value – addition and marketing channels particularly for *Sabai* grass (for furniture and utility items), *sal* leaves (for moulded plate – making), oils and medicinal plants. In addition to this, the project also hopes to promote the cultivation and processing of mushrooms.

d) Gender and Equity concerns in Biodiversity Conservation :

Inequalities between the sexes exist in all sections of society and all communities. Though unacknowledged, in most resource-dependent communities, women do the bulk of collection for commercial and domestic use, especially of resources like fuel, fodder and NTFP. Yet in most communities, women have very little say in decision-making with regard to the management of these resources.

Field observations have indicated the difference in the way men and women often view natural resources. According to an AKRSP study (1995), in Gujarat, western India, men wanted to sell off the entire bamboo harvest from their protected forests while women wanted the village requirements to be fulfilled first. Kothari, et. al. (1998) states that in some parts of the Indian Himalaya, where the Chipko Movement has been active, self-empowered women's committees have successfully opposed the selling of the civil forests to the contractors, by their own menfolk. Das and Christopher (1998) describes that at Kailadevi Sanctuary, Rajasthan, western India, the decision not to allow axes in the village forest (in order to stop the cutting of live trees), was taken by the all-male village FPCs; for the women, this represents further hardship.

According to Narain, et. al.(1994) a survey of 72 FPCs in the Midnapur West Forest Division found that out of 8,158 members only 241 (less than 2 per cent) were women, most of whom were widows. The only exceptions where the local forest officers have taken personal interest in involving women or an NGO or women's organisation has facilitated women's participation. Sarin (1993) states that in many cases, they remain unaware that they have been made managing committee (MC) members as the men select the women members on their own simply to complete the formality. Banerjee's study (1996) indicates that male household 'heads' neither necessarily consults their household women nor 'represent' the women's priorities. They are often remarkably unaware about the negative impact of sudden and total forest closure on women's gendered responsibility for procuring firewood. Sarin (1995) shows that some FPCs in West Midnapore Division receive 25 per cent of *sal* multiple shoot (MS) cutting each year as firewood. Because husband and wife have 'joint' FPC membership in West Bengal, although it is primarily women who are responsible for firewood, it is mostly men who come to collect the household's share of the MS cutting. *However, about 80 per cent of the men sell off their firewood shares.*

Sarin (1998) in an paper highlights that an interesting grassroots initiative by a small *adivasi* women's NGO, Pragatisheel Mahila Sabha (PMS), has emerged in the Dumka district of Bihar to form all-women Village Forest Management and Protection Samitis (VFMPSs). Due to their men easily getting bribed with alcohol by vested interests to break group rules, PMS has decided not to permit men to become members. This represents a reversal of typical roles. On the contrary, according to Murmu (1995), in contrast to the dominant male view about women being reckless forest destroyers, the women's *samitis* 'do not want men to become members of their committees because they are the ones who destroy the forsts so mercilessly as they do not know the difference between timber and firewood'.

e) Diversity and Sustainability in Community-based Conservation :

Kothari et. al. (1989, 1996) state that top-down, imposed conservation all too often entails huge social and ecological costs in areas where rural people are directly dependent on natural resources for their livelihoods. A growing body of empirical evidence now indicates that the transfer of 'western' conservation approaches to developing countries has indeed had adverse effects on the food security and livelihoods of people living in and around protected areas (PAs) and wildlife management schemes.

Colchester (1994) reviewed that on several occasions, local communities have been expelled from their settlements without adequate provision for alternative means of work and income. In other cases, local people have faced restrictions in their use of common property resources for food gathering, harvesting of medicinal plants, grazing, fishing, collection of wood and other wild products from forests, wetlands and pastoral lands, often turning them practically overnight from hunters and cultivators to 'poachers' and 'squatters'.

VII
Objectives

Acknowledging the research gaps this research project attempts to explore the "Eco – system People's" cultural heritage in the conservation of biodiversity and proper linkages between "Eco–system Peoples" with other ongoing poverty alleviation schemes.

With this basic objectives in view, the present research project seeks :

1. To explore the existing available resources and its rational and optimal utilisation for sustainable development;
2. To find out the possible nature and scope of sustainable development;
3. To analyse the various level of people's attitude and perception which will enable us to arrive at how far peoples are well equipped with sustain themselves with available resources;
4. To make an explorative study regarding utilisation of available resources;
5. To study the various socio-religious customs of the tribal from the biodiversity conservation prospective;
6. To explore possible integration with other poverty alleviation schemes by involving the "Eco – systems People" with other implementing machinaries;
7. To identify various problems and constraints while integrating with other poverty alleviation schemes; and
8. To offer a set of recommendations.

VIII

Methodology

Sampling Procedure :

Study has been conducted in the state of West Bengal as because this state had been considered as one of the states in India in which during past many more works have been initiated in the field of biodiversity conservation.

For the present study purposes following three district/ecological zones in West Bengal has been made :

Sl. No.	*District*	*Ecological Zone*	*Divisional Forest Office*	*Range*	*Block*	*Beat*
1.	Bankura	Part of Chotanagpur Plateau	Bankura (South)	Ranibandh	Ranibandh	Ranibandh
2.	Jalpaiguri	Hilly	Jalpaiguri	Moraghata	Dhupguri	Khutimari Totapara Gosainhat
3.	South - 24 Parganas	Coastal	24 Parganas (South)	Sajnekhali Wildlife Sanctuary	Gosaba	Pakhirala

From each district 120 samples were taken through purposive sampling procedure. The total sample size was 360 which is shown below :

Sl. No.	*District*	*Sample Size*				
		Tribal	*Non – tribal*	*Govt. & Panchayat Officials*	*Total*	
1.	Bankura	50	50	20	120	
2.	Jalpaiguri	50	50	20	120	**360**
3.	South - 24 Parganas	50	50	20	120	

(b) Sources of Data Collection

Data has been collected from two major sources namely, (a) Primary Sources, and (ii) Secondary Sources. Primary sources of information pertaining to household information like socio–economic background of the selected households of the "Eco-system People", use of major and minor forest produces in their day to day life, people's attitude and perception regarding biodiversity conservation, various socio-religious customs of the tribals from biodiversity conservation prospective, assistance received by them under different rural development schemes, etc. has been collected through structured household questionnaire with the help of different social survey methods. Secondary sources of information pertaining to forest related information like total area of the forest, available resources in the forest, utilisation of forest resources, number, member and functioning of the forest protection groups, different Government records and earlier research monographs and study in the related field has been collected from Government as well as other sources.

Government, Non – Government and different Panchayat level Officials dealt with forest management programmes also has been interviewed to get their views regarding biodiversity conservation and possible scope of integration with other rural development schemes.

Tools and Techniques of Investigation :

The following tools and techniques have been used for rigorous micro-level data collection from primary sources :

- Interview with Participant Observation;
- Case Study Method;
- Participatory Rural Appraisal techniques (PRA);
- Focus Group Interview Method;
- Linear Programming; and
- Socio-metric Scale.

(d) Tabulation and Analysis of Data

All the collected information both from primary and secondary sources has been tabulated and analysed by using simple methods of statistical tools and techniques for writing the final report.

(e) Chapterisation

This book contains nine major chapters. Chapter – I deals with Introduction followed by other eight chapters, which deals with the topics like, Study Area, The People, Socio-economic Profile of the sample households, Concept of Sustainable Development, Facets of Biodiversity and its Utilisation, Approaches to Biodiversity Conservation: Lessons from field, Scope of Sustainable Development and Brief Recommendation and Policy prescription.

2
Study Area

Study has been conducted in the state of West Bengal as because this state had been considered as one of the states in India in which during past many more works have been initiated in the field of biodiversity conservation.

For the present study purposes following three districts in West Bengal has been made:

I

District Profile : Bankura

Table: 2.1.1 Geographical Location and Area

District	*Latitude*		*Longitude*		*Area in Sq.Km.*
	North	*South*	*East*	*West*	
Bankura	$23^0 38'$ N	$22^0 38'$ N	$87^0 46'$ E	$86^0 36'$ E	6882

Source :Census of India, 1961

Table : 2.1.2 Rainfall and Temperature

Item	*Normal*	*Year*	
		1996	*1997*
Annual rainfall (in millimetre)	1422	1374	1454
Temperature		45	44
(in Celsius) : Maximum		8	8
Minimum			

Source :Meteorological Deptt, Govt. of India.

Administrative Units

Table : 2.1.3 Administrative Units

Year	Sub-Division	Police Station	C.D. Blocks	Panchayat Samity	Panchayat Gram	Mouzas	Inhabited villages	Town Municipal	Town Non-municipal	Household (1991)
1997	3	20	22	22	190	3824	3565	3	4	497420

Source : (1) Census of India, 1991.

(2) Panchayat Office, West Bengal.

Population

Table :2.1.4 Rural and Urban Population by Sex, 1991

Sl. No.	*Item*		*1991 District*	*1991 West Bengal*
1.	Population	(a) Male	1437515	35510633
		(b) Female	1367550	32567332
		(c) Total	2805065	68077965
2.	Rural	(a) Male	1317516	25442210
		(b) Female	1255071	23928154
		(c) Total	2572587	49370364
3.	Urban	(a) Male	119999	10068423
		(b) Female	112479	8639178
		(c) Total	232478	18707601
4.	Density of Population Per Sq. Km		408	767
5.	Percentage of Urban to Total Population		8.29	27.48

Source : Census of India, 1991.

Table : 2.1.5 Scheduled Caste and Scheduled Tribe Population

Year	*Scheduled Caste Male*	*Scheduled Caste Female*	*Scheduled Caste Total*	*Scheduled Tribe Male*	*Scheduled Tribe Female*	*Scheduled Tribe Total*
1991	449078	430853	879931	147036	142870	289906

Source :Census of India, 1991.

Table : 2.1.6 Distribution of population according to different categories of workers and non-workers by sex, 1991

Categories	Population (number)			Percentage to total population
	Male	Female	Total	
a. Total main workers:	728895	192696	921591	32.85
1. Cultivators	329860	46138	375998	13.40
2. Agricultural labourers	193760	116513	310273	11.06
3. Household workers	21227	10473	31700	1.13
4. Others workers	184048	19572	203620	7.26
b. Marginal workers	15658	69998	85656	3.06
c. Non-workers	692962	1104856	1797818	64.09
Total (a + b + c)	1437515	1367550	2805065	100.00

Source : Census of India, 1991.

Agriculture

Table : 2.1.7 Some Land Utilization Statistics

Year	*Total area (according to Village papers)*	*Forest (according to State Forest Department)*	*Current fallow*	*Other fallow land*	*Net cropped area*
1996-97	688.10	148.35	21.13	4.12	364.31
1997-98	688.10	148.35	26.96	4.08	358.27

Source : Directorate of Agriculture, W.B.

Table : 2.1.8 Area and Production of Principal Crops

Crops	*Area ('000 hectares)*		*Production ('000 tonnes)*	
	1996-97	1997-98	1996-97	1997-98
Aus (rice)	38.9	38.2	91.8	88.1
Aman (rice)	354.2	354.5	860.8	973.6
Boro (rice)	28.3	44.6	86.1	135.7
Crops	*Area ('000 hectares)*		*Production ('000 tonnes)*	
	1996-97	*1997-98*	*1996-97*	*1997-98*
Wheat	6.3	7.2	14.7	12.2
Gram	(a)	0.1	(b)	(b)
Other pulses	3.6	2.4	2.0	1.2
Rape & Mustard	11.2	12.3	8.8	8.1
Jute (1)	0.1	0.6	2.3	11.6
Sugarcane (2)	0.5	0.5	37.9	39.5
Dry chillies	1.1	1.3	0.5	1.1
Potato	22.0	18.9	574.3	387.7
Ginger	0.1	0.1	0.1	0.1

(1) Production in terms of 1000 bales of 180 kg. Each

(2) Production in terms of Gur. (a) Less than 50 hects. (b) Less than 50 tonnes.

Source : 1. Directorate of Agriculture W.B

2. B.A.E & Statistics, Govt. of W.B.

Table : 2.1.9 Index number of Agricultural area, production and productivity

Items	*Year*	
	1996-97	*1997-98 (P)*
Area	118.60	122.20
Production	255.46	271.40
Productivity	215.40	222.10

Source : B.A.E & Statistics, Govt. of W.B

Table : 2.1.10 Consumption of Fertilizers

Year	*Name of fertilizer*			*Total (N + P +K)*
	N	*P*	*K*	
1996-97	21.1	11.9	7.1	40.1
1997-98	22.1	13.5	8.2	43.8

Source : Directorate of Agriculture, W.B.

Table : 2.1.11 Forest area and out-turn of Forest

Item	*Unit*	*Year*	
		1996-97	*1997-98*
1	2	3	4
i) Forest area	Thousand hectares	148.2	148.2
ii) Forest Production	Thousand Cubic metre		
a) Timber	,,	0.324 + 889953 No. of Poles	0.616 + 187953 No. of Poles
b) Fuel	,,	24.953 m^3	19.921m^3
iii) Revenue & Expenditure	Thousand rupees		
a) Revenue	,,	10988	25732
b) Expenditure	,,	101005	117101

Source : Divisional Forest Office (north + south), Bankura

Table : 2.1.12 Fisheries

Sl. No.	Item	Year 1996-97	1997-98
1.	Government Schemes :		
	No. of Schemes operated	10	07
	Expenditure ('000 rupees)	6544	5146
	Assistance to needy fishermen ('000 rupees)	---	---
	Distribution of fry & fingerlings (in lakhs)	13.85	8.40
2.	Tanks & Beels (Govt. owned) :		
	Area (hectares)	6800	6800
	Expenditure ('000 rupees)	---	---
	Production of fry & fingerlings (in lakhs)	---	---
3.	Fishermen Co-operated Societies :		
	No. of Societies	39	40
	No. of Members	3445	3504

Source :Asstt. Director of Fisheries, Bankura

Table : 2.1.13 Warehousing and cold storage facilities available to cultivators

Year	Warehouse		Cold Storage		
	Number	Capacity	Number	Capacity (in mt.)	Nos. of cultivators benefited
1996-97	02	19125	19	200284	130059
1997-98	02	19125	26	331782	520435

Source :State Warehouse and different Cold Storage, Bankura

Table : 2.1.14 Area irrigated by different sources

(in '000 hectares)

Year	Govt. canal	Private			Deep tube wells & shallow tube wells	Other sources	Total area irrigated
		Canal	Tanks	Well			
1996-97	141604	---	50401	5982	102671	22861	323519
1997-98	217319	---	52968	5285	66586	14262	356420

Sources : 1) P.A.O., Bankura

2) Irrigation & Waterways Directorate West Bengal Education and Culture

Table : 2.1.15 Educational facilities

(Number)

Type of Institution	*Institution*		*Students*		*Teachers*	
	1996-97	*1997-98*	*1996-97*	*1997-98*	*1996-97*	*1997-98*
1. Primary	3374	3374	318521	334654	8516	8186
2. Middle	129	127	29628	32690	848	916
3. Secondary	225	228	200112	204976	5163	5256
4. Higher Secondary	65	66	21263	21792	*	*
5. College (Degree)	12	12	10898	11022	319	318
6. Profes-sional & Technical (Schools & Colleges)	07	07	1224	1431	176	173
7. Other Institution	01	01	64	82	10	12

Sources: 1) D.1 of Schools (Pry. & Sec.), Bankura

2) Social Education Officer, Bankura

3) Respective Colleges, *Bankura*

Table : 2.1.16 Literacy by Sex, 1991

(Percentage)

Sub-division/ district	*Rural*			*Urban*			*Total*		
	Male	*Female*	*Total*	*Male*	*Female*	*Total*	*Male*	*Female*	*Total*
Bankura Sadar	66.08	33.42	50.17	84.67	65.20	75.37	68.30	37.10	53.14
Bishnu-pur	62.11	37.50	50.08	80.69	62.26	71.64	64.13	40.21	52.43
Khatra	66.94	31.54	49.73	88.02	52.90	71.30	67.30	31.89	50.09
District	65.17	34.06	50.01	83.35	63.36	73.70	66.75	36.75	52.04

Note : Literate population excludes children of age group 0 – 6 years.

Sources : Census of India, 1991

Table : 2.1.17 Medical Facilities

Year	Hospital	Health centres	Clinics	Dispensaries	Total	Total Beds	No. of Doctors	Patients treated Indoor	Outdoor	Total
1	2	3	4	5	6	7	8	9	10	11
1996	4	91	510	91	696	2525	239	354392	1931607	2285999
1997	4	91	510	91	696	2525	236	358658	1975428	2334086

Sources : 1) C.M.O.H., Bankura

2) Dist. Inspector of Health Statistics, Bankura

Table : 2.1.18 Family Welfare

Year (as on 31st March)	No. of Family Welfare Centres			Total no. of cases of		
	Rural	Urban	Total	Vasectomy	Tubectomy	I.U.D
1996	509	03	512	14	16355	4666
1997	510	03	513	09	16434	3877

Sources: 1) Dist. Family Welfare Office, Bankura

2) Dy. C.M.O.H (III), Bankura

Table : 2.1.19 Commercial Banks

Year (as on 30th June)	No. of Bank Offices	Average Population served per office (in '000 Nos.)
1996	165	19
1997	165	19

Sources: 1) Reserve Bank of India

2) Basic Statistical Return (Summary results)

3) Economic Review

Table : 2.1.20 Co-operative Societies

Year	No. of Co-operative Societies	Membership (in '000 Nos.)	Working Capital (Rs. in lakhs)
1	2	3	4
1996-97	815	181	10873
1997-98	869	197	15757

Table : 2.1.21 Sale of Electricity and Town & Villages Electrified

Items	*Year*	
	1996-97	*1997-98*
A. Sale of Electricity (in '000 K.W.H)		
1. Domestic and Residential Consumption	42324	49615
2. Commercial Light and Power	32255	23599
3. Industrial Power	29286	24268
4. Public Lighting	1227	1260
5. Railway Traction	--	--
6. Irrigation	7908	44270
7. Public Waterworks and Sewerage Pumping	820	1790
B. No. of Towns & Villages Electrified upto the year (31st March)	--	1458
1. Towns	07	07
2. Villages	2369	2398

Sources : 1) Divisional Engr. (0+M), Bankura
2) State Electricity Board (R.E), Bankura

Transport and Communication

Table : 2.1.22 Roads Maintained by Different Organisation

(in Km)

Year	*P.W.D*		*Local Bodies*		*Municipalities*	
	Surfaced	*Un-surfaced*	*Surfaced*	*Un-surfaced*	*Surfaced*	*Un-surfaced*
1996-97(P)	1033.00	43.00	318.91	756.60	117.73	69.35
1997-98	1035.00	41.00	318.91	6211.00	120.93	69.35

Sources : 1) Local Bodies, Municipalities
2) P.W.D Office, Bankura

Table : 2.1.23 Post and Telegraph Offices

(Number)

Year (as on 31st March	*Post Offices*	*Combined Offices*	*Department of Telegraph Offices*
1997	463	26	01
1998	477	26	01

Sources : P.M.G, W.B (Bankura)

Table :2.1.24 Distribution of Vested Land for Agricultural purpose to the Landless & Small Cultivators

District/ State (as on 30.06.1997)	Area of Vested land distributed (in hectares)	No. of beneficiaries				Institu - tions & Societies
		Sche- duled Caste	Sche- duled Tribe	Others	Total	
Bankura	20579.25	76779	30848	36182	143809	--
West Bengal	394904.14	878279	485095	1143315	2506689	--

Sources : Board of Revenue, W.B

Table : 2.1.25 Recording of Bargadars

District / State (as on 31.10.97)	Schedule Caste		Scheduled Tribe		Others		Total	
	No.	Area	No.	Area	No.	Area	No.	Area
1	2	3	4	5	6	7	8	9
District	31585	7417.11	12481	3354.66	72147	16280.11	116213	27051.88
West Bengal	450267	146157.07	163552	62567.00	867206	235238.57	141025	443962.64

Source : Land & Land Reforms Dept., West Bengal

II

District Profile : Jalpaiguri

Geographical Location, Area, Rainfall and Temperature

Table : 2.2.1 Geographical location and Area

District	Latitude		Longitude		Area in sq. km.
	North	South	East	West	
Jalpaiguri	27^0 0"	26^0 10"	89^0 53"	88^0 25"	5758.9

Source : Census of India, 1991

Table : 2.2.2 Rainfall and Temperature

Item	Normal	Year	
		1994	1995
Annual rainfall (in millimetre)	3319	2521	4173
Temperature (in Celsius) :			
Maximum		38	37
Minimum		9	23

Source : Meteorological Deptt, Govt. of India

Administrative Units

Table : 2.2.3 Administrative Units

Year	Sub-Division	Police Station	C.D. Blocks	Panchayat Samity	Panchayat Gram	Mouzas	Inhabited village (1981)	Town Municipal	Town Non-municipal	Household 1991 (P)
1995	2	16	13	13	125	756	736	3	12	507356

Source: 1. Census of India, 1991
2. Zilla Parishad, Jalpaiguri

Population

Table : 2.2.4 Rural and Urban Population by Sex, 1991

Sl. No.	Item		1991 District	1991 West Bengal
1.	Population	a) Male	1453194	35510633
		b) Female	1347349	32567332
		c) Total	2800543	68077965
2.	*Rural*	a) Male	1214149	25442210
		b) Female	1128147	23928154
		c) Total	2342296	49370364
3.	Urban	a) Male	239045	10068423
		b) Female	219202	8639178
		c) Total	458247	18707601
4.	Density of Population Per Sq. Km		450	767
5.	Percentage of Urban to Total Population		16.36	27.48

Source : Census of India, 1991

Table : 2.2.5 Scheduled Caste and Scheduled Tribe Population

Year	Scheduled Caste Male	Scheduled Caste Female	Scheduled Caste Total	Scheduled Tribe Male	Scheduled Tribe Female	Scheduled Tribe Total
1991	539127	496687	1035814	301413	287525	588938

Source: Census of India, 1991

Table : 2.2.6 Distribution of population according to different categories of workers and non-workers by sex, 1991

Industrial categories	*Population (number)*			*Percentage to*
	Male	*Female*	*Total*	*total population*
a. Total main workers :	720802	162658	883460	31.55
1. Cultivators :	241637	16911	258548	9.23
2. Agricultural labourers :	119573	29971	149544	5.34
3. Household workers	7190	2752	9942	0.36
4. Others workers :	352402	113024	465426	16.62
b. Marginal workers :	15112	48450	63562	2.27
c. Non-workers :	717280	1136241	1853521	66.18
Total (a + b + c)	1453194	1347349	2800543	100.00

Source: Census of India, 1991

Agriculture

Table : 2.2.7 Some Land Utilization Statistics

Year	*Total area (according to D.D.R.W.B*	*Forest (according to State Forest Department)*	*Current fallow*	*Other fallow land*	*Net cropped area*
1993-94	--------	173.10	--------	--------	--------
1994-95	--------	173.95	33.99	--------	321.53

Source : Directorate of Agriculture, W.B.

Table : 2.2.8 Area and Production of principal crops

Crops	*Area ('000 hectares)*		*Production ('000 tonnes)*	
	1993-94	*1994-95*	*1993-94*	*1994-95*
Aus (rice)	59.6	62.5	62.2	53.2
Aman (rice)	191.5	176.3	255.4	212.0
Boro (rice)	2.0	2.8	4.4	6.1
Crops	*Area ('000 hectares)*		*Production ('000 tonnes)*	
	1993-94	*1994-95*	*1993-94*	*1994-95*
Wheat	15.0	19.7	23.2	29.2
Gram	--	--	--	--
Other pulses	3.0	3.8	1.9	1.5
Rape & Mustard	7.3	7.7	3.4	3.7
Jute (1)	37.6	41.3	155.5	355.0
Sugarcane (2)	0.1	--	0.3	--
Dry chillies	3.4	4.7	2.4	0.6
Potato	7.5	10.2	74.8	156.5
Ginger	1.2	1.2	2.8	2.7

Source : Directorate of Agriculture W.B

1) Production in terms of 1000 bales of 1000 Kg.

2) Production in terms of Gur.

Table : 2.2.9 Index number of Agricultural area, production and productivity

Year	*Name of fertilizer*			*Total (N + P +K)*
	N	*P*	*K*	
1993-94	14.5	6.4	4.2	25.1
1994-95	15.9	5.6	11.5	26.0

Source : B.A.E & Statistics, Govt. of W.B

Table : 2.2.10 Consumption of Fertilizers (in '000 tonnes)

Items	*Year*	
	1993-94	*1994-95*
Area	93.90	109.93
Production	128.48	134.68
Productivity	136.83	122.51

Source : Directorate of Agriculture, W.B P.A.O. Jalpaiguri

Table : 2.2.11 Forest area and out-turn of Forest

Item	*Unit*	*Year*	
		1993-94	*1994-95*
i) Forest area	Thousand hectares	173103	173103
ii) Forest Production	Thousand Cubic metre		
a) Timber	,,	900	982
b) Fuel	,,	192	67368*
iii) Revenue & Expenditure	Thousand rupees		
a) Revenue	,,	211483	242164
b) Expenditure	,,	105228	120434

Source : DFO

(1) Jalpaiguri, (2) Buxa (3) Baikunthapur (4) Coochbehar.

Table : 2.2.12 Fisheries

Sl. No.	*Item*	*Year* 1993-94	1994-95
1.	Government Schemes :		
	No. of Schemes operated	05	03
	Expenditure ('000 rupees)	729	378
	Assistance to needy fishermen ('000 rupees)	529	066
	Distribution of fry and fingerlings (in lakhs)	150	228
2.	Tanks and Beels (Govt. owned) :		
	Area (hectares)	05	05
	Expenditure ('000 rupees)	---	0.8
	Production of fry and fingerlings (in lakhs)	---	---
3.	Fishermen Co-operated Societies :		
	No. of Societies	13	11
	No. of Members	2572	2700

Source : Asstt. Director of Fisheries, Jalpaiguri

Table : 2.2.13 Warehousing and Cold Storage Facilities Available to Cultivators

Year	*Warehouse*		*Cold Storage*		
	Number	*Capacity*	*Number*	*Capacity (in mt.)*	*Nos. of cultivators benefited*
1	2	3	4	5	6
1993-94	03	23900	02	7500	1550
1994-95	03	23900	02	7500	1926

Source : State Warehouse and different Cold Storage, Jalpaiguri

Table : 2.2.14 Area Irrigated by Different Sources (in '000 hectares)

Year	*Govt. canal*	*Canal*	*Private Tanks*	*Well*	*Deep tube wells & shallow tube wells*	*Other sources*	*Total area irrigated*
1993-94	6.50	15.55	0.70	0.55	13.04	2.59	25.80
1994-95	10.20	21.57	0.70	0.55	13.04	4.25	37.27

Sources : 1) P.A.O.,

2) Irrigation and Waterways Directorate West Bengal

3) Jalpaiguri Zilla Parisad, Jalpaiguri

4) Assistant Engineer Agricultural Irrigation.

Education and Culture

Table : 2.2.15 Educational facilities

(Number)

Type of Institution	Institution 1993-94	Institution 1994-95	Students 1993-94	Students 1994-95	Teachers 1993-94	Teachers 1994-95
1. Primary	1908	1908	322460	327127	6238	6990
2. Middle	92	92	23948	24212	540	543
3. Secondary	137	142	95828	104245	1949	2022
4. Higher Secondary	37	37	41034	42282	1037	1058
5. College (Degree)	8	8	9740	10056	190	188
6. Professional & Technical (Schools & Colleges)	15	15	2452	2497	106	185
7. Other Institution	40*	-----	-----	162010	86	-----

Sources: 1) D.I of Schools (Pry. & Sec.),
2) Social Education Officer
3) Respective Colleges, Jalpaiguri,
4) T.L.C

Table : 2.2.16 Literacy by Sex, 1991

(Percentage)

Sub-division/ district	Rural Male	Rural Female	Rural Total	Urban Male	Urban Female	Urban Total	Total Male	Total Female	Total Total
Sadar sub-div.	41.70	21.80	31.77	64.79	50.64	58.05	46.13	26.66	36.78
Alipurduar	41.82	22.54	32.53	73.51	61.86	67.88	45.74	27.42	36.91
District	36.83	41.75	21.70	32.09	67.42	54.09	61.04	45.97	36.83

Sources : Census of India, 1991

Table : 2.2.17 Medical Facilities

Year	Hospital	Health centres	Clinics	Dispensaries	Total	Total Beds	No. of Doctors	Patients treated Indoor	Patients treated Outdoor	Patients treated Total
1993	08	52	53	60	173	1354	160	122929	1463884	1767422
1994	08	52	53	60	173	1434	160	124667	1463884	1588551
1995	08	52	53	60	173	1434	181	147514	1973391	2120905

Source : 1) C.M.O.H. Jalpaiguri
2) Dist. Inspector of Health Statistics

Table : 2.2.18 Family Welfare

Year (as on 31st March	*No. of Family Welfare Centres*			*Total no. of cases of*		
	Rural	*Urban*	*Total*	*Vasectomy*	*Tubectomy*	*I.U.D*
1993-94	522	4	526	968	19169	2819
1994-95	522	4	526	679	18897	1947

Sources : 1) Dist. Family Welfare Office,

2) Dy. C.M.O.H (III)

Table : 2.2.19 Commercial Banks

(Number)

Year (as on 30th June)	*No. of Bank Offices*	*Average Population served per office (in '000 Nos.)*
1994	133	23
1995	134	23

Sources : 1) Reserve Bank of India

2) Basic Statistical Return (Summary results)

Table : 2.2.20 Sale of Electricity and Town & Villages Electrified

Items	*Year*	
	1993-94	*1994-95*
A) Sale of Electricity (in '000 K.W.H)		
1. Domestic and Residential Consumption	34652	42390
2. Commercial Light and Power	19209	17950
3. Industrial Power	12212	22730
4. Public Lighting*	627*	905
5. Railway Traction	--	--
6. Irrigation	986	1950
7. Public Waterworkes and Sewrage Pumping	347	1850
B. No. of Towns & Villages Electrified upto the year (31st March)		
1. Town	12	12
2. Villages	725	725

* Includes consumption under Agricultural Irrigation and Public Waterworks of Jalpaiguri division

Sources : 1) Divisional Engr. (0+M), Jalpaiguri

2) State Electricity Board, Jalpaiguri, Alipurduar & Siliguri

Table : 2.2.21 Co-operative Societies

Year	*No. of Co-operative Societies*	*Membership (in '000 Nos.)*	*Working Capital (Rs. in lakhs)*
1993-94	413	88	113
1994-95	567	83	73

Source : A.R.C.S., Jalpaiguri & Coochbehar

Transport and Communication

Table : 2.2.22 Roads Maintained by Different Organisation

(in Km)

Year	*P.W.D*		*Local Bodies*		*Municipalities*	
	Surfaced	*Un-surfaced*	*Surfaced*	*Un-surfaced*	*Surfaced*	*Un-surfaced*
1993-94	1272	11.00	228.34	376.55	142.90	51.86
1994-95	1272	11.00	228.34	376.55	142.90	51.86

Sources: (1) P.W.D (Roads) W.B

(2) Local Bodies, Municipalities

(3) P.W.D Office, Jalpaiguri

Table : 2.2.23 Post and Telegraph Offices

(Number)

Year (as on 31st March	*Post Offices*	*Combined Offices*	*Department of Telegraph Offices*
1994	279	32	1
1995	279	32	1

Sources : P.M.G, W.B (Jalpaiguri)

Table : 2.2.24 Distribution of Vested Land for Agricultural purpose to the Landless & Small Cultivators

District/ State (as on 30th June)	*Area of Vested land distributed (in hectares)*	*No. of Beneficiaries* Scheduled Caste	*Scheduled Tribe*	*Others*	*Total*	*Instit-ution & Societies*
Jalpaiguri	37950.25	62610	26491	31143	120244	--
West Bengal	386842.84	830914	464108	974937	2269959	--

Sources : Board of Revenue, W.B.

Table : 2.2.25 Recording of Bargadars

Year	W.B.E.A Act		Bargadars recorded in W.B.L.R Act, 1985		Operation Barga	
	Number	Area (acres)	Number	Area (acres)	Number	Area (acres)
Sept. 1993	16985	27246.46	19318	21812.99	24343	46672.17

Sources : *Board of Revenue, W.B*

Table : 2.2.26 Production in Sericulture Industries

Year	Cocoons Production (in '000 Kahan)	Value (in '000 Rs.)
1994 – 95	19.90	1088.40

Note— One (1) *Kahan* is equivalent to 900 gms. (approx.)

Source: 1) Dy. Director, Sericulture, Jalpaiguri

2) Suptd. , Sericulture, Coochbehar

Table 2.2.27 Area, Production and Employment in Tea Industry

Year	No. of Tea garden	Total land under cultivation (hect.)	No. of persons employed in Factory	Plantation	Total	Production ('000 kg)	Average yield per hect. in kg
1994	163	68200	16238	146110	162348	120299	1905

Source : *I.T.P.A Jalpaiguri*

III
District Profile : South 24 Paraganas

Geographical Location, Area, Rainfall and Temperature

Table 2.3.1 Geographical location and Area

District	Latitude		Longitude		Area in sq. km
	North	South	East	West	
24 Parganas (S)	$22^0 33'$ N	$21^0 29'$ N	$89^0 4'$ E	$88^0 3'$ E	9960.00

Source : Census of India, 1961

Table 2.3.2 Rainfall and Temperature

Item	Normal	Year 1994	1995
Annual rainfall (in millimeter)	1609.13	1944	1840
Temperature (in Celsius)	Maximum	38	35
	Minimum	15	14

Source : Meteorological Dept., Govt. of India.

Administrative Units

Table 2.3.3 Administrative Units

Year	Sub-Division	Police Station	C.D. Blocks	Panchayat Samity	Panchayat Gram	Mouzas	Inhabited village (1981)	Town Municipal	Town Non-muni-cipal	No. of Household 1991
1997	5	26	29	29	312	2167	2119	14	35	1011522

Source : *Census of India*, 1991, Dept. of Panchayat, West Bengal.

Population

Table 2.3.4 Rural population by Sex, 1981 & 1991

Sl. No.	*Item*		*1991 District*	*1991 West Bengal*
		a) Male	2962214	35510633
1.	Population	b) Female	2752816	32567332
		c) Total	5715030	68077965
		a) Male	2557023	25442210
2.	Rural	b) Female	2397630	23928154
		c) Total	4954653	49370364
		a) Male	405191	10068423
3.	Urban	b) Female	355186	8639178
		c) Total	760377	18707601
4.	Density of Population		574	767
5.	% Urban to total Poupulation		6.50	27.48

Source : *Census of India, 1991*

Table 2.3.5 Distribution of population according to different categories of workers and non-workers by sex, 1991

	Categories	*Population (number) Male*	*Female*	*Total*	*Percentage to total population*
a.	Total main workers:	1411582	79613	1491195	26.09
	1. Cultivators :	401125	12750	413875	7.24
	2. Agricultural labourers :	425876	18816	444692	7.78
	3. Household workers :	51305	11194	62499	1.09
	4. Others workers :	533276	36853	570129	9.98
b.	Marginal workers :	35264	90425	125689	2.20
c.	Non-workers :	1515368	2582778	4098146	71.71
	Total (a + b + c)	2962214	2752816	5715030	100.00

Table 2.3.6 Scheduled Caste and Scheduled Tribe Population

Year	*Scheduled Caste*			*Scheduled Tribe*		
	Male	*Female*	*Total*	*Male*	*Female*	*Total*
1991	1019471	949343	1968814	35706	34793	70499

Source : *Census of India, 1991*

Agriculture

Table 2.3.7 Some Land Utilization Statistics

('000 hectares)

Year	*Total area (according to Village papers)*	*Forest (according to State Forest Department)*	*Current fallow*	*Other fallow land*	*Net cropped area*
1996-97	966.17	426.30	4.39	1.04	405.19
1997-98	966.17	426.30	4.57	1.11	397.35

Source : *Directorate of Agriculture, W.B.*

Table 2.3.8 Area and Production of Principal Crops

Crops	*Area ('000 hectares)*		*Production ('000 tonnes)*	
	1996-97	*1997-98*	*1996-97*	*1997-98*
Aus (rice)	2.4	2.4	4.6	5.3
Aman (rice)	372.1	373.2	635.3	494.2
Boro (rice)	51.6	54.7	150.7	135.7
Crops	*Area ('000 hectares)*		*Production ('000 tonnes)*	
	1996-97	*1997-98*	*1996-97*	*1997-98*
Wheat	0.1	1.1	0.3	1.5
Gram	0.1	-	(b)	-
Other pulses	6.8	5.1	4.9	3.1
Rape & Mustard	2.0	4.5	1.8	3.3
Jute (1)	1.0	0.9	14.5	10.3
Sugarcane (2)	a	a	0.2	2.3
Dry chillies	14.4	18.0	10.6	8.9
Potato	1.2	1.4	26.4	27.5
Ginger	0.1	0.1	b	b

1) Production in terms of 1000 bales of 180 Kg. Each

2) Production in terms of Gur.

3) Less than 50 hects. (b) Less than 50 tonnes.

Source : *(1) Directorate of Agriculture W.B.*

(2) B.A.E. & Statistics, Govt. of W.B.

Table 2.3.9 Index number of Agricultural area, production and productivity

(base : Triennium ending Crop year 1981-82 = 100) (All Combined)

Items	*Year*	
	1996-97	*1997-98 (P)*
Area	113.62	117.91
Production	256.90	192.14
Productivity	226.10	162.95

Source : *B.A.E. & Statistics, Govt. of W.B.*

Table 2.3.10 Consumption of Fertilizers

(in '000 tonnes)

Year	*Name of fertilizer*			*Total*
	N	*P*	*K*	*(N + P +K)*
1996-97	27.2	11.6	8.3	47.1
1997-98	21.8	13.1	10.3	51.2

Source : *Directorate of Agriculture, W.B.*

Table 2.3.11 Forest area and out-turn of Forest

Item	*Unit*	*Year*	
		1996-97	*1997-98*
1	*2*	*3*	*4*
i) Forest area	Thousand hectares	165389.08	165389.08
ii) Forest Production	Thousand Cubic metre		
a) Timber	,,	N. A.	N.A
b) Fuel	,,	N.A.	N.A
iii) Revenue & Expenditure	Thousand rupees		
a) Revenue	,,	2071	1487
b) Expenditure	,,	12864	21860

Source : *Divisional Forest Office, South 24 Parganas.*

Table 2.3.12 Warehousing and Cold Storage Facilities Available to Cultivators

Year	*Warehouse*		*Cold Storage*		*Nos. of cultivators benefited*
	Number	*Capacity*	*Number*	*Capacity (in mt.)*	
1996-97	N.A.	N.A	N.A.	N.A	N.A.
1997-98	N.A.	N.A	N.A.	N.A	N.A.

Source : *State Warehouse and different Cold Storage, South 24 Parganas*

Table 2.3.13 Fisheries

Sl. No.	*Item*	*Year* 1996-97	*Year* 1997-98
1.	Government Schemes :		
	No. of Schemes operated	90	221
	Expenditure ('000 rupees)	---	----
	Assistance to needy fishermen ('000 rupees)	---	---
	Distribution of fry & fingerlings (in lakhs)	N.A.	N.A
2.	Tanks & Beels (Govt. owned) :		
	Area (hectares)	N.A.	N.A
	Expenditure ('000 rupees)	N.A.	N.A
	Production of fry & fingerlings (in lakhs)	N.A.	N.A
3.	Fishermen Co-operated Societies :	N.A.	N.A
	No. of Societies	N.A.	N.A
	No. of Members	N.A.	N.A

Source : *Asstt. Director of Fisheries, South 24 Parganas*

Table 2.3.14 Area Irrigated by Different Sources

Year	Govt. canal	Private Canal	Private Tanks	Private Well	Deep tube wells & shallow tube wells	Other sources	Total area irrigated
1996-97	34.22	---	27.68	---	16 5393	19.79	81.69
1997-98	47.55	---	30.57	---	29 4869	22.73	100.85

Sources :*(1) P.A.O., South 24 Parganas*

(2) Irrigation & Waterways Directorate, West Bengal

Education and Culture

Table 2.3.15 Educational Facilities

Type of Institution	*Institution* 1996-97	*Institution* 1997-98	*Students* 1996-97	*Students* 1997-98	*Teachers* 1996-97	*Teachers* 1997-98
1. Primary	3429	3429	722510	704479	11136	9491
2. Middle	311	311	66331	67657	2015	2015
3. Secondary	387	385	239000	242380	5760	5710
4. Higher Secondary	79	81	84460	87549	2258	2308
5. College (Degree)	20	21	32230	32876	680	695
6. Professional & Technical Schools & Colleges)	20	20	2162	2202	203	196
7. Other Institution	12	12	1560	1557	146	140

Sources :*(1) D.I. of School (Pry. & Sec.), South 24 Parganas, (2) Social Education Officer, South 24 Parganas, (3) Respective Colleges, South 24 Parganas.*

Table 2.3.16 Literacy by Sex, 1991 (Percentage)

Sub-division/ district	*Rural*			*Urban*			*Total*		
	Male	*Female*	*Total*	*Male*	*Female*	*Total*	*Male*	*Female*	*Total*
Alipur	63.75	35.03	49.94	77.90	62.69	70.86	67.05	41.15	54.70
Diamond Harbour	69.96	39.06	54.05	82.23	63.326	73.09	70.57	39.72	55.69
Baruipur	67.63	40.31	54.54	79.60	57.71	69.37	67.97	40.78	54.95
Canning	59.21	25.38	42.81	73.10	51.41	62.55	61.76	30.19	46.45
Kakdwip	67.22	36.14	52.14	---	---	---	67.22	36.14	52.14
District	66.60	36.89	52.30	79.26	63.66	72.04	68.45	40.57	55.10

Note : (1) Literate population excludes children of age group 0-6 years.

Sources: *Census of India, 1991.*

Table 2.3.17 Medical Facilities

Year	Hospital	Health centres	Clinics	Dispensaries	Total	Total Beds	No. of Doctors	Patients treated		
								Indoor	Outdoor	Total
1996	15	83	50	31	179	1307	172	731180	2678312	3409492
1997	15	83	50	31	179	1307	141	64626	1981971	2046597

Sources: *1) C.M.O.H., South 24 Parganas*

2) Dist. Inspector of Health Statistics, South 24 Parganas

Table 2.3.18 Family Welfare

Year (as on 31st March)	*No. of Family Welfare Centres*			*Total no. of cases of*		
	Rural	*Urban*	*Total*	*Vasectomy*	*Tubectomy*	*I.U.D*
1996	-	-	30	11	16050	7663
1997	-	-	30	18	15340	6297

Sources: *1) Dist. Family Welfare Office, South 24 Parganas*

2) Dy. C.M.O.H. (III), South 24 Parganas

Table 2.3.19 Commercial Banks (in Numbers)

Year (as on 30th June)	*No. of Bank Offices*	*Average Population served per office (in '000 Nos.)*
1996	222	253
1997	222	253

Sources: *(1) Reserve Bank of India (2) Basic Statistical Return (Summary results) (3) Economic Review.*

Table 2.3.20 Co-operative Societies

Year	*No. of Co-operative Societies*	*Membership (in '000 Nos.)*	*Working Capital (Rs. in lakhs)*
1996-97	308	220	813.96
1997-98	304	209	1185.10

Source: *Asstt. Registrar of Co-operative Societies, South 24 Parganas.*

Table 2.3.21 Sale of Electricity and Town & Village Electrified

Items	*Year*	
	1996-97	*1997-98*
(A) Sale of Electricity (in '000 K.W.H)		
1. Domestic and Residential Consumption	101301	121558
2. Commercial Light and Power	29068	29960
3. Industrial Power	41446	38220
4. Public Lighting	962	2360
5. Railway Traction	1110	1080
6. Irrigation	775	1215
7. Public Waterworks and Sewerage Pumping	757	1432
(B) No. of Towns & Villages Electrified upto the year (31st March)		
1. Towns	N.A.	N.A.
2. Villages	1729	1713

Source: *(1) Divisional Engr. (0+M), South 24 Parganas*
(2) State Electricity Board (R.E.), South 24 Parganas

Transport and Communication

Table 2.3.22 Roads Maintained by Different Organisation

Year	*P.W.D*		*Local Bodies*		*Municipalities*	
	Surfaced	*Un-surfaced*	*Surfaced*	*Un-surfaced*	*Surfaced*	*Unsurfaced*
1996-97(P)	2376	20	1555.50	1680.47	N.A.	N.A.
1997-98	2381	15	2294.00	2158.00	N.A.	N.A.

Sources: *(1) Local Bodies, Municipalities*
(2) P.W.D. Office, South 24 Pargans

Table : 2.3.23 Post and Telegraph Offices

(Number)

Year (as on 31st March	*Post Offices*	*Combined Offices*	*Department of Telegraph Offices*
1997	791	123	02
1998	777	123	02

Sources : P.M.G, W.B (South 24 Parganas)

Table : 2.3.24 Distribution of Vested Land for Agricultural purpose to the Landless and Small Cultivators

District/ State (as on 30.6.1997 June)	*Area of Vested land distributed (in hectares)*	*No. of Beneficiaries*				*Instit-ution & Societies*
		Scheduled Caste	*Scheduled Tribe*	*Others*	*Total*	
South 24 Parganas	26480	55990	11278	76534	143802	--
West Bengal	394904.14	878279	485095	1143315	2506689	--

Source :Boarc of Revenue, W.B.

Table : 2.3.25 Recording of Bargadars

District / State (as on 31.10.97)	Schedule Caste		Scheduled Tribe		Others		Total	
	No.	Area	No.	Area	No.	Area	No.	Area
District	N.A.	N.A.	N.A.	N.A.	N.A.	N.A.	N.A.	N.A.
West Bengal	450267	146157.07	163552	62567.00	867206	235238.57	141025	443962.64

Source : *Land and Land Reforms Dept., West Bangal.*

Table : 2.4. Infrastructure Facilities Available in the Surveyed Mouzas in the State of West Bengal

Sl. No.	Facilities available in the village	Bankura District Ranibandh Block								Jalpaiguri District Dhupguri Block										South 24 Parganas District Gosaba Block			
		Ranibandh		Moula		Katiam		Birkham		Mela Forest Village		Khoklong Forest Village		Chanadipa		Madyha Salbari		Purba Duramari		Dayapur		Jamespur	
		Yes	No	Yes	No	Yes	No	Yes	No	Yes	No	Yes	No	Yes	No	Yes	No	Yes	No	Yes	No	Yes	No
1.1	**Educational Facilities**																						
i)	ICDS (Angan Wadi)	✓		✓		✓		✓		✓			✓	✓		✓		✓		✓		✓	
ii)	Primary School	✓		✓		✓		✓			✓	✓		✓		✓		✓		✓		✓	
iii)	Junior High School	✓			✓		✓		✓		✓		✓		✓		✓		✓		✓		✓
iv)	High School	✓			✓		✓		✓		✓		✓		✓		✓		✓	✓			✓
v)	Higher Secondary School	✓			✓		✓		✓		✓		✓		✓		✓		✓		✓		✓
vi)	ICJCKs	✓			✓		✓	✓		✓		✓			✓		✓		✓	✓		✓	
1.2	**Medical Facilities**																						
i)	Sub-centre (S.C)	✓			✓		✓	✓			✓		✓	✓			✓	✓		✓		✓	
ii)	P.H.C.	✓			✓		✓		✓		✓		✓		✓		✓		✓		✓		✓
iii)	B.P.H.C.	✓			✓		✓		✓		✓		✓		✓		✓		✓		✓		✓

Cont/......

Sl. No.	Facilities available in the village	Bankura District Ranibandh Block								Jalpaiguri District Dhupguri Block										South 24 Parganas District Gosaba Block			
		Ranibandh		Moula		Katiam		Birkham		Mela Forest Village		Khoklong Forest Village		Chanadipa		Madyha Salbari		Purba Duramari		Dayapur		Jamespur	
		Yes	No	Yes	No	Yes	No	Yes	No	Yes	No	Yes	No	Yes	No	Yes	No	Yes	No	Yes	No	Yes	No
1.3	**Veterinary Facilities**																						
i)	Sub-centre		✓		✓		✓		✓		✓		✓		✓		✓		✓		✓		✓
ii)	Dispensary		✓		✓		✓		✓		✓		✓		✓		✓		✓		✓		✓
iii)	Hospital		✓		✓		✓		✓		✓		✓		✓		✓		✓		✓		✓
iv)	Artificial Insemination Centre	✓			✓		✓		✓		✓		✓		✓		✓		✓		✓		✓
1.4	**Financial Institutions**																						
i)	Nationalised Banks	✓			✓		✓		✓		✓		✓		✓		✓		✓		✓		✓
ii)	Co-operative Banks	✓			✓		✓		✓		✓		✓		✓		✓		✓		✓		✓
iii)	Central Co-op. Banks		✓		✓		✓		✓		✓		✓		✓		✓		✓		✓		✓
iv)	Gramin/Rural Banks	✓			✓		✓		✓		✓		✓		✓		✓		✓		✓	✓	

Cont/......

Sl. No.	Facilities available in the village	Bankura District Ranibandh Block								Jalpaiguri District Dhupguri Block										South 24 Parganas District Gosaba Block			
		Ranibandh		Moula		Katiam		Birkham		Mela Forest Village		Khoklong Forest Village		Chanadipa		Madyha Salbari		Purba Duramari		Dayapur		Jamespur	
		Yes	No	Yes	No	Yes	No	Yes	No	Yes	No	Yes	No	Yes	No	Yes	No	Yes	No	Yes	No	Yes	No
1.5	**Co-operative Societies**																						
i)	Agricultural Co-operative Society		✓		✓		✓		✓		✓		✓		✓		✓		✓	✓			✓
ii)	LAMPS	✓			✓	✓			✓		✓		✓		✓		✓		✓		✓		✓
i)	Rickshaw / Tracer/Boat	✓		✓		✓		✓			✓		✓	✓		✓		✓		✓		✓	
ii)	Roadway (Bus Stand)	✓			✓	✓			✓		✓		✓		✓	✓		✓			✓		✓
iii)	Railway (Railway Station)		✓		✓		✓		✓		✓		✓		✓		✓		✓		✓		✓
iv)	Metalled Road	✓			✓	✓			✓		✓		✓		✓		✓	✓			✓		✓
1.7	**Electricity**																						
i)	Electrification	✓		✓		✓			✓		✓		✓		✓		✓		✓		✓		✓
1.8	**Drinking Water Facility**					✓		✓															
i)	Drinking Water facility	✓		✓						✓		✓		✓		✓		✓			✓		✓

Cont/......

Sl. No.	Facilities available in the village	*Bankura District Ranibandh Block*								*Jalpaiguri District Dhupguri Block*												*South 24 Parganas District Gosaba Block*			
		Ranibandh		*Moula*		*Katiam*		*Birkham*		*Mela Forest Village*		*Khoklong Forest Village*		*Chanadipa*		*Madyha Salbari*		*Purba Duramari*		*Dayapur*		*Jamespur*	
		Yes	*No*	*Yes*	*No*	*Yes*	*No*	*Yes*	*No*	*Yes*	*No*	*Yes*	*No*	*Yes*	*No*	*Yes*	*No*	*Yes*	*No*	*Yes*	*No*	*Yes*	*No*
1.9	**Communication Facilities**																						
i)	Post Office	✓			✓		✓	✓			✓		✓		✓		✓		✓	✓		✓	
iii)	Telegraphic Office		✓		✓		✓		✓		✓		✓		✓		✓		✓		✓		✓
iv)	Telephone Office / Booth	✓			✓		✓		✓		✓		✓		✓		✓		✓	✓			✓
1.10	**Market**																						
i)	Marketing Facilities (Shandies)	✓			✓	✓			✓				✓		✓		✓		✓	✓			✓
ii)	Private Traders	✓		✓		✓		✓		✓		✓		✓		✓		✓		✓		✓	
1.11	**Fair Price Shop (PDS)**																						
i)	Fair Price Shop (Ration Shop)	✓			✓		✓	✓			✓		✓		✓	✓		✓		✓		✓	
ii)	If yes, it is functioning?	✓						✓								✓		✓		✓		✓	

Cont/......

Sl. No.	Facilities available in the village	Bankura District, Ranibandh Block: Ranibandh		Moula		Katiam		Birkham		Jalpaiguri District, Dhupguri Block: Mela Forest Village		Khoklong Forest Village		Chanadipa		Madyha Salbari		Purba Duramari		South 24 Parganas District, Gosaba Block: Dayapur		Jamespur	
		Yes	No	Yes	No	Yes	No	Yes	No	Yes	No	Yes	No	Yes	No	Yes	No	Yes	No	Yes	No	Yes	No
1.12	**Recreational Centres**																						
i)	Cinema / Video Hall	✓			✓		✓		✓		✓		✓		✓	✓			✓		✓		✓
ii)	Playground	✓		✓		✓		✓			✓	✓			✓		✓	✓		✓		✓	
iii)	Park		✓		✓		✓		✓		✓		✓		✓		✓		✓		✓		✓
1.13	**Irrigation Facilities**																						
i)	Irrigation Facilities		✓	✓			✓		✓	✓		✓		✓		✓		✓			✓		✓
1.14	**Administrative Facilities**																						
i)	Police Station / Outpost (Phanri)	✓			✓	✓			✓		✓		✓		✓		✓		✓		✓		✓
ii)	Panchayat Office	✓			✓		✓		✓		✓		✓		✓		✓		✓		✓		✓
iii)	Panchayat Member	✓		✓			✓	✓		✓		✓		✓		✓		✓		✓		✓	

Cont/......

Table 2.1a Block Profile Ranibandh

Total area of the Block	:	428.40 sq. k.m.
Total no. of Gram Panchayats	:	8
Police Station	:	1
Total No. of Mouzas	:	186
Total no. of habitated mouzas	:	169
Electrified Villages (upto 1998)	:	79
Population (1991 Census)	:	
Total	:	93,748
Male	:	48,098
Female	:	45,653
Scheduled Castes		
Total	:	10,595
Male	:	5,481
Female	:	5,114
Scheduled Tribes		
Total	:	44833
Male	:	22755
Female	:	22078
Population Density	:	219 per sq. k.m.
Literacy Rate		
Total	:	43.90%
Male	:	62.96%
Female	:	23.76%
Population Features of Farmers		
Bargadars	:	1467
Pattaholders	:	3518
Small Farmers	:	4565
Marginal Farmers	:	6537
Agricultural Labours	:	9772
(1) Distribution of Main workers		
Total	:	36632
Male	:	25280
Female	:	11352

Cont/.......

(A) Total Cultivators	:	21510
Male	:	15331
Female	:	6179
(B) Total Agricultural labours	:	9772
Male	:	5426
Female	:	4346
(C) Household Industrial Labours	:	1005
Male	:	746
Female	:	259
(D) Others	:	4345
Male	:	3777
Female	:	568
(2) Total Marginal Workers	:	4466
Male	:	451
Female	:	4015
(3) Total Non-workers	:	54861
Male	:	20826
Female	:	34035
Utilisation and Distribution of Land (in hec.)		
a) Net area under cultivation	:	15536
b) Pasture & Orchard	:	1392
c) Cultivable waste land	:	1058
d) Homestead land	:	7652
e) Forest land	:	16477
Sources of Irrigation and Area Irrigated (in hec.)		
i) Canal	:	750
ii) Tank	:	8000
iii) River Lift Irrigation	:	360
iv) Shallow Tubewell	:	-
v) Others	:	510
Educational Institutions (in no.)		
i) Primary School	:	151
ii) Middle School	:	05
iii) Secondary School	:	08
iv) Higher Secondary	:	03
Health Institutions (in no.)		
a) Hospital	:	-
b) Health Centres	:	04
c) Clinics	:	24

Cont/.......

d) Dispensary	:	04
Veterinary Facilities (in no.)		
i) Artificial Insemination Centres	:	04
ii) Dispensary	:	04
iii) Veterinary Personnel	:	09
Financial Institutions (in no.)	:	
a) Commercial Banks	:	03
b) Gramin Banks	:	02
c) Co-operative Societies	:	31
Post & Telegraph (in no.)		
i) Post Office	:	24
ii) Telegraphic office	:	-

Table 2.2a Block Profile Dhagpuri

Total area of the Block	:	561.60 sq. k.m.
Total no. of Gram Panchayats	:	18
Police Station	:	02
Total No. of Mouzas	:	108
Electrified Villages	:	65
Population (1991 Census)		
Total	:	285780
Male	:	149230
Female	:	136550
Scheduled Caste		
Total	:	115042
Male	:	57930
Female	:	57112
Scheduled Tribe		
Total	:	62858
Male	:	32252
Female	:	30606
Total no. of households	:	53475
Literacy Rate		
Total	:	40.93%
Male	:	52.69&
Female	:	28.24%
Population Features of Farmers		
Bargadars	:	2897
Pattaholders	:	12590
Small Farmers	:	4345
Marginal Farmers	:	11597
Agricultural Labours	:	16585
Total Cultivators	:	33033
Others	:	57486
Utilisation and Distribution of Land (in hec.)		
a) Net area under cultivation	:	20640
b) Orchard	:	748
c) Cultivable waste land	:	1950
d) Homestead land	:	211
No. of Tea Gardens	:	08

Educational Institutions (in no.)		
i) Primary School	:	199
ii) Middle School	:	07
iii) Secondary School	:	15
iv) Higher Secondary	:	04
v) College	:	01
Health Institutions (in no.)		
a) B.P.H.C	:	01
b) P. H.C	:	01
c) S.H.C	:	03
d) Sub-Centres	:	07
Veterinary Facilities (in no.)		
i) Artificial Insemination Centres	:	01
ii) Dispensary	:	02
iii) Veterinary Hospital	:	01
Financial Institutions (in no.)		
a) Commercial Banks	:	14
b) Co-operative Banks	:	01
c) Co-operative Societies	:	01
Regulated Market	:	01
Sandy	:	12
Post & Telegraph (in no.)		
i) Post Office	:	40
ii) Telegraphic office	:	-

Table 2.3a Block Profile Gosaba

Total area of the Block	:	285.05 sq. k.m.
Total no. of Gram Panchayats	:	14
Police Station	:	01
Total no. of Mouzas	:	51
Total no. Islands	:	11
Population (1991 Census)		
Total	:	200506
Male	:	103307
Female	:	97199
Scheduled Castes		
Total	:	130355
Male	:	67543
Female	:	62812
Scheduled Tribes		
Total	:	19435
Male	:	9819
Female	:	9617
Population Density	:	703.40 sq.k.m.
Population Features of Farmers (in no.)		
Bargadars	:	5170
Pattaholders	:	17151
Marginal Farmers	:	14031
No of Land less family	:	4462
No. Homeless family	:	09
No. of Fishermen family	:	450
(1) Distribution of Main workers		
(A) Total Cultivators	:	27457
Male	:	26154
Female	:	1303
(B) Total Agricultural labour	:	22874
Male	:	20102
Female	:	2772
(C) Household Industrial Labour	:	560
Male	:	490
Female	:	70
(D) Others	:	7205
Male	:	6312
Female	:	893

Utilisation and Distribution of Land (in hec.)		
a) Orchard	:	525.00
b) No. of *Bheri*	:	04
Market		
i) Daily	:	04
ii) Weekly	:	14

3
The People

The present chapter deals with the people selected for the study.

The Kheria

The Kherias/Kharias mainly inhabit in Jharkhand, Chattisgarh, Orissa and West Bengal. A few Kheria individuals and some families can be found in Assam and Andaman Islands. They live with high concentration in Jharkhand only. In the state of West Bengal, the Kherias are distributed in the districts of Purulia, Bankura and Midnapore with high concentration. Hinduised Kherias are recorded from Midnapore, while a considerable number of Kherias are immigrant to 24 Parganas and Jalpaiguri and North Bengal part.

The Kherias have been classed on racial and cultural – particularly linguistic grounds among the Munda group of the aborigines of India. Though in point of numerical strength the Kherias are inferior to the better-known Munda group of tribes, in point of ethnological interest they do not yield to any of those allied tribes. In fact, a special interest would appear to attach to the Kheria tribe. The three distinctive divisions of the tribe, known respectively as the *Pahari Kheria* or Hill Kheria (sometimes called the *Erenga Kheria* or the Wild Kheria), the *Dhelki Kheria* and the *Dudh Kheria* represent different grades of primitive culture.

The traditions of the Dudh Kherias and the Dhelki Kherias still retain memories of the time when they together formed one compact tribe and their migrations from their home in the Vindhya and Kaimur ranges to Chhotanagpur lay along practically the same route, whereas the Hill Kherias regard themselves as the autochthones of the Mayurbhanj hills.

The Hill Kherias are still found mostly in the food gathering and hunting stage of economic culture, with occasional practice of a rude system of shifting cultivation. The next division of the tribe, the Delki or

Dhelki Kherias, as they are called, though they have long been food-producers and have taken to regular plough cultivation and evolved a more advanced social and religious system than the Hill Kherias, are still in a somewhat lower level of material culture than the Dudh kherias. The Dudh Kheria section of the tribe is in point of culture more progressive than the other sections, and ranks with the Munda, the Ho and the Santal among the most advanced of the Mundari-speaking tribes of India. As may be naturally expected, the agricultural and land-owning Dudh and Dhelki sections of the tribe are in a better economic condition than the Hill or *Paharia* section that have practically no cultivation. Better economic organisation and co-operation have further helped the Delki or Dhelki, and more so the Dudh section in improving their economic condition. But in the practical absence of artificial irrigation, their crops are always at the mercy of the monsoon rains, which can never be depended upon. So in years of drought or of excess rain damaging or destroying their crops, many Kheria families are obliged to emigrate for a time to work in the tea gardens of Assam or the Duars, or elsewhere.

The religion of the Kheria, though essentially a cult of 'powers', is not a religion of mere crouching fear of the baffling mysterious Powers of the dark. In spite of a haunting fear of evil powers, the Kherias reverent awe of an inscrutable Providence symbolised by the Sun, and a modicum of something of the nature of the filial devotion to Mother-Goddess, and of natural love and a feeling of respectful comradeship towards the Ancestor-Spirits, would appear to have elevated his religion to a somewhat higher level than that of the more primitive savage. Apart from the Ancestor-cult and a belief in a Supreme Creator, the Kheria believes in a host of spirits presiding over natural objects such as hills, trees and plants, and even over living creatures such as cattle.

Kheria social organisation with its body of traditions, that constitutes the social environment of the individual, produces appropriate social sentiments. This moulds the character and behaviour of the individual in society, and mark off members of Kheria society from other societies. Traditional usage crystallised into customary law. It is the business of the tribal government to enforce obedience to such law and custom. The machinery of tribal government varies in size and complexity with the size and culture of a particular tribe or group. The village council or *Panchayat* settles all social (including socio-religious and socio-political) matters of local interest, particularly violations of minor social or religious taboos, and disputes about partition. The headman in consultation with the elders of the settlement also arranges for raising contribution from the villagers for periodical public worship and religious feast, and for the propitiatry sacrifices to the spirits in times of epidemic to men or cattle.

The Bhumij

A non-Aryan tribe of Jharkhand, and West Bengal classed by Dalton (1872) and others, mainly on linguistic grounds, as Kolarian. There can be no doubt that the Bhumij are closely allied to, if not identical with, the Mundas, but there is little to show that they ever had a distinct language of their own.

Bhumij are nothing more than a branch of the Mundas, who have spread to the eastward, mingled with the Hindus, and thus for the most part severed their connexion with the parent tribe. This hypothesis seems on the whole to be borne out by the facts observable at the present day. The Bhumij of Purulia in West Bangal are beyond doubt pure Mundas. They inhabit the tract of the country which lies on both sides of the Subarnarekha river, bounded on the west by the edge of the Chhotanagpur Plateau, on the east by the hill range of which Ajodhya is the crowning peak, on the south by the Singbhum hill, and on the north by the hills forming the boundary between Lohardanga, Hazaribagh and Purulia district.

On the eastern side of the Ajodhya range, which forms a complete barrier to ordinary communication, all is changed. Both the Mundari language and the title of Munda have dropped out of use, and the aborigines of this eastern tract call themselves Bhumij or Sarda, and talk Bengali. The physical characteristics of the race, however, remain the same; and although they have adopted Hindu customs and are fast becoming Hindus, there can be no doubt that they are the descendants of Mundas who first settled in the country, and were given the name of *Bhumij* (autochthon) by the Hindu immigrants who found them in possession of the soil.

The Bhumij possess any independent traditions of migration. Those who live in proximity to Chhotanagpur recognise no distinction between themselves and the Mundas. They intermarry and associate and coalesce in all matters indicating identity of race; for, though it may be said that they are not much troubled with caste prejudices, there is no portion of the old Indian population, which is quite free from it. The Bhumij farther east have become too Hiduised to acknowledge the relationship. The Dhalbhum Bhumij consider themselves autochthones, and will not admit that they are in any way connected with the Mundas, Hos, or Santals.

The Bhumij recognise polygamy, and in theory at least impose no limitation on the number of wives a man may have. When a man has no children by his first wife, he usually marries again if he can afford to do so; and it frequently happens that the second wife is a young widow, whom he marries by the *sanga* ritual, paying a nominal bride-price and incurring far less expenditure than would be necessary in the event of his marrying a virgin. Widow-marriage is freely permitted by the *sanga* ritual, in which a widow smears on the bride's forehead vermilion, which the bridegroom has previously touched with his great toe. It is deemed right for a widow to marry her late husband's younger brother or cousin, if such an arrangement be feasible; and in the event of her marrying an outsider, she forfeits all claim to a share in her husband's property and to the custody of any children she may have had by him.

The religion of the Bhumij varies, within certain limits, according to the social position and territorial status of the individuals concerned. Zamindars and well-to-do tenure-holders employ Brahmans as their family priests, and offer sacrifices to Kali or *Mahamaya*. The mass of the people revere the sun under the names of *Sing-Bonga* and *Dharm*, as the giver of harvests to men and the cause of all changes of seasons affecting their agricultural fortunes.

With the Bhumij, as with other non-Aryan tribes of Chhotanagpur, the *Karam* festival, Colonel Dalton's description of which is quoted in the article *Oraon*, seems to be especially popular. The Bhumij of Bankura district celebrate this feast in the later half of the month Bhadra, corresponding roughly to the first half of September. A branch o the karam-tree (*Nauclea parvifolia*) is planted by the laya in the centre of the village dancing ground (*akra*). At the foot of this branch is a vessel partly filled with earth, into which, on the first day of the festival, the unmarried girls of the village throw various kinds of seed grain. These are carefully tended and watered from time to time so as to germinate by the *sankranti* (last day of the month), when the girls give the sprouting blades to each other, and wear them in their hair at the dance, which usually lasts the whole of that night.

The original occupation of the Purulia Bhumij is believed by them to have been military service, and there can be little doubt that the bands of Chuars or plunderers, who repeatedly overran the Midnapore district towards the end of last century, were largely recruited from this tribe. The circumstance, however, that they took a more or less prominent part in a series of marauding attacks on an unarmed and unwarlike population affords no ground for a belief in the existence among them of any real military instinct; and in fact they are conspicuous for the dislike of discipline, which is one of the prominent characteristics of the Kolarian races. For many years agriculture and post-agriculture has been the sole profession of the tribes. A few have aged in petty trade and some have immigrated to the tea districts of Assam.

The Rabha

Ethnically Rabhas in Jalpaiguri district of West Bengal belong to Koch-Rabha and Pati-Rabha group. According to Hodgson, Rabhas are a branch of the great Mech family; Risley treats them as branch of the Bodo group.

Racially they (Rabhas) may be classified into mongoloid stock. Dalton (1872) states "The Rabhas ...... are also branches of the Kachari race, and connected with the Garos". Their stature is short to medium, skin colour is yellowish having flat nose, straight to slightly wavy hair. Face is also round, check bones are more or less prominent. All of these features show a kin affinity with the Mongoloid traits.

Linguistically, Rabha language has been included in the Bodo group of language of Assam-Burmese group of Assam branch, by Grierson (1903). But Shafers (1953) has included this language under Koch sub-group. Datta's (1969) view is that the Rabha speech should be included in Garo sub-group had especially with Garo of Jalpaiguri. Though the Census of 1961 returns all this Rabhas of this state as the speakers of the Rabha language but in fact many of the village Rabhas of the district of Jalpaiguri and Coach Behar does not know the Rabha language. The younger generations of the villages have almost forgotten their old mother tongue. At present they speak in local Bengali (Rajbanshi), which is mixed with some Rabha words when they speak amongst themselves. The Forest Rabhas of course, have retained the Rabha language as their mother tongue. The males and some females know Bengali.

Cultivation has long been the traditional occupation of the Rabha. From time immemorial, agriculture has been the main source of their livelihood. The Forest Rabhas are mostly employed as forest labourers. The village Rabhas find it rather difficult to subsist by cultivation alone. Many of them keep poultry birds and domestic animals (cattle, pigs, sheep's, fowls, etc.). Weaving was a traditional occupation of the Rabha women and still now the practice is on vogue. The opening and expansion of markets in their areas and transaction with cash economy have made them more and more conscious about them and made the economic pursuits more male man-power oriented. The involvement of males in decision-making, economic pursuit has given rise to the village Rabhas household's masculinity and more authority to the male folk, particularly to the patri-kins, which helped the village Rabhas to move towards patriarchalisation. This is not seen in case of the Forest Rabhas.

The Rabhas are divided into a number of exogamous clans, known as the *husuks*. This social unit exists in both ecological groups of the Rabhas – the Forest Rabhas and the village Rabhas and identical *husuks* are present in both. In both cases these are unilateral, exogamous, matrilineal descent groups.

Both movable and immovable belongings of an individual, which he or she earns or acquires by his or her own efforts or receives from his or her ancestors or ancestress or gets as donations are considered by the Forest as well as the village Rabhas as their property. The forest Rabhas have only the movable property (which includes utensils, furniture, ornaments, domestic animals and poultry birds, etc.), but they do not have any immovable property (e.g., land, house, etc.) of their own in true sense. The land, house and other constructions in their possession are all actually owned by the Forest Department of the State Government. The Forest Department gives the (only the official forest labourers) a plot of land for cultivation and house and a house building and repairing materials free of cost in exchange of their labour for forest works. The land, house-site, house, etc. are never given to them permanently, and as a result he has no right on the land, house, house-site, etc., nor can he / she sell, mortgage or lease out or in any way dispose of it.

Among the village Rabha the movable and immovable property are owned by a person. A village Rabha may have land, house and other personal belonging such as utensils, furniture, ornaments, clothing, cash, etc., or his own. And on these he / she has every right like other people.

The Forest and the Village Rabhas follow rules of inheritance and of the ownership of the property. Among the Forest Rabha rule of inheritance, right on ancestral property flows from the deceased mother to the surviving daughter. But among the present day village Rabhas, on the other land, "the males are the owner of the property both ancestral and acquired" (Das & Raha, 1967).

The traditional village council or council of elders *(marab sen)* still persists among the Forest Rabhas only, the same among the village Rabhas has almost been replaced by the statutory panchayat system. Here only a relic of *marab sen* is seen. Only in a few cases the village Rabha elders assemble together to discuss about some very important social or religious issues. Even in those cases also the elders, particularly the members of the statutory village *panchayat* (gram sabha) are also invited to attend. The latter that mostly belong to the Rajbanshi or other Bengalee refugee even take part in the deliberations and help the body to come to conclusion. Among the Forest Rabha the situation is quite different. The *marab sen* works in full swing and no statutory panchayat system exists there. The outsiders are also not allowed to participate in the deliberations. They also have traditional means to solve the inter-*bastee* dispute. But the mechanism to solve inter-village dispute among the village Rabha is not that strong.

The Rabhas were once a full-fledged matrilineal tribe but at present both patrilineal and matrilineal characters are prevalent in their social systems. Those who live in forest have maintained many of their traditional culture, but their counterpart living in settled villages have been subjected to many changes and have imbibed Hindu way of life due to influence of neighbouring Rajbanshi community.

Though "the present day Rabha religion may be characterised as a mixed type of Hinduism and animism" (Das & Raha, 1967 : 130) still an important difference is noticed in the religion of the two Rabha divisions of Jalpaiguri district – the Forest Rabhas and Village Rabhas. This difference is in the degree of admixture of the Hinduism with the traditional animism of the Rabhas. The number of people turning to Christianity is not that significant though in the recent years it has much increased.

4

Socio-Economic Profile of Sample Households

The present chapter makes an attempt to discuss the socio-economic profile of the sample households in the selected three districts namely (1) Bankura (2) Jalpaiguri and (3) South 24 Parganas of West Bengal.

The socio-economic profile could be explained under the following :

a) Age sex composition.

b) Level of education.

c) Marital status

d) Occupational distribution.

e) Occupational mobility.

f) Size of land holding.

g) Sources of income.

h) Income pattern.

i) Pattern of household expenditure.

j) Pattern of expenditure on agricultural pursuits.

k) Nature of indebtedness.

l) Loan received from the government.

I

Ranibandh Block of District Bankura

The table 4.1.1 shows the age-sex composition of the sample households of Ranibandh block in the district Bankura. There are altogether total 529 numbers of populations out of surveyed communities. In the case of Scheduled Tribe the total number of male population was 134

Table—4.1.1– Age-Sex Composition of the Sample Household of Ranibandh Block in The District of Bankura

Community (No. of Surveyed Household)	*Age Group (yrs.)*										*Total Population*		
	0-4		*5-14*		*15-44*		*45-59*		*60+*		*Population*		*Total (%)*
	M	*F*	*M*	*F*	*M*	*F*	*M*	*F*	*M*	*F*	*M*	*F*	
Scheduled Tribes (50)	12	10	42	33	58	60	16	14	06	02	134	119	253 (47.83)
Non-Scheduled Tribes (50)	08	15	23	31	66	67	18	20	15	13	130	146	276 (52.17)
Total (%)	20 7.58	25 9.43	65 24.62	64 24.15	124 46.97	127 47.92	34 12.88	34 12.83	21 7.95	15 5.66	264 100.00	265 99.99	529 (100.00)

followed by female population 119. In the respect of Non Scheduled Tribe there are altogether 130 males followed by 146 female members. Age group wise it has been noticed that in the age group between 0 – 5 in the case of Scheduled Tribe there are 12 nos. of male and 10 female. In the same age group with reference to non Scheduled Tribe there are 8 nos. of male followed by 15 nos. of female. Next in the age group between 6 – 14 in the case of Scheduled Tribe there are 42 nos. of male and 33 nos. of female persons. In the case of non-Scheduled Tribe community there are 23 nos. of male and 31 nos. of female persons. In the age group between 15 – 44 in the case of non-scheduled tribe there are 66 nos. of male and 67 nos. of female persons. In the same age group in case of scheduled tribe communities there are 58 nos. of male followed by 60 female members. In the age group between 45 – 59 with reference to the scheduled tribe communities there are 16 nos. of male and 14 nos. of female members. In the same age group with reference toe non-Scheduled Tribes there are 18 nos. of male followed by 20 nos. of female members. Finally in the age group between 60 and above with reference to scheduled tribe communities there are 6 nos. of male followed by 2 female members. In the same age group with reference to non-scheduled tribe communities there are 15 nos. of male and 13 nos. of female members.

The table 4.1.2 gives detail about the level of education of the sample households. The level of education has been considered above 6 years age of the surveyed households. Community wise in the case of scheduled tribe out of total 116 nos. of male and 107 female persons 39 nos. of male 80 nos. of female person are illiterate followed by 6 nos. of male and 5 nos. of female members are functionally literate i.e. who knows reading and writing and having functional knowledge of arithmetic. With reference to formal education it has been noticed in the same community that out of total 116 nos. of male and 107 nos. of female persons there are 32 nos. of male and 16 nos. of female persons studied up to class IV followed by 26 nos. of female persons studied up to class VIII, 8 nos. of male and 1 female person studied up to class X, 1 male person studied up to XII and 4 male persons studied up to graduate level. No female person was found to be studied either in XI – XII or up to graduate. With reference to non-scheduled tribe communities out of total 120 nos. of male and 128 nos. of female persons there are 13 males and 35 females are illiterate followed by 9 nos. of male and 11 nos. of female persons are functionally literate. Regarding formal

Table—4.1.2 Level of Education of the Sample Households of Ranibandh Block in the District of Bankura

Community (No. of Surveyed Household)	*Illiterate*		*Functional Literate*		*Formal Education*										*Population (above 6 yrs.)*	
					I - IV		*V - VIII*		*IX - X*		*XI - XII*		*Graduate or Others*			
	M	*F*	*M*	*F*	*M*	*F*	*M*	*F*	*M*	*F*	*M*	*F*	*M*	*F*	*M*	*F*
Scheduled Tribes (50)	39	80	06	05	32	16	26	05	08	01	01	-	04	-	116	107
Non-Sche-duled Tribes (50)	13	35	09	11	22	31	48	39	17	09	07	01	04	02	120	128
Total	52	115	15	16	54	47	74	44	25	10	08	01	08	02	236	235
(% to the total population of above 6 yrs. age)	22.03	48.94	6.36	6.81	22.88	20.00	31.36	18.72	10.59	4.26	3.39	0.42	3.39	0.85	100.00	100.00

education in the same community out of total 120 nos. of male and 128 nos. of female persons there are 22 nos. of male and 31 nos. of female persons are studied up to class IV followed by 48 male and 39 female persons studied up to class VIII, 17 nos. of male and 9 nos. of female persons studied up to class X, 7 nos. of male and 1 female person studied up to class XII and finally 4 nos. of male and 2 nos. of female persons studied up to graduate level. Community wise in all the cases by taking together the majority of 74 nos. of male persons (31.36) and 44 nos. of female persons (18.72) are found to be studied up to class VIII.

Table 4.1.3 shows the marital status of the sample households. In respect of 50 nos. of surveyed households of schedule tribe communities it has been noticed that in the age group of 14 yrs there 53 nos. of male and 43 nos. of females are unmarried. In the age group between 15-29, 16 nos. of male and 10 nos. of female persons are unmarried followed by 9 male persons and 20 nos. of female persons are found to be widow. In the age group between 30-44 there are only 2 nos. of male persons are unmarried followed by 29 male and 25 female persons are found to be married. One male person is widowers followed by 2 female persons are widow. One male person is found to be married in the age group between 45 –59 followed by 14 male and 10 female persons in this age group are found to be married only. In this age group 2 male persons are widower followed by 5 female persons are widow. Lastly in the age group between 60 and above nobody is found to be unmarried followed by 6 male persons are married and 2 female persons are widow only. Next out of 50 nos. of surveyed households of non-scheduled tribe communities in the age group of 14 years 30 male and 47 female persons are found to be unmarried. In the age group between 15-29 there are 31 nos. of male and 19 nos. of female persons are unmarried followed by 10 male and 22 female persons are married. In the age group between 30 – 44 there are 25 nos. of male and 24 nos. of female persons found to be married. In this age group 2 female persons are found to be widow only. One male person is found to be unmarried in the age group between 45 –59 followed by 17 male and 14 female persons are married. Five female persons are found to be widow followed by one female person is found to be separated. Lastly, in the age group of 60 and above 14 nos. of male and 6 nos. of female persons are found to be married followed by one male persons is widower and 7 female persons are widow only.

Table—4.1.3 Marital Status of the Population of The Sample Households of Ranibandh Block in the District of Bankura

Community (No. of Surveyed Household)	*Age- group (In years)*	*Marital Status*								*Total*	
		Unmarried		*Married*		*Widower/Widow*		*Separated*			
		Male	*Female*	*Male*	*Female*	*Male*	*Female*	*Male*	*Female*	*Male*	*Female*
Scheduled Tribe (50)	Up to 14	53	43	-	-	-	-	-	-	53	43
	15 – 29	16	10	09	20	-	02	-	-	25	32
	30 – 44	02	-	29	25	01	02	-	-	32	27
	45 – 59	01	-	14	10	02	05	-	-	17	15
	60 +	-	-	06	-	-	02	-	-	06	02
	Sub-total	**72**	**53**	**58**	**55**	**03**	**11**	-	-	**133**	**119**
Non – Scheduled Tribe (50)	Up to 14	30	47	-	-	-	-	-	-	30	47
	15 – 29	31	19	10	22	-	-	-	-	41	41
	30 – 44	-	-	25	24	-	02	-	-	25	26
	45 – 59	01	-	17	14	-	05	-	01	18	19
	60 +	-	-	14	06	01	07	-	-	15	13
	Sub-total	**62**	**66**	**66**	**66**	**01**	**14**	-	**01**	**129**	**147**
TOTAL		**134**	**119**	**124**	**121**	**04**	**25**	-	**01**	**262**	**266**

Table 4.1.4 gives detail about the occupational distribution of the sample households. Out of 50 surveyed households of the scheduled tribe communities there are altogether 82 nos. of male and 75 nos. of female working population there are 28 nos. of males and 25 nos. of female persons are agricultural labour followed by 9 male and 2 female persons are non-agricultural labour, 21 nos. of male and 25 nos. of female persons are in cultivation. One male person is found to be engaged in petty business. In the animal husbandry there are only 3 female persons are found to be engaged in this profession followed by 2 male persons are engaged in service. Six male and 15 female persons are found to be engaged in the collection of forest produce. Lastly 15 nos. of male and 5 nos. of female persons are found to be engaged in others category like masonry, carpentry and maidservant. In the case of 50 surveyed households of non-scheduled tribe communities there are altogether 88 nos. of male and 94 nos. of female persons found to be total working force. Out f total 88 nos. of male and 94 nos. of female working force there are only 4 nos. of male and 3 nos. of female persons are agricultural labour followed by 14 nos. of male and 3 nos. of female persons are found to be non-agricultural labour. There are 45 nos. of male and 59 nos. of female persons are found to be engaged in cultivation followed by 2 male and one female person is found to be engaged in petty business, five female persons are engaged in animal husbandry, 7 male persons are in service, 3 nos. of male and 8 nos. of female persons are found to be engaged in forest collection produce and 13 male and 15 female persons are found to be engaged in others profession.

Table 4.1.5 gives detail about the occupational mobility of the sample household's generation wise. In the respect of scheduled tribe communities generation wise so far respondent is concerned it has been noticed that 14 persons major occupation is cultivation followed by fathers generation 13 persons are in cultivation and one person is having others. In respect to son's category there are 2 persons each who are agricultural labour and non-agricultural labour and one each is having occupation like service and others. The majority of 22 respondents are having occupation like agricultural labour followed by their father generation it has been found that the majority of 13 persons are having cultivation and 9 persons are engaged in agricultural labour. In respect to son there are three each persons is having occupation like agricultural labour, non- agricultural labour and others. Regarding non-agricultural labour it has been noticed that 6 nos.

Table—4.1.4 Occupational Distribution of the Sample Households of Ranibandh Block in the District of Bankura

Community (no of surveyed households)	*Type of Occupation **																			
	Agril. Labour		*Non-agril. Labour*		*Cultivation*		*Petty Business*		*Animal Husbandry*		*Service*		*Fishing or Aqua-culture*		*MFP/NTF/ TFP Collection*		*Others***		*Total Working Population*	
	M	*F*	*M*	*F*	*M*	*F*	*M*	*F*	*M*	*F*	*M*	*F*	*M*	*F*	*M*	*F*	*M*	*F*	*M*	*F*
Scheduled Tribe (50)	28	25	09	02	21	25	01	-	-	03	02	-	-	-	06	15	15	05	82	75
Non-Scheduled Tribes (50)	04	03	14	03	45	59	02	01	-	05	07	-	-	-	03	08	13	15	88	94
Total	32	28	23	05	66	84	03	01	-	08	09	-	-	-	09	23	28	20	170	169
(%)	18.82	16.57	13.53	2.96	38.82	49.70	1.76	0.59	-	4.73	5.29	-	-	-	5.29	13.61	16.48	11.83	99.99	99.99

Table—4.1.5 Occupational Mobility of the Sample Households of Ranibandh Block in the District of Bankura

Occupation of the Respondent		*Occupation of the Respondent's Father*									*Occupation of the Respondent's Son*								
		I	*II*	*III*	*IV*	*V*	*VI*	*VII*	*VIII*	*IX*	*I*	*II*	*III*	*IV*	*V*	*VI*	*VII*	*VIII*	*IX*
Scheduled Tribe																			
I. Cultivation	14	13	-	-	-	-	-	-	-	01	-	02	02	-	-	01	-	-	01
II. Agril. Labour	22	13	09	-	-	-	-	-	-	-	-	01	01	-	-	-	-	-	01
III. Non-Agril. Labour	06	03	01	02	-	-	-	-	-	-	-	-	-	-	-	-	-	-	-
IV. Petty Business	-	-	-	-	-	-	-	-	-	-	-	-	-	-	-	-	-	-	-
V. Animal Husbandry	01	-	01	-	-	-	-	-	-	-	-	-	-	-	-	-	-	-	-
VI. Service	-	-	-	-	-	-	-	-	-	-	-	-	-	-	-	-	-	-	-
VII. Fishing or Aquaculture	-	-	-	-	-	-	-	-	-	-	-	-	-	-	-	-	-	-	-
VIII. *Forest Produce collection*	-	-	-	-	-	-	-	-	-	-	-	-	-	-	-	-	-	-	-
IX. Others*	07	01	06	-	-	-	-	-	-	-	-	01	-	-	-	-	-	-	-

Occupation of the Respondent		*Occupation of the Respondent's Father*									*Occupation of the Respondent's Son*								
		I	*II*	*III*	*IV*	*V*	*VI*	*VII*	*VIII*	*IX*	*I*	*II*	*III*	*IV*	*V*	*VI*	*VII*	*VIII*	*IX*
Non - Scheduled Tribe																			
I. Cultivation	30	28	-	-	-	-	01	-	-	01	03	02	04	-	-	02	-	-	-
II. Agril. Labour	-	-	-	-	-	-	-	-	-	-	-	-	-	-	-	-	-	-	-
III. Non-Agril. Labour	04	03	-	01	-	-	-	-	-	-	-	-	-	-	-	-	-	-	-
IV. Petty Business	02	02	-	-	-	-	-	-	-	-	-	-	01	-	-	-	-	-	-
V. Animal Husbandry	-	-	-	-	-	-	-	-	-	-	-	-	-	-	-	-	-	-	-
VI. Service	03	02	-	-	-	-	-	-	-	01	02	-	-	-	-	-	-	-	-
VII. Fishing or Aquaculture	-	-	-	-	-	-	-	-	-	-	-	-	-	-	-	-	-	-	-
VIII. MFP /NTFP/ TFP collection	-	-	-	-	-	-	-	-	-	-	-	-	-	-	-	-	-	-	-
IX. Others*	11	03	01	-	-	-	01	-	01	05	02	-	02	-	-	-	-	-	02

of persons engaged themselves with this profession. Against that their father generation is concerned it has been observed that 3 persons are having cultivation followed by one engaged agricultural labour and two persons are non-agricultural labour. So far petty business is concerned nobody is found to be in this profession. Regarding animal husbandry only one respondent is found to be engaged in this profession and against that regarding father generation only one person is found to be engaged in agricultural labour. Regarding others profession with reference to the respondent the total 7 persons engaged themselves in this profession. Against that regarding father generation the majority of 6 nos. of persons engaged in agricultural labour followed by one person engaged in cultivation. Regarding respondents son only one person is found to be engaged in agricultural labour. In the respect of non-scheduled tribe community generation wise the majority of 30 respondents who are found to be engaged themselves in cultivation followed by their father's generation the majority of 28 persons and involved in some profession and each one is found to be involved in occupation like service and others. In the case of son's generation the majority of 4 persons are involved in non-agricultural labour followed by 3 persons involved in cultivation and each two persons are engaged themselves in agricultural labour and in service. In the case of respondent the 4 nos. of persons are found to be engaged in non-agricultural labour followed by their father generation 3 persons are found to be engaged in cultivation and one person engaged in non-agricultural labour. Again in the respondent category 2 nos. of persons are found to be engaged in petty business. Against to that there father generation 2 nos. of persons is found to be engaged in cultivation and in respect to their son one person is found to be engaged in non-agricultural labour. Three persons of respondent category are found to be engaged in service. Against to that in respect to their father's category two persons are found to be engaged in cultivation followed by one person engaged in other category and in respect to their son two persons are found to be engaged in cultivation. Lastly the 11 nos. of persons in the respondent category are found to be engaged in others category. Against that in respect to their fathers category 3 nos. of persons are followed by 5 nos. of persons are found to be engaged in other category and each one is found to be engaged in agricultural labour, animal husbandry and collection of forest produce. In respect of son's category each two persons are found to be engaged in cultivation, non-agricultural labour and others category. From the above table generation wise no such type of occupational mobility has been noticed.

Table 4.1.6 shows the size of land holding of the sample households. With reference to scheduled tribe communities the majority of 14 persons are having land up to 0.49 followed by 13 persons are found to be landless, 6 persons possessed land 4.01 and above followed by 5 persons who possessed land 0.50 – 1.00, each 3 persons are having land between 1.01 – 1.50 and 3.01 – 3.50 and finally each 2 persons are having land between 2.51 – 3.00 and 3.51 – 4.00. In respect to non-scheduled tribe communities the majority of 10 persons are having land in between 0.50 – 1.00 followed by 8 persons who possessed land between 1.01 - 1.50, 7 persons possessed land between 2.01 – 2.50, 6 persons are having land between 4.01 and above, 3 persons are having land between 3.01 – 3.50, 4 persons are having land between 1.51 – 2.00, 2 persons possessed land between 2.51 – 3.00, one person possess land between 3.51 – 4.00 and 4 persons are found to be land less. No of landless was found more among the scheduled tribe communities.

Table 4.1.7 A. gives detail about sources of income of the sample households. In the case of scheduled tribe community it has been noticed that source from agriculture out of total 34 households the majority of 15 nos. of households are having annual income of Rs. up to 2400 followed by 9 persons whose annual income of Rs. 2401 – 5400, 4 persons are having annual income of Rs. 5401 – 8400, each 2 persons are having annual income of Rs. 11401 – 14400 and Rs. 21401 and above and each one is having annual income of Rs. 8401 – 11400 and Rs. 17401 to 21400. Source from agricultural labour out of total 46 households the majority of 14 persons whose annual income of Rs. 2401 – 5400 followed by 11 persons are having annual income of Rs. up to 2400, 7 persons annual income of Rs. 5401 – 8400, 9 persons annual income of Rs. 11401 – 14400 and 5 persons annual income of Rs. 8401 – 11400. From the source like non-agricultural labour the majority of 19 persons whose annual income of Rs. up to 2400 followed by 5 persons whose annual income of Rs. 2401 – 5400, 4 persons annual income of Rs. 5401 – 8400 and each one is having annual income of Rs.8401-11400 and Rs.17401-21400. Only 2 persons' annual income of Rs.21401 and above from the source like service only. From the source like business it has been noticed that each one is having their

Table—4.1.6 Size of Land Holding of The Sample Households of Ranibandh Block in The District of Bankura

Community	*Size of Land (in Acres)*										*Total no of surveyed households*
	*Landless**	*Up to 0.49*	*0.50-1.00*	*1.01-1.50*	*1.51-2.00*	*2.01-2.50*	*2.51-3.00*	*3.01-3.50*	*3.51-4.00*	*4.01 +*	
Scheduled Tribes	13	14	05	03	01	03	02	01	02	06	50
Non-scheduled Tribes	04	05	10	08	04	07	02	03	01	06	50
Total	17	19	15	11	05	10	13	04	03	12	100

Table—4.1.7 A. Sources of Income of Sample Households of Ranibandh Block in the District of Bankura

Source of Income	Community																	
	Scheduled Tribes Amount of Income (annually in Rs.)									Non-Scheduled Tribes Amount of Income (annually in Rs.)								
	Upto 2400	2401-5400	5401-8400	8401-11400	11401-14400	14401-17400	17401-21400	21401+	Total households	Upto 2400	2401-5400	5401-8400	8401-11400	11401-14400	14401-17400	17401-21400	21401+	Total house-holds
Agriculture	15	09	04	01	02	-	01	02	34	04	09	09	12	02	04	03	03	46
Agrilabour	11	14	07	05	09	-	-	-	46	05	03	02	-	01	-	-	-	11
Non-agril. labour	19	05	04	01	-	-	01	-	30	02	04	05	02	02	-	-	-	15
Service	-	-	-	-	-	-	-	02	02	-	-	-	-	-	-	01	06	07
Business	-	01	-	-	01	-	-	-	02	02	03	-	-	01	-	-	-	06
A. Husbandry	21	01	-	-	-	-	-	-	22	15	02	01	-	-	-	-	-	18
Fishery	-	-	-	-	-	-	-	-	-	01	-	-	-	-	-	-	-	01
Collection of F. produce	11	32	02	-	-	-	-	-	45	27	17	03	01	-	-	-	-	48
Others*	02	07	02	01	-	-	01	-	13	02	05	05	01	-	-	-	-	13

'others' includes pottery, driving, carpentary, bonded labour, private tution.

annual income of Rs. 2401-5400 and Rs.11401-14400. From the animal husbandry the majority of 21 persons whose annual income of Rs. up 2400/= and only one person whose annual income of Rs. 2401 – 5400. From collection of forest produce the majority of 32 persons whose annual income of Rs. 2401 – 5400 followed by 11 persons whose annual income of Rs. up to 2400/= and 2 persons whose annual income of Rs. 5401 – 8400. From the source like others the 7 persons whose annual income of Rs. 2401 – 5400 followed by 2 each whose annual income of Rs. up to 2400/= and Rs. 5401 – 8400 and each one whose annual income of Rs. 8401 – 11400 and Rs. 17401 – 21400. In the case of non-scheduled tribe community from the source like agriculture the majority of 12 persons whose annual income of Rs. 8401 – 11400 followed by each 9 persons whose annual income of Rs. 2401 – 5400 and 5401 – 8400, each 4 persons whose annual income of Rs. up to 2400/ and Rs. 4401 – 17400, each 3 persons whose annual income of Rs. 17401 – 21400 and Rs. 21401 and above and 2 persons whose annual income of Rs. 11401 – 1400. Next from the source like agricultural labour out of total 11 households the majority of 5 persons whose annual income of Rs. up to 2400/ followed by 3 persons whose annual income of Rs. 2401 – 5400, 2 persons whose annual income of Rs. 5401 – 8400 and only 1 person who is having annual income of Rs. 11401 – 14400. From the source like non-agricultural labour the majority of 5 persons whose annual income of Rs. 5401 – 8400 followed by 4 persons whose annual income of Rs. 2401 – 5400 and each 2 persons are having annual income of Rs. up to 2400/, Rs. 8401 – 11400 and Rs. 11401 – 14400. From the source like service the majority of 6 persons whose annual income of Rs. 21401 and above and 1 person who is having annual income of Rs. 17401 – 21400. From the business the 3 persons whose annual income of Rs. 2401 – 5400 followed by 2 persons whose annual income of Rs. up to 2400/ and only 1 person who is having annual income of Rs. 11401 – 14400. From the source like animal husbandry the majority of 15 persons whose annual income of Rs. up to 2400/ followed by 2 persons whose annual income of Rs. 2401 – 5400 and only 1 person who is having annual income of Rs. 5401 – 8400. From the fishery only one person whose annual income of Rs. up to 2400/=. From the source like collection of forest produce the majority of 27 persons whose annual income of Rs. up to 2400/ followed by 17 persons whose annual income of Rs. 2401 – 5400, 3 persons whose annual income of Rs. 5401 – 8400 and only one person who is having annual income of Rs. 8401 – 11400. Finally, from the source like others the majority of each 5 persons whose annual income of Rs. 2401 – 5400 and Rs. 5401 – 8400 and only one person who is having annual income of Rs. 8401 – 11400.

The table 4.1.7B gives detail about the distribution of income pattern of the surveyed households community wise. In the case of scheduled tribe communities out of total 50 surveyed households the majority of 14 persons whose annual income range of Rs. 14401 – 17400 followed by 13 persons who belongs to the income range of Rs. 11401 – 14400, 11 persons annual income of Rs. 21401 and above, 6 persons whose annual income of Rs. 17401 – 21400, 4 persons whose annual income of Rs. 8401 – 11400 and 2 persons whose annual income of Rs. 5401 – 8400. In the case of total 50 surveyed households of non-scheduled tribe communities the majority of 19 persons whose annual income of Rs. 21401 and above followed by 11 persons whose annual income of Rs. 17401 – 21400. 7 persons annual income of Rs. 8401 – 11400, 6 persons annual income of Rs. 11401 – 14400, 4 persons annual income of Rs. 1401 – 17400 and 3 persons annual income of Rs. 5401 – 8400.

Table 4.1.8A deals with the pattern of household expenditure of the surveyed households. In the case of scheduled tribe communities out of 50 surveyed households towards food the majority of 12 households who used to spend annually Rs. 3401 – 5400 followed by 10 who spends annually of Rs. 5401 – 7400, 9 spends annually Rs. 7401 – 9400, each 7 nos. spend annually of Rs. 9401 – 11400 and Rs. 11401 – 13400 and only 5 nos. who spend annually of Rs. 1401 – 3400. Towards clothing and footwear the majority of 31 persons who spends annually of Rs. 401 – 1400 followed by 13 nos. who spends annually Rs. 1401 – 3400, 4 persons spends Rs. up to 400/= and only 2 persons who spends annually of Rs. 3401 – 5400. Towards health the majority of 30 persons who spends annually of Rs. 401 –1400 followed by 10 persons who spends annually of Rs. up to 400/= and each one who spends annually of Rs. 5401 – 7400 and Rs. 11401 – 13400. The majority of 8 persons who spends annually of Rs. up to 410/= towards education followed by 4 persons who spends of Rs. 401 –1400, 2 persons spends annually of Rs. 1401 – 3400 and 1 person who spend annually of Rs. 11401 – 13400. Next towards housing the majority of 25 persons who spends annually of Rs. up to 400/= followed by 22 persons who spends annually of Rs. 401 – 1400. Towards rituals the 5 persons who spends

Table—4.1.7 B. Distribution of Income Pattern of The Sample Households of Ranibandh Block in The District of Bankura

Community	Amount of Total Income (In Rs.)							Total no. of Household
	Upto 5400	5401-8400	8401-11400	11401-14400	14401-17400	17401-21400	21401+	
Scheduled Tribes	-	02	04	13	14	06	11	50
Non- Scheduled Tribes	-	03	07	06	04	11	19	50
Total	-	05	11	19	18	17	30	100

Table—4.1.8 A. Pattern of Household Expenditure (Annually) of the Sample Houdeholds of Ranibandh Block in the District of Bankura

Item of the Expen-diture	Community																	
	Scheduled Tribes									Non-Scheduled Tribe								
	Upto 400	401 -1400	1401-3400	3401-5400	5401-7400	7401-9400	9401-11400	11401-13400	13401+	Upto 400	401-1400	1401-3400	3401-5400	5401-7400	7401-9400	9401-11400	11401-13400	13401+
Food	-	-	05	12	10	09	07	07	-	-	-	-	02	13	11	11	04	09
Clothing & Footwear	04	31	13	02	-	-	-	-	-	02	18	27	03	-	-	-	-	-
Health	10	30	-	-	01	-	-	01	-	12	33	05	-	-	-	-	-	-
Education	08	04	02	-	-	-	-	01	-	06	14	05	03	01	-	-	-	01
Housing	25	22	-	-	-	-	-	-	-	06	34	10	-	-	-	-	-	-
Rituals	05	03	-	-	-	-	-	-	-	03	10	-	-	-	-	-	-	
Social Functions	09	40	01	-	-	-	-	-	-	08	34	08	-	-	-	-	-	-
Fuel & Lighting	-	21	22	05	-	-	-	-	-	05	25	11	08	01	-	-	-	-
Smoking & Alcohol	21	25	-	-	-	-	-	-	-	03	26	02	01	-	-	-	-	-

annually of Rs. up to 400/= followed by 3 persons who spends annually of Rs. 401 – 1400. Next towards social functions the majority of 40 persons who spends annually of Rs. 401 –1400 followed by 9 persons who spends annually of Rs. up to 400/= and only 1 persons who spend annually of Rs. 1401 – 3400. Next the majority of 22 persons who spends annually of Rs. 1401-3400 followed by 21 persons who spends annually of Rs. 401 –1400, 5 persons who spends annually of Rs. 3401 –5400 and only 2 persons who spends annually of Rs. up to 400/=. Finally, towards smoking and alcohol the majority of 25 persons who spends annually of Rs. 401 – 1400 and 21 persons who spends annually of Rs. up to 400/=. In the case of non-scheduled tribe communities out of total 50 surveyed households the majority of 13 persons who spends annually of Rs. 5401 – 7400 followed by each 11 persons who spends annually of Rs. 7401 – 9400 and Rs. 9401 – 11400, 9 persons who spends of Rs. 13401 and above, 4 persons who spends annually of Rs. 11401 – 13400 and only 2 persons who spends annually Rs. 3401 – 5400. Next towards clothing and footwear the majority of 27 persons who spends annually of Rs. 1401 – 3400 followed by 18 persons who spends annually of Rs. 401 – 1400, 3 persons who spends annually of Rs. 3401 – 5400 and 2 persons who spends annually of Rs. up to 400/=. Towards health the majority of 33 persons who spends annually of Rs. 401 – 1400 followed by 12 persons who spends annually of Rs. up to 400/= and 5 persons who spends annually of Rs. 1401-3400. The majority of 14 persons who spends annually of Rs. 401 – 1400 towards education followed by 6 persons who spends annually of Rs. up to 400/=, 5 persons spends of Rs. 1401 – 3400, 3 persons who spends annually of Rs. 3401 – 5400 and only 1 person who spend annually of Rs. 5401 – 7400. Next towards housing the majority of 34 persons who spends annually of Rs. 401 – 1400 followed by 10 persons who spends annually of Rs. 1401 – 3400 and only 6 persons who spends annually of Rs. up to 400/=. Towards rituals, the majority of 10 persons who spends annually of Rs. 401 – 1400 and 3 persons who spends annually of Rs. up to 400/=. Towards social functions the majority of 34 persons who spends annually of Rs. 401 – 1400 followed by each 8 who spends of Rs. up to 400/= and Rs. 1401 – 3400. Towards fuel and lighting the majority of 25 persons who spends annually of Rs. 401 – 1400 followed by 11 persons who spends of Rs. 1401 – 3400, 8 persons who spends annually of Rs. 3401 – 5400, 5 persons who spends annually of Rs. up to 400/= and one person who spends annually of Rs. 5401 – 7400. Finally, towards smoking and alcohol the majority of 26 persons who spends annually of Rs. 401 – 1400 followed by 3 persons who spends annually of Rs. up to 400/=, 2 persons who spends of Rs. 1401 – 3400 and only 1 person who spends of Rs. 3401 – 5400.

Table 4.1.8B gives detail distribution of household expenditure of the surveyed households. In the case of scheduled tribe community out of total 50 households the majority of 31 persons whose annual expenditure of Rs. 13401 and above followed by 8 persons whose expenditure range of Rs. 11401- 13400, 5 persons expenditure range of Rs. 7401 – 9400, 4 persons whose expenditure range of Rs. 9401 – 11400 and only 2 persons whose annual expenditure range of Rs. 5401 – 7400. In the case of non-scheduled tribe community the majority of 33 persons whose annual expenditure range of Rs. 13401 and above followed by 7 persons whose annual expenditure of Rs. 941 –11400 and each 5 persons whose annual expenditure range of Rs. 7401 – 9400 and Rs. 11401 – 13400.

Table 4.1.9A gives detail pattern of expenditure on agricultural per suit of the sample households. In the case of scheduled tribe community towards agricultural implements the only 2 persons who spends annually of Rs. up to 500/=. Towards ploughing the majority 27 persons spends annually of Rs. 500/= followed by 5 persons who spends of Rs. 501 –1000, 4 persons spends of Rs. 1001 – 1500 and only 1 person spend of Rs. 1501 – 2000. The majority of 31 persons who spends annually of Rs. up to 500/ = towards purchasing of seeds followed by 1 person who spends of Rs. 501 – 1000. Towards sowing the majority of 30 persons who spends annually of Rs. up to 500/= followed by 6 persons who spends of Rs. 501 – 1000 and only 1 person who spends of Rs. 1001 – 1500. Towards wedding the majority of 25 persons who spends up to Rs. 500/= and 2 persons who spend of Rs. 501 – 1000. Next the majority of 10 persons who spends annually of Rs. up to 500/= towards fertilizers 8 pesticides and only 1 person who spends of Rs. 501 – 1000. No body is found to be spending any amount towards irrigation. For harvesting the majority of 28 persons who spends annually of Rs. up to 500/= followed by each 4 persons who spends of Rs. 501 – 1000 and Rs. 1001 – 1500 and only 1 person who spend of Rs. 1501 – 2000. In the case of non-scheduled tribe community towards agricultural implements only one person who spends annually of Rs. 3501 and above. Towards ploughing the majority of 24 persons who spends annually of Rs. up to 500/= followed by 14 persons who spends of Rs. 501

Table—4.1.8 B. Distribution of Household Expenditure (Annually) of the Sample Houdeholds of Ranibandh Block in the District of Bankura

Community	Amount of Total Expenditure (In Rs.)						
	Upto 5400	5401-7400	7401-9400	9401-11400	11401-13400	13401 +	Total no. of Household
Scheduled Tribes	-	02	05	04	08	31	50
Non- Scheduled Tribes	-	-	05	07	05	33	50
Total	-	**02**	**10**	**11**	**13**	**64**	**100**

Table—4.1.9 A. Pattern of Expenditure (Annually) on Agricultural Pursuit of The Sample Houdeholds of Ranibandh Block in The District of Bankura

Item of the Expenditure	Community															
	Scheduled Tribes								Non- Scheduled Tribes							
	Upto 500	501-1000	1001-1500	1501-2000	2001-2500	2501-3000	3001-3500	3501+	Upto 500	501-1000	1001-1500	1501-2000	2001-2500	2501-3000	3001-3500	3501+
Agricultural Implements	02	-	-	-	-	-	-	-	-	-	-	-	-	-	-	01
Ploughing	27	05	04	01	-	-	-	-	24	14	03	02	03	-	-	-
Purchasing of Seeds	31	01	-	-	-	-	-	-	43	03	-	-	-	-	-	-
Sowing	30	06	01	-	-	-	-	-	28	11	02	02	01	02	-	-
Weeding	25	02	-	-	-	-	-	-	34	01	-	-	-	-	-	-
Fertilizers & pesticides	10	01	-	-	-	-	-	-	18	12	04	-	-	-	-	-
Irrigation	-	-	-	-	-	-	-	-	15	01	-	-	-	-	-	-
Harvesting	28	04	04	01	-	-	-	-	21	12	07	03	01	01	01	-

– 1000, each 3 persons who spends of Rs. 1001 – 1500 and Rs. 2001 – 2500 and 2 persons who spends of Rs. 1501 – 2000. Next the majority of 43 persons who spends of Rs up to 500/= towards purchasing of seeds and only 3 persons who spends of Rs. 501 – 1000. Towards sowing the majority of 28 persons who spends of Rs. up to 500/= followed by 11 persons who spends of Rs. 501 – 1000 and each 2 persons who spends annually of Rs. 1001 – 1500, Rs. 1501 – 2000 and Rs. 25001 – 3000 and only 1 person who spends of Rs. 2001 – 2500. Towards weeding the majority of 34 persons who spends of Rs. up to 500/= and only 1 person who spends of Rs. 501 – 1000. Towards fertilizers and pesticides the majority of 18 persons who spends annually of Rs. up to 500/= followed by 12 persons who spends of Rs. 501 – 1000 and only 4 persons who spends of Rs. 1001 – 1500. For irrigation in this community the majority of 15 persons who spends of Rs. up to 500/= and 1 person who spends of Rs. 501 – 1000. Lastly towards harvesting the majority of 21 persons who spends of Rs. up to 500/= followed by 12 persons who spends of Rs. 501 – 1000, 7 persons spends of Rs. 1001 – 1500, 3 persons spends of Rs. 1501 – 2000 and each 1 persons who spends of Rs. 2001 – 2500, Rs. 2501 – 3000 and Rs. 3001 – 3500.

Table 4.1.9B deals with the distribution of expenditure range annually of sample households on agricultural pursuits. In the case of scheduled tribe community the majority of 16 persons out of 37 total households who used to do agriculture are found to be spend annually of Rs. up to 500/= followed by 10 persons who spends annually of Rs. 501 – 1000, each 4 persons who spends of Rs. 1001 – 1500, Rs. 3501 and above, 2 persons spends of Rs. 3001 – 3500 and only 1 persons who spends of Rs. 1501 – 2000. In the case of non-scheduled tribe communities out of total 46 households the majority of 18 persons who spends of Rs. 3501 and above followed by 9 persons who spends of Rs. 501 – 1000, 6 persons who spends of Rs. 2001 – 2500, each 4 persons who spends of Rs. 1001 – 1500 and Rs. 2501 – 3000 and 3 persons who spends of Rs. 1501 – 2000 and 2 persons who spends of Rs. up to 500/=.

Table 4.1.10 gives detail about the nature of indebtedness among the sample households. In the case of scheduled tribe communities regarding debt it has been noted that there was no ancestor debt but 13 nos. of households who borrowed the loan amount from various sources for different purposes. From the table it has been noted the loan amount of 13 persons is Rs. up to 1000/=. Out of 13 the majority of each 6 persons

Table—4.1.9 B. Distribution of Expenditure (Annually) on Agricultural Pursuit of The Sample Households of Ranibandh Block in The District of Bankura

Community	Amount of Total expenditure (in Rs.)								Total House holds
	Upto 500	501-1000	1001-1500	1501-2000	2001-2500	2501-3000	3001-3500	3501+	
Scheduled Tribe	16	10	04	01	-	-	02	04	37
Non- Scheduled Tribe	02	09	04	03	06	04	-	18	46
Total	18	19	08	04	06	04	02	22	83

Table—4.1.10. Nature of Indebtedness among the Sample Households of Ranibandh Block in the District of Bankura

Community	Amount of borrowing	Source of borrowing			Purpose of borrowing					Repayment Status		Security			Debt	
		Neighbours	Local Traders	Friends & Relatives	Purchasing of food materials	Life cycle ceremonies	To pay bride price	Medical treatment	Others*	Due – fully	Due – partially	Land	Ornaments	Others	Ancestor	Respondent
Scheduled Tribes	Up to 1000	06	01	06	03	-	-	07	03	11	02	02	-	-	-	13
	1001 - 2000	-	-	-	-	-	-	-	-	-	-	-	-	-	-	-
	2001 - 3000	-	-	-	-	-	-	-	-	-	-	-	-	-	-	-
	3001 - 4000	-	-	-	-	-	-	-	-	-	-	-	-	-	-	-
	4001 – 5000	-	-	-	-	-	-	-	-	-	-	-	-	-	-	-
	5001 – 6000	-	-	-	-	-	-	-	-	-	-	-	-	-	-	-
	Sub-total	**06**	**01**	**06**	**03**	-	-	**07**	**03**	**11**	**02**	**02**	-	-	-	**13**

contd.......

Community	Amount of borrowing	Source of borrowing			Purpose of borrowing					Repayment Status		Security			Debt	
		Neighbours	Local Traders	Friends & Relatives	Purchasing of food materials	Life cycle ceremonies	To pay bride price	Medical treatment	Others*	Due – fully	Due – partially	Land	Ornaments	Others	Ancestor	Respondent
Non-Scheduled Tribes	Up to 1000	02	02	01	01	01	-	02	01	05	-	-	-	-	-	05
	1001 - 2000	04	-	-	03	-	01	-	-	04	-	02	-	-	-	04
	2001 - 3000	01	01	-	01	01	-	-	-	02	-	01	-	-	-	02
	3001 - 4000	-	-	-	-	-	-	-	-	-	-	-	-	-	-	-
	4001 – 5000	01	-	-	-	-	-	-	01	-	01	-	-	-	-	01
	5001 – 6000	02	-	-	-	-	01	-	01	01	01	01	-	-	-	02
	Sub-total	**10**	**03**	**01**	**05**	**02**	**02**	**02**	**03**	**12**	**02**	**04**	-	-	-	**14**
Total		**16**	**04**	**07**	**08**	**02**	**02**	**09**	**06**	**23**	**04**	**06**	-	-	-	**27**

* 'others' includes housing, agriculture, purchasing of bullocks and judicial purposes.

borrowed the amount from the source like neighbours, friends and relatives followed by 1 person who borrowed the amount from local traders. The majority of 7 persons who took the loan amount for medical purpose followed by each 3 persons who borrowed the amount for purchasing of food materials and others. Out of total 13 loanees the majority of 11 persons who did not pay at all followed by 2 persons who partly paid. Regarding security only 2 persons mortgaged their land for getting loan amount. In the case of non-scheduled tribe community altogether 14 nos. of persons borrowed the amount. Out of 14 the majority of 5 persons whose borrowed amount is up to Rs. 1000/= Out of 5 each 2 persons who took the loan amount from the source like neighbours and local traders followed by one who took the amount from friends and relatives. Each 3 persons borrowed the amount for the purpose like purchasing of food materials, life cycle ceremonies and other. All the 5 persons did not pay the loan amount. There are 4 nos. of persons whose borrowed amount of Rs. 1001 – 2000 from the source like neighbours. Out of 4, 3 persons took the loan for the purpose like purchasing food materials and only 1 person who took the loan for bride price. The total 4 persons did not pay the loan amount. Only 2 persons out of 4 mortgaged their land. The loan amount of 2 persons is Rs. 2001 – 3000. Out of two each one took the loan from the source like neighbours and local traders. Each one took the loan for the purpose like purchasing of food material and life cycle ceremonies. All the 2 persons did not pay the loan amount and one person mortgaged their land. Next one person whose loan amount is Rs. 4001 – 5000 from the source like neighbours for the purpose like others. And the person concerned paid the amount partially. Finally, the last 2 persons out of 14 whose loan amount of Rs. 5001 – 6000 from the source like neighbours for the purpose like bride price and others. And out of 2 persons each one is found to be defaulter and paid partially. From the analysis of this table it is point to be note that out of total 27 loanees the majority of 23 persons who did not repay the amount, 4 persons paid it partially.

Table 4.1.11 gives detail about the development loan received by the sample households from various sources like Nationalised Bank, Gramin Bank and co-operative societies. In the case of scheduled tribe communities out of total 50 surveyed households the total 8 persons are found to be received loan for various purposes like agriculture, business and animal husbandry. Out of 8 the 2 persons are found to receive loan of Rs. up to

Table—4.1.11. Loan Received by The Sample Households from Various Sources * of Ranibandh Block in The District of Bankura

Type of Loan	Community																					
	Scheduled Tribe											Non - Scheduled Tribe										
	Loan Amount				Loan Repayment			Security		Loan taken by		Loan Amount				Loan Repayment			Security		Loan taken by	
	upto 3000	3001- 6000	6001 - 9000	9001 +	Paid fully	Paid partially	Due totally	Land	Ornaments	Respondent	Ancestor	upto 3000	3001- 6000	6001 – 9000	9001 +	Paid fully	Paid partially	Due totally	Land	Ornaments	Respondent	Ancestor
Agri-culture	02	-	-	-	-	-	02	-	-	02	-	-	01	-	-	-	01	-	-	-	01	-
Busi-ness	01	02	-	-	-	-	03	-	-	03	-	07	04	01	01	01	02	10	-	-	13	-
Animal Hus-bandry	03	-	-	-	-	-	03	-	-	03	-	-	-	-	01	-	01	-	-	-	-	01
Total	06	02	-	-	-	-	08	-	-	08	-	07	05	01	02	01	04	10	-	-	14	01

3000/= for agricultural. And the persons concerned did not repay the loan. For business purposes one person is found to receive loan of Rs. up to 3000/= followed by 2 persons who received the loan amount of Rs. 3001 – 6000. They are also found to be defaulter. Another 3 persons who received the loan amount of Rs. up to 3000/= for the purpose of animal husbandry and did not repay the loan amount. Altogether total 8 persons who received the loan amount for various purposes are found to be defaulter. In the case of non – scheduled tribe community there are altogether 15 persons are found to receive the loan out of 50 surveyed households. Out of 15 loanees the 14 persons are respondents and 1 person is found to be their ancestor. Out of 14 the majority of 7 persons who took the loan amount of Rs. up to 3000/= followed by 4 persons who received the loan amount of Rs. 3001 – 6000, each two persons who received the loan amount of Rs. 6001 – 9000, and Rs.9001 and above. All the persons used the loan amount of business purposes. Among those only one is found to be paid fully followed by 2 persons who paid partially and 10 persons did not pay at all. Among their ancestor 1 person is found to receive the loan of Rs. 9001 and above for the purpose of animal husbandry and paid the amount partially.

II

Dhupguri Block of District Jalpaiguri

Table 4.2.1 gives detail about age-sex composition of the sample households. From the table it has been noticed that in the case of scheduled tribe community there are 240 population of out 50 surveyed households. Out of total 240 there are male population consists of 117 followed by female population 123. In the case of non –scheduled tribe communities the total number of population is 260 out of 50 surveyed households. Out of total 260, male population consists of 144 followed by female population 116. Age and sex composition wise in the case of scheduled tribe communities in the age group between 0 –4 there 10 males followed by 16 females. In the age group of 5 – 14 there are 29 males and 26 females. Next in the age group of 15 – 44 there are 57 males and 60 females. In the age group between 45 –59 there are 13 males and 10 females. Lastly in the age group between 60 and above there are 8 males and 11 females. With reference to non-scheduled tribe community in the age group between 0 – 4 there are 9 male members followed by 12 female members. There are 46

Table—4.2.1. Age-sex composition of the sample households of Dhupguri Block in the District of Jalpaiguri

Community (No. of surveyed households)	Age Group (yrs.)										Total Population		
	0-4		5-14		15-44		45-59		60+		Population		Total (%)
	M	F	M	F	M	F	M	F	M	F	M	F	
Scheduled Tribes (50)	10	16	29	26	57	60	13	10	08	11	117	123	240
Non-Scheduled Tribes (50)	09	12	46	29	63	58	18	12	08	05	144	116	260
Total	19	28	75	55	120	118	31	22	16	16	261	239	500
(%)	07.28	11.71	28.73	23.01	45.98	49.38	11.88	09.20	06.13	06.69	100	99.99	99.99

male and 29 female members in the age group between 5 – 14. In the age group between 15 – 44 there are 63 male and 58 female members. There are 18 male and 12 female members are found to be in the age group between 45-59. Lastly, in the age group of 60 and above there are 8 male and 5 female members.

Table 4.2.2. gives detail about the education background of the sample households. Educational background of persons has been considered above 6 years of age onwards. In the case of scheduled tribe community out of total 105 male populations there are 44 male members are found to be illiterate followed by 64 female illiterates out of total 105 female populations. There are 4 male members and 1 female member is found to be functionally literate. So far formal education is concerned in the class between I – IV, there are 26 male and 25 female members followed by in the class between V – VIII, there 24 male and 14 female members, in the class between IX – X, there are 6 male and 1 female members in the class between XI – XII, there are only one male member. No body is found to be in graduate and others level. In the case of non-scheduled tribe community out of 134 male and 103 female members there are 29 male and 47 female members are found to be illiterate and only one female member is found to be functionally literate. Regarding formal education in the class between I – IV there are 54 male and 30 female members followed by in the class of V – VIII there are 35 male and 19 female members, 15 male and 5 female persons are in the class of IX – X, one female person is found to be in class XI – XII and finally 1 male member is found to be in graduate level.

Table 4.2.3 deals with the marital status of the population of the surveyed households community wise. In the case of scheduled tribe community 39 male and 42 female members are found to be unmarried in the age group up to 14. In the age group between 15 – 29 there are 14 male and 9 female members are found to be unmarried followed by 19 male and 25 female members are married. In the age group between 30- 44 there are one male and one female member who are found to be unmarried followed by 23 male and 25 female members to be married and only 2 female members are widow. In the age group between 45 – 59 there are no body found to be unmarried followed by 12 male and 7 female members are found to be married and only 3 female members are widow. Lastly, in the age group 60 years and above 9 male and 5 female members are found to be married one followed by 6 female members are found to be widow. With reference to

Table—4.2.2. Level of Education of the sample households of Dhupguri Block in the District of Jalpaiguri

Community (No of surveyed households)	Illiterate		Functional Literate		Formal Education										Population (above 6 yrs.)	
					I - IV		V - VIII		IX - X		XI - XII		Graduate or Others			
	M	F	M	F	M	F	M	F	M	F	M	F	M	F	M	F
Scheduled Tribes (50)	44	64	04	01	26	25	24	14	06	01	01	-	-	-	105	105
Non-scheduled Tribes (50)	29	47	-	01	54	30	35	19	15	05	-	01	01	-	134	103
Total (% to the total population of above 6 yrs. age)	73	111	04	02	80	55	59	33	21	06	01	01	01	-	239	208
	30.54	53.36	1.67	0.96	33.47	26.44	24.69	15.86	08.79	02.88	0.42	0.49	0.42	-	100.00	99.99

Functional Literate : Who knows reading, writing and Arithmetic.

Table—4.2.3. Martial Status of the Population of the sample households of Dhupguri Block in the District of Jalpaiguri

Community (No of surveyed household)	Age- group (In years)	Marital Status								Total	
		Unmarried		Married		Widower/Widow		Separated			
		Male	Female	Male	Female	Male	Female	Male	Female	Male	Female
Scheduled Tribe (50)	Up to 14	39	42	-	-	-	-	-	-	39	42
	15 – 29	14	09	19	25	-	-	-	-	33	34
	30 – 44	01	01	23	25	-	02	-	-	24	28
	45 – 59	-	-	12	07	-	03	-	-	12	10
	60 +	-	-	09	05	-	06	-	-	09	11
	Sub-total	**54**	**52**	**63**	**62**	-	**11**	-	-	**117**	**125**
Non – Scheduled Tribe (50)	Up to 14	56	43	-	-	-	-	-	-	55	43
	15 – 29	21	08	11	27	-	-	-	-	32	35
	30 – 44	04	-	25	24	01	-	-	-	30	24
	45 – 59	-	-	17	08	01	04	-	-	18	12
	60 +	-	-	05	02	02	03	01	-	07	05
	Sub-total	**81**	**51**	**58**	**61**	**04**	**07**	**01**	-	**142**	**119**
TOTAL		**135**	**103**	**113**	**123**	**04**	**18**	**01**	-	**259**	**244**

non-scheduled tribe community up to 14 yrs age there are 56 male and 43 female members are found to be unmarried. In the age group between 15 – 29 there are 21 male and 8 female members are found to be unmarried followed by 11 male and 27 female members are found to be married. Next in the age group between 30 – 44 only 4 male members are found to be unmarried followed by 25 male and 24 female members are found to be married one. In the age group between 45 – 59 no body is found to be unmarried one followed by 17 male and 8 female members are found to be married one. 1 male is widower and 4 female members are widow. Lastly, in the age group of 60 and above there are 5 male and 2 female members are found to be married one followed by 2 male members who are found to be widower and 3 female members are widow.

Table 4.2.4 gives detail regarding occupational distribution of the sample households. In the case of scheduled tribe communities there are altogether 68 male and 66 female members are happened to be fall under working group. Out of those there are each 2 male and female persons are agricultural labour followed by 11 male and 4 female members are found to be non-agricultural labour, 42 male and 40 female members are having cultivation, 3 male members are having petty business, 11 female members are found to be involved in animal husbandry, 5 male members are in service, 1 male member is found to be engaged in fishing, 1 male and 9 female members are involved in the process of collection of minor forest produce and 3 members are found to be engaged in others occupation. In the case of non-scheduled tribe community out of 81 male and 61 female working force there are 13 female and 9 male members are found to be agricultural labours followed by 13 male and 1 female members are involved in non-agricultural labour, the majority of 43 male and 41 female members are having cultivation, 10 male members are having petty business, 2 female members are engaged with animal husbandry, 1 male member is in service, no body is found to be engaged in fishing, 4 female members and, male member are involved in the process of collection of minor forest produce and 4 male members are involved in others occupation.

The table 4.2.5 deals with occupational mobility of the sample households of the surveyed block. Respondent wise it has been observed that the 38 persons whose major occupation is cultivation. Against the respondent their father generation is concerned the majority of 37 persons are having cultivation and 1 person was found to be non-agricultural

Table—4.2.4. Martial Status of the Population of the sample households of Dhupguri Block in the District of Jalpaiguri

Comm-unity (No of surveyed household	Type of Occupation *																			
	Agril. Labour		Non-agril. Labour		Cultivation		Petty Business		Animal Husbandry		Service		Fishing or Aqua-culture		MFP/NTF/ TFP Collection		Others**		Total Working Population	
	M	F	M	F	M	F	M	F	M	F	M	F	M	F	M	F	M	F	M	F
Scheduled Tribe (50)	02	02	11	04	42	40	03	-	-	11	05	-	01	-	01	09	03	-	68	66
Non-Scheduled Tribes (50)	09	13	13	01	43	41	10	-	-	02	01	-	-	-	01	04	04	-	81	61
	11	15	24	05	85	81	13	-	-	13	06	-	01	-	02	13	07	-	149	127
Total (%)	07.38	11.81	16.11	03.94	57.05	63.77	08.72	-	-	10.24	04.03	-	0.67	-	01.34	10.24	04.70	-	100.00	100.0

* Working force : 15-59 age group

** Other include: Priest, Tuition, Carpentry, Kobiraj, Forest guard.

Table—4.2.5. Occupational Mobility of the sample households of Dhupguri Block in the District of Jalpaiguri

Occupation of the Respondent		Occupation of the Respondent's Father									Occupation of the Respondent's Son								
		I	II	III	IV	V	VI	VII	VIII	IX	I	II	III	IV	V	VI	VII	VIII	IX
Scheduled Tribe																			
I. Cultivation	38	37	-	01	--	-	-	-	-	-	02	-	03	01	-	-	-	-	-
II. Agril. Labour	-	-	-	-	-	-	-	-	-	-	-	-	-	-	-	-	-	-	-
III. Non-Agril. Labour	05	02	01	02	-	-	-	-	-	-	-	-	-	-	-	-	01	-	-
IV. Petty Business	02	02	-	-	-	-	-	-	-	-	-	-	-	-	-	-	-	-	-
V. Animal Husbandry	01	-	-	01	-	-	-	-	-	-	-	-	-	-	-	-	-	-	-
VI. Service	02	01	-	01	-	-	-	-	-	-	-	-	-	-	-	-	-	-	-
VII. Fishing or Aquaculture	-	-	-	-	-	-	-	-	-	-	-	-	-	-	-	-	-	-	-
VIII. Forest Produce collection	01	-	-	-	-	-	-	-	01	-	-	-	-	-	-	-	-	-	-
IX. Others*	01	01	-	-	-	-	-	-	-	-	-	-	-	-	-	-	-	-	-

Occupation of the Respondent		Occupation of the Respondent's Father									Occupation of the Respondent's Son								
		I	II	III	IV	V	VI	VII	VIII	IX	I	II	III	IV	V	VI	VII	VIII	IX
Non – Scheduled Tribe																			
I. Cultivation	25	23	-	01	01	-	-	-	-	-	04	01	01	01	-	-	-	-	-
II. Agril. Labour	06	01	05	-	-	-	-	-	-	-	-	-	-	-	-	-	-	-	-
III. Non-Agril. Labour	07	03	03	-	-	-	-	-	-	-	-	-	01	-	-	-	-	-	-
IV. Petty Business	08	02	03	01	03	-	-	-	-	-	01	-	-	-	-	-	-	-	-
√. Animal Husbandry	-	-	-	-	-	-	-	-	-	-	-	-	-	-	-	-	-	-	-
VI. Service	01	01	-	-	-	-	-	-	-	-	-	-	-	-	-	-	-	-	-
VII. Fishing or Aquaculture	-	-	-	-	-	-	-	-	-	-	-	-	-	-	-	-	-	-	-
VIII. MFP /NTFP/ TFP collection	-	-	-	-	-	-	-	-	-	-	-	-	-	-	-	-	-	-	-
IX. Others*	03	01	01	-	-	-	-	-	-	01	-	-	-	-	-	-	-	-	01

labour. So far their son's generation is concerned against the same respondents the majority of 3 persons who are non-agricultural labour, 2 persons are having cultivation and only one is having petty business. In the second category of occupation like agricultural labour nobody is found to be in this category. Regarding non-agricultural labour 5 respondents are found to be in this category. Against those their father generation is concerned each 2 persons are having cultivation and non-agricultural labour and only one is found to be agricultural labour. So far their son's generation is concerned only one is having fishing. In the next category of petty business the 2 nos. of respondents are having this occupation followed by their father generation the 2 nos. of persons are having same occupation. One respondent is having animal husbandry. Against the respondent next their father generation is concerned one person is found to be non-agricultural labour. In the next category of service there are 2 nos. of respondents a found to be in service followed by their father's generation it is found to each one who is having cultivation and non-agricultural labour. In the category of forest produce collection one respondent is found to be in this occupation followed by one person is happens to be father's generation is having same occupation. Finally, in the others category each one the respondent is having others occupation and the father is having cultivation. With reference to non-scheduled tribe community occupation wise firstly the 25 nos. of respondents are having cultivation followed by the 23 nos. of their father's generation are having the same occupation and each one is found to be non-agricultural labour and is having petty business. Regarding their son's occupation is concerned the majority of 4 persons are having cultivation and each one is found to be an agricultural labour, non-agricultural labour and is having petty business. In the category of agricultural labour respondent wise 6 persons are found to be in this occupation followed by their father's generation the majority of 5 persons are found to be non-agricultural labour and one is having cultivation. In the next category of non-agricultural labour 6 nos. of respondents are found to be in this category followed by their father's generation each 3 is found to be in cultivation and agricultural labour. So far there son's generation is concerned there is 1 person who is found to be non-agricultural labour. No body is involved in the category of animal husbandry. So far service is concerned each one respondent and his father is in service. Regarding occupation like fishing and collection of forest produce generation wise no body is found to be in those categories. Finally, in the category of others 3 respondents are found to be in this category followed by their father's generation each 3 nos. of persons are found to be in cultivation, agricultural labour and others. In the case of son's generation 1 person is found to be in other's category.

Table 4.2.6. deals with the size of land holding of the sample households of the surveyed block. From the table it has been noticed that in the case of scheduled tribe communities out of 50 surveyed households the majority of 27 household who possess the land between 1.01 – 1.50 acres followed by 8 persons who is having land between 2.01 – 2.50. 6 persons do not have any land. 4 persons possess land between 0.50 – 1.00, 3 person's size of land is between 2.51 – 3.00 and finally 2 persons who possess land between 1.51 – 2.00. In the case of non-scheduled tribe community out of 50 surveyed households the majority of 16 persons does not possess any amount of agricultural land followed by 9 persons who possess land between 1.01 – 1.50, followed by 8 persons whose size of land is between 2.01 – 2.50, 5 persons who possess land between 4.01 and above, 3 persons possess land is between 2.51 – 3.00, 2 person's size of land between 1.51 – 2.00 and each 3 persons are having land between up to 0.49, 3.01 – 3.50 and 3.51 – 4.00.

Table 4.2.7A gives detail about the sources of income of the surveyed households. In the case of Scheduled tribe community out of total 44 persons having agriculture as source of income the majority of 19 persons have annual income of Rs. 5401 – 8400 followed by 11 persons whose annual income of Rs. 5401 – 8400 followed by 11 persons whose income of Rs. 8401 – 11400, each 6 persons annual income of Rs. 2401 – 5400 and Rs. 11401 – 14400 and each 1 person is having annual income of Rs. up to 2400/= and Rs. 17401 – 21400. From agricultural labour the majority of 7 persons whose annual income of Rs. 2401 – 5400 followed by 5 persons who annually earns of Rs. up to 2400/= and 3 persons annual income of Rs. 5401 – 8400. Next from non-agricultural labour the majority of 8 persons whose annual income of Rs. 2401 – 5400 followed by 6 persons whose annual income of Rs. up to 2400/=, 4 persons annual income of Rs. 5401 – 8400 persons and each one is having annual income of Rs. 8401 – 11400 and Rs. 11401 – 14400. From the source like service the majority of 2 persons whose annual income of Rs. 8401 – 11400 followed by each one who is having annual income of Rs. 11401 – 14400 and Rs. 21401 and

Table—4.2.6. Size of Land Holding of the sample households of Dhupguri Block in the District of Jalpaiguri

Community	Size of Land (in Acres)										Total no of surveyed households
	Landless*	Up to 0.49	0.50-1.00	1.01-1.50	1.51-2.00	2.01-2.50	2.51-3.00	3.01-3.50	3.51-4.00	4.01 +	
Scheduled Tribes.	06	-	04	27	02	08	03	-	-	-	50
Non-scheduled Tribes	16	01	04	09	02	08	03	01	01	05	50
Total	22	01	08	36	04	16	06	01	01	05	100

* Not having agricultural land other than homestead land.

Table—4.2.7. A. Sources of Income of the sample households of Dhupguri Block in the District of Jalpaiguri

Source of Income	Community																	
	Scheduled Tribes Amount of Income (annually in Rs.)									Non-Scheduled Tribes Amount of Income (annually in Rs.)								
	Upto 2400	2401-5400	5401-8400	8401-11400	11401-14400	14401-17400	17401-21400	21401+	Total house-holds	Upto 2400	2401-5400	5401-8400	8401-11400	11401-14400	14401-17400	17401-21400	21401+	Total house-holds
Agri-culture	01	06	19	11	06	-	01	-	44	02	07	08	06	06	02	-	03	34
Agri-labour	05	07	03	-	-	-	-	-	15	10	16	03	-	-	-	-	01	30
Non-agril.labour	06	08	04	01	01	-	-	-	20	01	13	02	-	01	-	-	-	17
Service	-	-	-	02	01	-	-	01	04	-	-	-	-	-	-	-	01	01
Busi-ness	-	01	02	-	-	-	-	-	03	-	01	03	01	02	-	01	01	09
A. Husbandry	09	16	02	02	-	-	01	-	30	30	05	-	-	-	-	-	-	35
Fishery	01	03	-	-	-	-	-	-	04	01	-	-	-	-	-	-	-	01
Collection of F. produce	15	31	02	-	-	01	-	-	49	42	04	-	-	-	-	-	-	46
Others*	03	03	01	01	-	-	-	-	08	01	01	01	-	-	-	01	01	05

* Others includes Priest, Tuition, Carpentry, Kobiraj, Forest guard, nut cultivation.

above. From the business source the majority of 2 persons whose annual income of Rs. 5401 – 8400 and one person is having annual income of Rs. 2401 – 5400. From the source like animal husbandry the majority of 16 persons whose annual income of Rs. 2401 – 5400 followed by 9 persons who earn annually of Rs. up to 2400/=, each 2 persons are having annual income of Rs. 5401 – 8400 and Rs. 8401 – 11400 and only 1 person is having annual income of Rs. 17401 – 21400. The majority of 3 persons whose annual income of Rs. 2401 – 5400 from fishery and 1 person who earns annually of Rs. up to 2400/= from the same source. From collection of forest produce the majority of 31 persons whose annual income of Rs. 2401 – 5400 followed by 15 persons who earn annually of Rs. up to 2400/ =, 2 persons annual income of Rs. 5401 – 8400 and 1 person who earn annually of Rs. 14401 – 17400. Finally, from other sources each 3 persons whose annual income of Rs. up to 2400/= and Rs. 2401 – 5400 and each one is having annual income of Rs. 5401 – 8400 and Rs. 8401 – 11400. In the case of non-scheduled tribe community from the source like agriculture the majority of 8 persons whose annual income of Rs. 5401 – 8400 followed by 7 persons whose annual income of Rs. 2401 – 5400, each 6 persons are having annual income of Rs. 8401 – 11400 and Rs. 11401 – 14400, each 2 persons are having annual income of Rs. up to 2400/= and Rs. 14401 – 17400 and 3 persons annual income of Rs. 21401/= and above. Next from the source like agricultural labour the majority of 16 persons whose annual income of Rs. 2401 – 5400 followed by 10 persons who earn annually of Rs. up to 2400/=, 3 persons annual income of Rs. 5401 – 8400 and only 1 person is having annual income of Rs. 21401/= and above. Next from non-agricultural labour the majority of 13 persons whose annual income of Rs. 2401 – 5400 followed by 2 persons who earn annually of Rs. 5401 – 8400, and 1 person who earn annually of Rs. 11401 – 14400. One person whose annual income of Rs. 21401 and above from the source like service. From the business the majority of 3 persons whose annual income of Rs. 5401 – 8400 followed by 2 persons who annually earn of Rs. 11401 – 14400, and each one is having annual income of Rs. 2401 – 5400, Rs. 8401 – 11400, Rs. 17401 – 21400 and Rs. 21401 and above. Next from the source like animal husbandry the majority of 30 persons whose annual income of Rs. up to 2400/= and 5 persons who earn annually of Rs. 2401 – 5400. From the fishery only one person is found to be earn of Rs. up to 2400/=. From the collection of forest produce the majority of 42 persons' annual income of

Rs. up to 2400/= and 4 persons who earn annually of Rs. 2401 – 5400. Lastly from other sources each one is found to be earn of Rs. up to 2400/ =, Rs. 2401 – 5400, Rs. 5401 – 8400, Rs. 17401 – 21400 and Rs. 21400 and above.

Table 4.2.7B gives detail about the distribution of income pattern of the sample households. In the case of scheduled tribe community out of 50 surveyed households the majority of 18 households who earn annually of Rs. 17401 – 21400 followed by 12 households whose annual income of Rs. 11401 – 14400, the income of 9 households of Rs. 14401 – 17400, 6 households annual income of Rs. 21401 and above and lastly 5 households annual income of Rs.8401 – 11400. With reference to surveyed non-scheduled tribe community out of total 50 surveyed households the majority of 17 persons whose annual income of Rs. 17401 – 21400 followed by 9 households whose annual income of Rs. 21401 and above, each 7 nos. of households whose annual income of Rs. 8401 – 11400, and Rs. 14401 – 17400 and each 5 persons annual income of Rs. 8401 – 11400 and Rs. 11401 – 14400.

Table 4.2.8A gives detail about the pattern of household expenditure of the sample households. With reference to surveyed scheduled tribe community towards food the majority of 17 persons whose annual expenditure of Rs. 5401 – 7400 followed by 13 persons who spends annually of Rs. 7401 – 9400, 8 persons annual expenditure of Rs. 13401 and above. Each 5 persons who spends annually of Rs. 3401 – 5400 and Rs. 9401 – 11400. Lastly 2 persons whose annual expenditure of Rs.11401 – 13400. Next towards clothing and foot wear the majority of 29 persons who spends annually of Rs. 401 – 1400 followed by 18 persons who spends annually of Rs. 1401 – 3400, 2 persons spend annually of Rs. up to 400/= and one person spend annually of Rs. 3401 – 5400. The majority of 42 persons whose annual expenditure of Rs. 401 – 1400 towards health followed by 7 persons who spends annually of Rs. up to 400/=. One person who spends annually of Rs. 1401 – 3400. Towards education the 13 persons who spends annually of Rs. up to 400/= followed by 12 persons whose annual expenditure of Rs. 401 – 1400, 4 persons annual expenditure of Rs. 1401 – 3400 and only 1 person who spends annually of Rs. 3401 – 5400. Next towards housing the majority of 25 persons whose annual expenditure of Rs. 401 –1400 followed by 19 persons whose annual expenditure of Rs. up to 400/=, 4 persons annual expenditure of Rs. 1401 – 3400 and one person

Table—4.2.7. B. Distribution of Income Pattern of the Sample Households of Dhupguri Block in the District of Jalpaiguri

Community	Amount of Total Income (In Rs.)							Total no. of Household
	Upto 5400	5401-8400	8401-11400	11401-14400	14401-17400	17401-21400	21401+	
Scheduled Tribes	-	-	05	12	09	18	06	50
Non- Scheduled Tribes	-	05	07	05	07	17	09	50
Total	-	05	12	17	16	35	16	100

Table—4.2.8. A. Pattern of Household Expenditure (Annually) of the Sample Households of Dhupguri Block in the District of Jalpaiguri

Item of the Expend-iture	Community																	
	Scheduled Tribes									Non-Scheduled Tribe								
	Upto 400	401 – 1400	1401-3400	3401-5400	5401-7400	7401-9400	9401-11400	11401-13400	13401 +	Upto 400	401-1400	1401-3400	3401-5400	5401-7400	7401-9400	9401-11400	11401-13400	13401+
Food	-	-	-	05	17	13	05	02	08	-	-	-	07	15	08	12	04	04
Clothing & Footwear	02	29	18	01	-	-	-	-	-	23	23	04	-	-	-	-	-	-
Health	07	42	01	-	-	-	-	-	-	15	30	03	01	-	-	-	01	-
Education	13	12	04	01	-	-	-	-	-	09	13	06	02	-	-	-	-	-
Housing	19	25	04	01	-	-	-	-	01	21	23	06	-	-	-	-	-	-
Rituals	09	02	-	-	-	-	-	-	-	20	13	-	-	-	-	-	-	-
Social Functions	08	41	01	-	-	-	-	-	-	15	28	06	01	-	-	-	-	-
Fuel & Lighting	-	32	11	07	-	-	-	-	-	01	44	05	-	-	-	-	-	-
Smoking & Alcohol	22	17	-	-	-	-	-	-	-	05	36	02	-	-	-	-	-	-

spends annually of Rs. 3401 – 5400. Towards rituals the 9 persons who spends annually of Rs. up to 400/= and another 2 persons who spends annually of Rs. 401 – 1400. For social functions the majority of 41 persons who spends annually of Rs. 401 – 1400 followed by 8 persons whose annual expenditure of Rs. up to 400/= and only one person who spends annually of Rs. 1401 – 3400. Towards fuel and lighting the majority of 32 persons whose annual expenditure of Rs. 401 – 1400 followed by 11 persons who spends annually of Rs. 1401 – 3400 and 7 persons annual expenditure of Rs. 3401 – 5400. Finally, towards smoking and drinking the majority of 22 persons whose annual expenditure of Rs. up to 400/= and 17 persons whose annual expenditure of Rs. 401 – 1400. In the case of non-scheduled tribe community towards food the majority of 15 persons whose annual expenditure of Rs. 5401 – 7400 followed by 12 persons who spends annually of Rs. 9401 – 11400, 8 persons annual expenditure of Rs. 7401 – 9400, 7 persons annual expenditure of Rs. 3401 – 5400 and each 4 persons who spends annually of Rs. 11401 – 13400 and Rs. 13401 and above. Towards clothing and footwear the majority of each 23 persons who spends annually of Rs. up to 400/= and Rs. 401 – 1400 and 4 persons whose annual expenditure of Rs. 1401 – 3400. Next the majority of 30 persons who spends annually of Rs. 401 – 1400 for health followed by 15 persons who spends annually of Rs. up to 400/=, 3 persons spends annually of Rs. 1401 – 3400, and each one who spends annually of Rs. 3401 – 5400 and Rs. 11401 – 13400. Towards education the majority of 13 persons whose annual expenditure of Rs. 401 – 1400 followed by 9 persons who spends annually of Rs. up to 400/=, 6 persons spends annually of Rs. 1401 – 3400 and 2 persons annual expenditure of Rs. 3401 – 5400. For housing the majority of 23 persons who spends annually of Rs. 401 – 1400 followed by 21 persons who spends annually of Rs. up to 400/= and 6 persons who spends annually of Rs. 1401 – 3400. Towards rituals the majority of 20 persons who spends annually of Rs. up to 400/= and 13 persons who spends annually of Rs. 401 – 1400. For social functions the majority of 28 persons who spends annually of Rs. 401 – 1400 followed by 15 persons whose annual expenditure of Rs. up to 400/=, 6 persons who spends annually of Rs. 1401 – 3400 and only 1 person who spends annually of Rs. 3401 – 5400. For fuel and lighting the maximum number of 44 persons who spend annually of Rs. 401 – 1400 followed by 5 persons who spends annually of Rs. 1401 – 3400 and one person who spend annually of Rs. up to 400/=. Finally, towards smoking and drinking the majority of 36 persons whose annual expenditure of Rs. 401 – 1400 followed by 5 persons who spends annually of Rs. up to 400/= and 2 persons who spends annually of Rs. 1401 – 3400.

Table 4.2.8B deals with the distribution pattern of household expenditure of the sample households. In the case of scheduled tribe community out of total 50 households the majority of 33 households whose annual expenditure of Rs. 13401 and above followed by 8 nos. of house holds who spends annually of Rs. 11401 – 13400, 5 households whose annual expenditure of Rs. 7401 – 9400 and 4 households annually expenditure of Rs. 11401 – 13400. In the case of non-scheduled tribe community out of 50 surveyed households the majority of 29 nos. of households whose annual expenditure of Rs. 13401 and above followed by 10 nos. whose annual expenditure of Rs. 9401 – 11400, 5 households annual expenditure of Rs. 11401 – 13400, 4 persons annual expenditure of Rs. 5401 – 7400 and 2 persons annual expenditure of Rs. 7401 – 9400.

Table 4.2.9A gives detail about pattern of expenditure annually on agricultural pursuits of the sample households. With reference to scheduled tribe community towards agricultural implements no body is found to spend. Towards ploughing the majority of 25 persons whose annual expenditure of Rs. up to 500/= followed by 17 persons who spends annually of Rs. 501 – 1000 and 2 persons who spends annually of Rs. 1001 – 1500. For purchasing of seeds the majority of 41 persons whose annual expenditure of Rs. up to 500/= followed by 2 persons who spends annually of Rs. 501 – 1000 and 1 person who spends annually of Rs. 1001 – 1500. Towards sowing the majority of 35 persons whose annual expenditure of Rs. up to 500/= followed by 6 persons who spends annually of Rs. 501 – 1000 and 3 persons whose annual expenditure of Rs. 1001 – 1500. For weeding the majority of 41 persons whose annual expenditure of Rs. up to 500/=. Towards fertilizer and pesticides the majority of 25 persons who spends annually of Rs. up to 500/= and 5 persons whose annual expenditure of Rs. 501 – 1000. Towards irrigation the only 5 persons who spends annually of Rs. up to 500/=. Finally, for harvesting the majority of 18 persons who spends annually of Rs. up to 500/= followed by 17 persons who spends annually of Rs. 501 – 1000, 8 persons annual expenditure of Rs. 501 – 1000 and one person who spends annually of Rs. 1501 – 2000. In the case of non-scheduled tribe community towards agricultural implements only one person who spends annually of Rs. 3501 and above.

Table—4.2.8. B. Distribution Pattern of Household Expenditure (Annually) of the Sample Households of Dhupguri Block in the District of Jalpaiguri

Community	Amount of Total Expenditure (In Rs.)						Total no. of Household
	Upto 5400	5401-7400	7401-9400	9401-11400	11401-13400	13401 +	
Scheduled Tribes	-	-	05	04	08	33	50
Non- Scheduled Tribes	-	04	02	10	05	29	50
Total	-	**04**	**07**	**14**	**13**	**62**	**100**

Table—4.2.9. A. Pattern of Expenditure (Annually) on Agricultural Pursuit of the Sample Households of Dhupguri Block in the District of Jalpaiguri

Item of the Expenditure	Community															
	Scheduled Tribes								Non- Scheduled Tribes							
	Upto 500	501-1000	1001-1500	1501-2000	2001-2500	2501-3000	3001-3500	3501+	Upto 500	501-1000	1001-1500	1501-2000	2001-2500	2501-3000	3001-3500	3501+
Agricultural Implements	-	-	-	-	-	-	-	-	-	-	-	-	-	-	-	01
Ploughing	25	17	02	-	-	-	-	-	21	08	03	01	-	01	-	-
Purchasing of Seeds	41	02	01	-	-	-	-	-	32	01	-	-	-	-	-	-
Sowing	35	06	03	-	-	-	-	-	22	07	03	01	-	01	-	-
Weeding	41	-	-	-	-	-	-	-	28	01	-	-	-	-	-	-
Fertilizers & pesticides	25	05	-	-	-	-	-	-	24	02	02	01	-	-	-	-
Irrigation	05	-	-	-	-	-	-	-	-	-	-	-	-	-	-	-
Harvesting	18	17	08	01	-	-	-	-	19	08	04	02	-	-	-	01

For ploughing the majority of 21 persons who spends annually of Rs. up to 500/= followed by 8 persons who spends annually of Rs. 501 – 1000, 3 persons spends annually of Rs. 1001 – 1500 and each one who spends annually of Rs. 1501 – 2000 and Rs. 2501 – 3000. Towards purchasing of seeds the majority of 32 persons who spends annually of Rs. up to 500/= and one person who spends annually of Rs. 501 – 1000. For sowing the majority of 22 persons who spends annually of Rs. up to 500/= followed by 7 persons who spends annually of Rs. 1001 – 1500 and each one who spends annually of Rs. 1501 – 2000 and Rs. 2501 – 3000. For weeding the majority of 28 persons who spends annually of Rs. up to 500/= and one person who spends annually of Rs. 501 – 1000. Next towards fertilizers and pesticides the maximum number of 24 persons who spends annually of Rs. up to 500/= followed by each 2 persons whose annual expenditure of Rs. 501 – 1000 and Rs. 1001 – 1500 and one person who spends annually of Rs. 1501 – 2000. Towards irrigation nobody is found to spend. Lastly, towards harvesting the majority of 19 persons who spends annually of Rs. up to 500/= followed by 8 persons who spends annually of Rs. 501 – 1000, 4 persons spend annually of Rs. 1001 – 1500, 2 persons annual expenditure of Rs. 1501 – 2000 and only one person who spends annually of Rs. 3501 and above.

Table 4.2.9B gives detail distribution pattern of expenditure of the sample households on agricultural pursuits. In the case of surveyed scheduled tribe communities the majority of 12 persons whose annual expenditure of Rs. 1501 – 2000 followed by 9 persons who spends annually of Rs. 1001 – 1500, 8 persons who spends annually of Rs. 501 – 1000, 6 persons annual expenditure of Rs. 3501 and above and each person who spends annually of Rs. 2001 – 2500, Rs. 2501 – 3000 and Rs. 3001 – 3500. Next with reference to non-scheduled tribe community the majority of 10 persons whose annual expenditure of Rs. 1001 – 1500 followed by each 8 persons who spends annually of Rs. 501 – 1000, and Rs.3501 and above, 3 persons who spends annually of Rs. 1501 – 2000 and each 2 persons who spends annually of Rs. 2001 – 2500 and Rs. 2501 – 3000 and only 1 person who spends annually of Rs. up to 500/=.

Table 4.2.10 gives details about the nature of indebtedness among the sample households of the surveyed block. In the case of scheduled tribe community altogether 13 persons are fond to be take a loan from various sources to meet their variety of demands. Out of total 12 persons

Table—4.2.9. B. Distribution Pattern of Expenditure (Annually) on Agricultural Pursuit of the Sample Households of Dhupguri Block in the District of Jalpaiguri

Community	Amount of Total Expenditure (in Rs.)								Total Households
	Upto 500	501-1000	1001-1500	1501-2000	2001-2500	2501-3000	3001-3500	3501+	
Scheduled Tribe	-	08	09	12	03	03	03	06	44
Non- Scheduled Tribe	01	08	10	03	02	02	-	08	34
Total	01	16	19	15	05	05	03	14	78

Table—4.2.10. Nature of Indebtedness among of the Sample Households of Dhupguri Block in the District of Jalpaiguri

Community	Amount of borrowing	Source of borrowing			Purpose of borrowing					Repayment Status		Security			Debt	
		Neighbours	Local Traders	Friends & Relatives	Purchasing of food materials	Life cycle ceremonies	To pay bride price	Medical treatment	Others *	Due – fully	Due – partially	Land	Ornaments	Others	Ancestor	Respondent
	Up to 1000	03	01	02	02	-	-	-	04	06	-	-	-	-	-	06
	1001 - 2000	03	-	-	01	-	-	-	02	02	01	-	-	-	-	03
	2001 - 3000	-	-	-	-	-	-	-	-	-	-	-	-	-	-	-
Scheduled Tribes	3001 - 4000	02	01	-	-	-	-	-	03	03	-	01	-	-	-	03
	4001 – 5000	-	-	-	-	-	-	-	-	-	-	-	-	-	-	-
	5001 – 6000	-	01	-	-	-	-	-	01	01	-	01	-	-	01	-
	Sub-total	**08**	**03**	**02**	**03**	-	-	-	**10**	**12**	**01**	**02**	-	-	**01**	**12**

Communi ty	Amount of borro-wing	Source of borrowing			Purpose of borrowing					Repayment Status		Security			Debt	
		Neigh -bours	Local Tra-ders	Friends & Rela-tives	Purcha-sing of food mate-rials	Life cycle cere-monies	To pay bride price	Medi-cal treat-ment	Others *	Due – fully	Due – par-tially	Land	Orna-ments	Others	Ancestor	Res-pondent
Non-Schedule d Tribes	Up to 1000	01	01	01	01	-	-	-	02	03	-	-	-	-	-	03
	1001 - 2000	-	02	02	01	-	-	02	01	04	-	-	-	-	01	03
	2001 - 3000	-	-	01	-	-	-	01	-	01	-	-	-	-	-	01
	3001 - 4000	-	-	-	-	-	-	-	-	-	-	-	-	-	-	-
	4001 – 5000	-	-	-	-	-	-	-	-	-	-	-	-	-	-	-
	5001 – 6000	-	-	-	-	-	-	-	-	-	-	-	-	-	-	-
	Sub-total	-	**03**	**04**	**01**	-	-	**03**	**02**	**08**	-	-	-	-	**01**	**07**
Total		**08**	**06**	**06**	**04**	-	-	**03**	**12**	**20**	**01**	**02**	-	-	**02**	**19**

the majority of 6 persons who borrowed the amount of Rs. up to 1000/=. Out of 6 three persons borrowed the amount from neighbours followed by 2 persons who took loan from friends and relatives and one person who took loan from local traders. Out of 6 the majority of 4 persons who borrowed the amount for other purposes followed by 2 who used the loan amount for purchasing of food materials and the 6 persons did not repay those loan amount. Next another 3 persons whose loan amount of Rs. 1001 – 2000 and all the three borrowed the amount from neighbours. Out of 3 two persons took loan for others purposes and 1 person took the loan amount for purchasing of food materials. Out of 3 the two persons did not pay the loan amount partly. Lastly another 3 persons whose loan amount happens to be of Rs. 3001 – 4000. Out of those 2 persons are found to be taken the loan from neighbours and one person took the loan from local traders. And all the 3 persons used their loan amount for other purposes. Three, persons did not repay the loan amount and out of those one person mortgaged his land as security. One person among the ancestor took the loan amount of Rs. 5001 – 6000 from local traders and used the loan amount for the purpose of other. Regarding repayment he is found to be defaulter and mortgaged his land as security. With reference to non-scheduled tribe community the total 18 persons are found to be loanees. Out of 18 persons there are 3 persons who took the loan amount of Rs. up to 1000/=. Out of the 3 persons each 1 is found to be taken loan from neighbours, local traders and friends and relatives. Two persons used the loan amount for others purposes and one person who used the loan amount for purchasing of food materials. All the three persons did not pay the loan amount. Next another 3 respondents whose loan amount of Rs. 1001 – 2000 followed 1 person is found to be ancestor side who also took the loan amount of Rs. 1001 – 2000. In this range out of total 4 each 2 persons are found to be taken loan from local traders, friends and relatives. Two persons used the loan amount for medical purpose followed by each one who used the loan amount for purchasing of food materials and other purposes and the 4 persons did not pay the loan amount. Lastly, 1 person who took the highest loan amount of Rs. 2001 – 3000 from friends and relatives for medical treatment. And he also did not pay the loan amount fully.

Table 4.2.11 gives detail aspect of loan received by the sample households from various credit institutions for development purposes. In the case of scheduled tribe community one each from respondent as well

Table—4.2.11. Loan Received by the Sample Households of Dhupguri Block in the District of Jalpaiguri

Type of Loan	Community																					
	Scheduled Tribe											Non - Scheduled Tribe										
	Loan Amount				Loan Repayment			Security		Loan taken by		Loan Amount				Loan Repayment			Security		Loan taken by	
	upto 3000	3001 - 6000	6001 - 9000	9001 +	Paid fully	Paid partially	Due totally	Land	Ornaments	Respondent	Ancestor	upto 3000	3001 - 6000	6001 – 9000	9001 +	Paid fully	Paid partially	Due totally	Land	Ornaments	Respondent	Ancestor
Agri-culture	-	02	-	-	-	-	02	-	-	01	01	-	02	-	-	01	01	-	-	-	02	-
Busi-ness	01	-	-	-	-	01	-	-	-	01	-	-	01	02	01	01	02	01	01	-	04	-
Animal Hus-bandry	03	01	-	-	-	-	04	-	-	03	01	02	03	-	-	04	01	-	-	-	05	-
Total	**04**	**03**	-	-	-	**01**	**06**	-	-	**05**	**02**	**02**	**06**	**02**	**01**	**06**	**04**	**01**	**01**	-	**11**	-

* Source of Loan : Generally the households take loan from any Nationalised Bank, Gramin Bank and Co-operative Societies.

as ancestor side took the loan amount of Rs. 3001- 6000. Both of the persons used the loan amount for agriculture. They did not pay the loan amount fully. Another 1 person who took the loan amount of Rs. up to 3000/= for the purpose of business and the amount was paid by him partially. Finally, 3 respondents and who took the loan amount of Rs. up to 3000/= followed by one ancestor who took the same amount. All of them used the loan amount for the purpose of animal husbandry. They did not repay the loan amount. In the case of non-scheduled tribe community all the total 11 respondents took the loan amount from various credit institution. Out of 11 persons 2 persons who took the loan amount of Rs. 3001 – 6000 for the purpose of agriculture followed by total 4 persons out of which the majority of 2 persons who took the loan amount of Rs. 6001 – 9000 and each one who took the loan amount of Rs.3001-6000 and Rs. 9001 and above. All of them used the loan amount for business purpose. Out of those 2 persons are found to be paid partially and each one is found to be paid fully and did not pay the amount. Lastly total 5 persons out of which 3 persons who took the loan amount of Rs. 3001 – 6000 followed by 2 persons who took the loan amount of Rs. up to 3000/=. All of them took the loan for the animal husbandry purpose. Out of 5 it is found to be that 4 persons paid fully and 1 person paid partially.

III

Gosaba Block of District South 24-Parganas

Table 4.3.1 gives detail account of age-sex composition of the sample households of the surveyed block. In the case of scheduled tribe communities out of total 50 surveyed households there are altogether 125 male and 123 female populations. Their age-sex composition wise it has been noticed that in the age group between 0-5 there are 14 male and 12 female members followed by 34 male and 34 female members in the age group between 6 – 14, 56 male and 60 female persons are in the age group of 15 – 44, 15 male and 12 female members are in the age group of 45 –59 and lastly 6 male and 5 female members are in the age group of 60 and above. In the case of non-schedule tribe community out of 50 surveyed households there are altogether 133 male and 110 female members. Their age – sex composition wise it has been noticed that there are 14 male and 12 female members are in the age group of 0-5 followed by 35 male and 23

Table—4.3.1. Age-Sex Composition of the Sample Households of Gosaba Block in the District of South 24-Parganas

Community (No. of surveyed households)	Age Group (yrs.) 0-5		6-14		15-44		45-59		60+		Total Population Population		Total (%)
	M	F	M	F	M	F	M	F	M	F	M	F	
Scheduled Tribes (50)	14	12	34	34	56	60	15	12	06	05	125	123	248 (50.51)
Non-Scheduled Tribes (50)	14	12	35	23	64	60	11	07	09	08	133	110	243 (49.49)
	28	24	69	57	120	120	26	19	15	13	258	233	
Total (%)	10.85	10.34	26.74	24.46	46.51	51.50	10.08	8.19	5.81	5.60	52.54	47.45	491 (100.00)

female members are in the age group of 6 – 14, 64 male and 60 female members are in the age group of 15 –44, 11 male and 7 female members are in the age group of 45 – 59, 9 male and 8 female members are in the age group of 60 and above.

Table 4.3.2 deals with level of education of sample households. The level of education has been considered above 6 years age on wards. In this age group in the case of scheduled tribe communities there are altogether 108 male and 109 female members. Education wise it has been noticed that there are altogether 29 male and 65 female members are illiterate followed by 10 male and 3 female persons are functionally literate. So far formal education is concerned there are 36 male and 27 female members who read up to IV th standard followed by 22 male and 12 female members who read up to VIII th standard, 10 male and 1 female members studied up to X th class, each one male and female is found to studied up to XII th and nobody is found in graduate level. In the case of non-scheduled tribe community there are 40 male and 43 female members are illiterate followed by 9 male and 5 female members are found to be functionally literate. So far formal education is concerned there are 42 male and 26 female members studied up to IV th standard followed by 37 male and 21 female members who studied up to VIII th standard, 9 male and 3 female members who studied up to X th standard up to XII th standard 2 male members studied and each one male and female are found to be studied up to graduate level.

Table 4.3.3 gives detail marital status of the sample households. Community wise in the case of scheduled tribe communities up to 14 yrs 48 male and 46 female members are found to be unmarried followed by in the age group between 15 – 29 there are 16 male and 8 female members who are found to be unmarried. In the same age group there are 8 male and 24 female members who are found to be married one. In the age group between 30-44 there are 32 male and 24 female members who are married one. In the same age group 4 female members are widow. One female member is found to be unmarried in the age group between 45 –59 followed by 14 male and 7 female members are found to be married one, One male member is widower and 4 female persons are widow. Lastly, in the age group of 60 and above 3 male and female persons are found to be married one followed by 1 male who is widower and 4 female persons who are widow. In the case of non-scheduled tribe community up to 14 yrs there are 47 male and 34 female persons are unmarried. In the age group between 15-29 there are 21 male

Table—4.3.2. Level of Education of the Sample Households of Gosaba Block in the District of South 24-Parganas

Community (No. of surveyed households)	Illiterate		Functional Literate		Formal Education										Population (above 6 yrs.)	
					I-IV		V-VIII		IX-X		XI-XII		Graduate or Others			
	M	F	M	F	M	F	M	F	M	F	M	F	M	F	M	F
Scheduled Tribes (50)	29	65	10	03	36	27	22	12	10	01	01	01	-	-	108	109
Non-scheduled Tribes (50)	40	43	09	05	42	26	37	21	09	03	02	-	01	01	114	99
Total	43	108	19	08	78	53	59	33	19	04	03	01	01	01	222	208
(% to the total population of above 6 yrs. age)	19.37	51.92	8.55	3.84	35.13	25.48	26.57	15.86	8.55	1.92	1.35	0.48	0.45	0.48	51.63	48.37

Functional Literate: Who knows reading, writing and Aritmetic.

Table—4.3.3. Marital Status of the Population of the Sample Households of Gosaba Block in the District of South 24-Parganas

Community (No. of surveyed household)	Age-group (In years)	Marital Status								Total	
		Unmarried		Married		Widower/Widow		Separated		Male	Female
		Male	Female	Male	Female	Male	Female	Male	Female		
Scheduled Tribe (50)	Up to 14	48	46	-	-	-	-	-	-	48	46
	15 – 29	16	08	08	24	-	-	-	-	24	32
	30 – 44	-	-	32	24	-	04	-	-	32	28
	45 – 59	-	01	14	07	01	04	-	-	15	12
	60 +	-	-	03	01	02	04	01	-	06	05
	Sub-total	**64**	**55**	**57**	**56**	**03**	**12**	**01**	-	**125**	**123**
Non – Scheduled Tribe (50)	Up to 14	47	34	-	-	-	-	-	-	49	35
	15 – 29	21	06	11	22	-	-	-	-	33	28
	30 – 44	-	-	31	32	-	-	-	-	31	32
	45 – 59	-	-	11	06	-	01	-	-	11	07
	60 +	-	-	08	04	-	05	-	-	09	08
	Sub-total	**68**	**40**	**61**	**64**	-	**06**	-	-	**131**	**111**
TOTAL		**132**	**95**	**118**	**120**	**03**	**18**	**01**	-	**256**	**234**

and 6 female members who are found to be unmarried followed by 11 male and 22 female members are found to be married one. There are 31 male and 32 female members who are found to be married one in the age group between 30-44. In the age group between 45-59 there are 11 male and 6 female members are married. One female member is widow. Lastly, in the age group 60 and above there are 8 male and 4 female persons are found to be married one followed by 5 female members who are widow.

Table 4.3.4. gives detail occupational distribution of the sample households. Community wise with reference to scheduled tribe community there are altogether 69 male and 70 female members who are found to be working force. Occupational distribution wise there are 6 male and 11 female members who are agricultural labour followed by 37 male and 11 female members who are found to be non-agricultural labour, 22 male and 41 female members are having cultivation, 2 male and 1 female persons are having petty business. One male person is in service and lastly 1 male and 6 female persons are having others occupation. In the case of non-scheduled tribe community there are altogether 75 male and 71 female members who are found to be the working force. Occupational distribution wise there are 6 male and 2 female members are agricultural labour followed by 3 male and 1 female members are non-agricultural labour, 18 male and 36 female members are having cultivation, 13 male members are having petty business, 1 female member is having animal husbandry, 23 male and 21 female members are having fishing, 1 female member is found to be collect minor forest produce and lastly 12 male and 9 female members are having others occupation.

Table 4.3.5 gives detail about occupational mobility of the sample household's generation wise. In the first category of cultivation 17 respondents are found to be in this occupation followed by their fathers generation the majority of 15 persons who are having cultivation and 2 persons are agricultural labour. So far son's generation is concerned in this category one member is found to be in cultivation followed by 5 persons who are non –agricultural labour. In the second category of agricultural labour 2 respondents are found to be in this profession followed by their father's generation each one is found to be in cultivation and agricultural labour and in their son's generation one is having others occupation. In the third category of non-agricultural labour there are 27 respondents who are in this profession followed by their fathers generation

Table—4.3.4. Occupational Distribution of the Sample Households of Gosaba Block in the District of South 24-Parganas

Comm-unity (No. of surveyed house-hold)	Type of Occupation *																			
	Agril. Labour		Non-agril. Labour		Cultivation		Petty Business		Animal Husbandry		Service		Fishing or Aqua-culture		MFP/NTF/ TFP Collection		Others**		Total Working Population	
	M	F	M	F	M	F	M	F	M	F	M	F	M	F	M	F	M	F	M	F
Scheduled Tribe (50)	06	11	37	11	22	41	02	01	-	-	01	-	-	-	-	-	01	06	69	70
Non-Scheduled Tribes (50)	06	02	03	01	18	36	13	-	-	01	-	-	23	21	-	01	12	09	75	71
Total	12	13	40	12	40	77	15	01	-	01	01	-	23	21	-	01	13	15	144	141
(%)	**8.33**	**9.22**	**27.78**	**8.51**	**27.78**	**54.61**	**10.42**	**0.71**	-	**0.71**	**0.69**	-	**15.97**	**14.89**	-	**0.71**	**9.03**	**10.64**	**50.53**	**49.47**

* Working force: 15-59 age group.

** Others includes: mansonry, carpentry, maid servant

Table—4.3.5. Occpational Mobility of the Sample Households of Gosaba Block in the District of South 24-Parganas

Occupation of the Respondent		Occupation of the Respondent's Father									Occupation of the Respondent's Son								
		I	II	III	IV	V	VI	VII	VIII	IX	I	II	III	IV	V	VI	VII	VIII	IX
S.T																			
I. Cultivation	17	15	02	-	-	-	-	-	-	-	01	-	05	-	-	-	-	-	-
II. Agril. Labour	02	01	01	-	-	-	-	-	-	-	-	-	-	-	-	-	-	-	01
III. Non-Agril. Labour	27	11	03	12	01	-	-	-	-	-	-	01	01	-	-	-	-	-	-
IV. Petty Business	02	02	-	-	-	-	-	-	-	-	-	-	-	-	-	-	-	-	-
V. Animal Husbandry	-	-	-	-	-	-	-	-	-	-	-	-	-	-	-	-	-	-	-
VI. Service	01	01	-	-	-	-	-	-	-	-	-	-	-	-	-	-	-	-	-
VII. Fishing or Aquaculture	-	-	-	-	-	-	-	-	-	-	-	-	-	-	-	-	-	-	-
VIII. Forest Produce collection	-	-	-	-	-	-	-	-	-	-	-	-	-	-	-	-	-	-	-
IX. Others*	01	01	-	-	-	-	-	-	-	-	-	-	-	-	-	-	-	-	-

Occupation of the Respondent		Occupation of the Respondent's Father									Occupation of the Respondent's Son								
		I	II	III	IV	V	VI	VII	VIII	IX	I	II	III	IV	V	VI	VII	VIII	IX
Non – S.T																			
I. Cultivation	13	11	01	-	-	-	-	01	-	-	01	-	-	01	-	-	04	-	01
II. Agril. Labour	05	02	03	-	-	-	-	-	-	-	-	-	-	-	-	-	-	-	-
III. Non-Agril. Labour	-	-	-	-	-	-	-	-	-	-	-	-	-	-	-	-	-	-	-
IV. Petty Business	07	03	04	-	-	-	-	-	-	-	-	-	-	01	-	-	-	-	-
V. Animal Husbandry	-	-	-	-	-	-	-	-	-	-	-	-	-	-	-	-	-	-	-
VI. Service	-	-	-	-	-	-	-	-	-	-	-	-	-	-	-	-	-	-	-
VII. Fishing or Aquaculture	15	07	06	-	-	-	-	02	-	-	-	-	-	-	-	-	01	-	-
VIII. MFP /NTFP/ TFP collection	-	-	-	-	-	-	-	-	-	-	-	-	-	-	-	-	-	-	-
IX. Others*	10	-	01	01	-	-	-	-	01	07	01	02	02	-	-	-	-	-	-

the majority of 12 persons who are non-agricultural labour. 11 persons are having cultivation, 3 persons are agricultural labour and 1 person is found to be in petty business. So far their son's generation is concerned each one is found to be in occupation like agricultural labour and non-agricultural labour. There are 2 respondents who are having petty business followed by their father's generation 2 persons are having cultivation. No body is found to be in the category of animal husbandry. In the service sector one respondent is found to be in service followed by his father's generation one member is found to be in cultivation. Lastly, in other's category one respondent is found to be in this category followed by his father's generation one person is found to be in cultivation. In the case of non-scheduled tribe community occupational mobility is concerned in the first category of cultivation 13 respondents are found to be in this category followed by their father's generation there are 11 persons who are having cultivation and each one is found to be in agricultural labour and fishing is concerned each one is found to be in cultivation and each one is found to be in agricultural labour and fishing and so far their son's generation is concerned each one is found to be in cultivation, petty business and others and 4 persons are found to be in fishing. In the next category of agricultural labour 5 respondents are found to be in this profession followed by their father's generation the major 3 persons are found to be agricultural labour and 2 persons are in cultivation. Category like petty business 7 respondents are found to be in this profession followed by their father's generation the majority of 4 persons who are found to be agricultural labour and 3 persons are having cultivation and with reference to their son's generation one person is found to be in petty business. In the category of fishing the 15 respondents are found to be in this profession followed by their father's generation 7 persons are found to be in cultivation followed by 6 persons who are agricultural labour and 2 persons in fishing and in their son's generation 1 person is having fishing. Lastly in others category 10 respondents are found to be in this profession followed by their father's generation the majority of 7 persons are having others and each one is found to be agricultural labour, non-agricultural labour and fishing. So far respondent's sons is concerned it has been noticed that each 2 persons are found to be agricultural and non-agricultural labour and only one is having cultivation.

Table 4.3.6 gives detail about size of land holding of the sample households. Community wise out of 50 surveyed households the majority

Table—4.3.6. Size of Land Holding of the Sample Households of Gosaba Block in the District of South 24-Parganas

Community	Size of Land (in Acres)										Total no of surveyed households
	Landless*	Up to 0.49	0.50-1.00	1.01-1.50	1.51-2.00	2.01-2.50	2.51-3.00	3.01-3.50	3.51-4.00	4.01 +	
Scheduled Tribes	03	16	13	04	05	03	02	02	01	01	50
Non-scheduled Tribes	11	14	09	12	01	02	-	01	-	-	50
Total	14	30	22	16	06	05	02	03	01	01	100

* Not having agricultural land other than homestead land.

of 16 households are having land up to 0.49 followed by 13 members whose size of land between 0.50 – 1.00, 5 members are having land between 1.51 – 2.00, 4 member's size of land is between 1.01 – 1.50, 3 members possess land between 2.01 – 2.50, each 2 members are having land between 2.51 – 3.00 and 3.01 – 3.50, each one is having land between 3.51 – 4.00 and 4.01 and above and 3 members are found to be landless. Out of 50 surveyed households of non-schedule tribe community the majority of 14 members who possess land up to 0.49 followed by 12 persons whose size of land between 1.01 – 1.50, 9 persons who possess land between 0.50-1.00, 2 persons are having land between 2.01-2.50, and each one member is having land between 1.51 – 2.00 and 3.01 – 3.50.

Table 4.3.7A deals with source of income of the sample households. Community wise in the case of scheduled tribe community the majority of 14 persons whose source of income annually of Rs. 2401 – 5400 from agriculture followed by 10 persons who earn annually of Rs. up to 2400/=, each 4 persons earn annually of Rs. 5401 – 8400 and Rs. 11401 – 14400 and only 1 person who earn annually of Rs. 17401 – 21400. From the source like agricultural labour the majority of 18 persons who earn annually of Rs. 2401 – 5400 followed by 7 persons whose annual source of income of Rs. 5401 – 8400, 5 persons earn annually of Rs. 8401 – 11400 and 4 persons earn annually of Rs. up to 2400/=. The majority of 17 persons who earn annually of Rs. 5401 – 8400 from source like non-agricultural labour followed by 11 persons whose annual income of Rs. 8401 – 11400, 9 person's annual income of Rs. 2401 – 5400, 3 persons who earn annually of Rs. 11401 – 14400 and 1 person who earn annually of Rs. 14401 – 17400. Only one person annually earn of Rs. 21401 and above. From business also one person is found to be earn Rs. 8401 – 11400. From animal husbandry source the majority of 10 persons who earn annually of Rs. up to 2400/=. Only one person is found to earn annually of Rs. up to 2400/=. Lastly, from other sources each 2 persons are found to earn annually of Rs. up to 2400/= and Rs. 5401 – 8400 and 3 persons earn annually of Rs. 2401 – 5400. In the case of non-scheduled tribe community it has been noted that from agriculture source the majority of 15 persons whose annual income of Rs. 2401 – 5400 followed by 10 persons who earn annually of Rs. 5401 – 8400, 9 persons annual income of Rs. up to 2400/=, each 2 persons whose annual income of Rs. 8401 – 11400, Rs. 11401 – 1440 and only 1 person who earn annually of Rs. 14401 – 17400. Next from agricultural labour the majority of

Table—4.3.7.A. Sources of Income of the Sample Households of Gosaba Block in the District of South 24-Parganas

Source of Income	Community: Scheduled Tribes Amount of Income (annually in Rs.)									Non-Scheduled Tribes Amount of Income (annually in Rs.)								
	Upto 2400	2401-5400	5401-8400	8401-11400	11401-14400	14401-17400	17401-21400	21401+	Total households	Upto 2400	2401-5400	5401-8400	8401-11400	11401-14400	14401-17400	17401-21400	21401+	Total households
Agri-culture	10	14	04	-	04	03	01	-	36	09	15	10	02	02	01	-	-	39
Agri-labour	04	18	07	05	-	-	-	-	34	04	09	04	-	-	-	-	-	17
Non-agril.labour	02	09	17	11	03	01	02	-	45	03	-	02	-	-	-	-	-	05
Service	-	-	-	-	-	-	-	01	01	-	-	-	-	-	-	-	-	-
Busi-ness	-	-	-	01	-	-	-	-	01	-	-	01	01	03	01	01	01	08
A. Husbandry	10	-	-	-	-	-	-	-	10	05	-	02	-	-	-	-	-	07
Fishery	-	-	-	-	-	-	-	-	-	02	06	10	04	-	01	01	-	24
Collection of F. produce	01	-	-	-	-	-	-	-	01	32	06	02	-	-	-	-	-	40
Others*	02	03	02	-	-	-	-	-	07	-	08	03	02	-	01	-	-	14

* Others include masonary, carpentry, mat weaving, quick doctor, and tuition.

9 persons whose annual income of Rs. 2401 – 5400 followed by each 4 persons who earn annually of Rs. up to 2400/= and Rs. 5401 – 8400. From the source like non-agricultural labour the 3 persons whose annual income of Rs. up to 2400/= and 2 persons who earn annually of Rs. 5401 – 8400. In this community no body did not earn from service. From the business the majority of 3 persons whose annual income of Rs. 11401 – 14400 followed by each 1 who earn annually of Rs. 5401 – 8400, Rs. 8401 – 11400, Rs. 14401 – 17400, Rs. 17401 – 21400 and Rs. 21401 and above. From the source like animal husbandry the majority of 5 persons whose annual income of Rs. up to 2400/= and 2 persons annual income of Rs. 5401 – 8400. From fishery the majority of 10 persons whose annual income of Rs. 5401 – 8400 followed by 6 persons Rs. 2401 – 5400. 4 persons annual income of Rs. 8401 – 11400, 2 persons annual income of Rs. up to 2400/= and each one who earn annually of Rs. 14401 – 21400 and Rs. 17401 – 21400. From the collection of forest produce the majority of 32 persons whose annual income of Rs. up to 2400/= followed by 6 persons who earn annually of Rs. 2401 – 5400 and 2 persons annual income of Rs. 5401-8400. Lastly, from other sources the majority of 8 persons whose annual income of Rs. 2401-5400 followed by 3 persons who earn annually of Rs. 5401 – 8400, 2 persons earn annually of Rs. 8401 – 11400 and one person earn annually of Rs. 14401 – 17400.

Table 4.3.7B deals with distribution income pattern of the sample households community wise in the case of scheduled tribe community out of 50 surveyed households the majority f 18 persons whose annual income range of Rs. 14401 – 17400 followed by 13 members who fall under the range of Rs. 11401 – 14400, 9 members fall under the range of Rs. 17401 – 21400, 6 members annual income range of Rs. 8401 – 11400, 3 members annual income range of Rs. 21400 and above and only 1 member who earn annually of Rs. 5401 – 8400. Next in the case of non-scheduled tribe community out of 50 surveyed households the majority of 15 persons whose annual income range of Rs. 11401 – 1440 followed by 14 persons who earn annually of Rs. 8401 – 11400, 10 members fall under the range of Rs. 17401 – 21400, each 5 members who earn annually of Rs. 14401 – 17400 and Rs. 21400 and above and 1 member is found to earn of Rs. 5401 – 8400.

Table 4.3.8A gives detail about pattern of household expenditure annually of the sample households. Community wise in the case of scheduled tribe community it has been observed that towards food the majority of 20 who spends annually of Rs. 5401 – 7400 followed by 11

Table—4.3.7.B. Distribution of Income of the Sample Households of Gosaba Block in the District of South 24-Parganas

Community	Amount of Total Income (In Rs.)							
	Upto 5400	5401-8400	8401-11400	11401-14400	14401-17400	17401-21400	21401+	Total no. of Household
Scheduled Tribes	-	01	06	13	18	09	03	50
Non- Scheduled Tribes	-	01	14	15	05	10	05	50
Total	-	02	20	28	23	19	08	100

Table—4.3.8.A. Pattern of Household Expenditure (Annually) of the Sample Households of Gosaba Block in the District of South 24-Parganas

Item of the Expenditure	Community																	
	Scheduled Tribes									Non-Scheduled Tribe								
	Upto 400	401 - 1400	1401-3400	3401-5400	5401-7400	7401-9400	9401-11400	11401-13400	13401+	Upto 400	401-1400	1401-3400	3401-5400	5401-7400	7401-9400	9401-11400	11401-13400	13401+
Food	-	-	-	04	20	11	09	02	04	-	-	-	06	16	18	05	02	03
Clothing & Footwear	02	41	07	-	-	-	-	-	-	-	21	27	02	-	-	-	-	-
Health	05	43	01	-	-	-	01	-	-	16	31	02	01	-	-	-	-	-
Education	10	20	01	02	-	-	-	-	-	08	16	05	01	01	-	-	-	-
Housing	45	05	-	-	-	-	-	-	-	01	45	04	-	-	-	-	-	-
Rituals	-	05	-	-	-	-	-	-	-	04	06	-	-	-	-	-	-	-
Social Functions	04	43	03	-	-	-	-	-	-	17	28	05	-	-	-	-	-	-
Fuel & Lighting	39	11	-	-	-	-	-	-	-	01	48	01	-	-	-	-	-	-
Smoking & Alcohol	31	12	-	-	-	-	-	-	-	17	09	01	-	-	-	-	-	-

persons who spends annually of Rs. 7401 – 9400, 9 persons spend annually of Rs. 9401 – 11400, each 4 who spends annually of Rs. 3401 – 5400 and Rs. 13401 and above and 2 persons spend annually of Rs. 11401 – 13400. Towards clothing and footwear the majority of 41 household members whose annual expenditure of Rs. 401 – 1400 followed by 7 members who spends annually of Rs. 1401 – 3400 and only 2 persons who spends annually of Rs. up to 400/=. Towards health the majority of 43 members who spend annually of Rs. 401 – 1400 followed by 5 members whose annual expenditure of Rs. up to 400/= and each 1 member who spend annually of Rs. 1401 – 3400 and Rs. 9401 – 11400. The majority of 20 household members who spends annually of Rs. up to 401 – 1400 for health followed by 10 members who spends annually of Rs. up to 400/=, 2 members who spend annually of Rs. 3401 – 5400 and only 1 member who spend annually of Rs. 1401 – 3400. For housing the majority of 45 household members who spend annually of Rs. up to 400/= and 5 members whose annual expenditure of Rs. 401 – 1400. Only 5 household members are found to spend annually of Rs. 401 – 1400 for rituals. Towards social functions the majority of 43 household members who spend annually of Rs. 401 – 1400 followed by 4 members who spend annually of Rs. up to 400/= and 3 members whose annual expenditure of Rs. 1401 – 3400. Towards fuel and lighting the majority of 39 house hold members who spend annually of Rs. up to 400/= and 11 members who spend annually of Rs. 401 – 1400 and lastly towards smoking and drinking the majority of 31 members whose annual expenditure of Rs. up to 400/= and 12 members who spend annually of Rs. 401 – 1400. Next in the case of non-scheduled tribe community it has been observed that towards food the majority of 18 household members whose annual expenditure of Rs. 7401 – 9400 followed by 16 members who spend annually of Rs. 5401 – 7400, 6 members who spend annually of Rs. 3401 –5400, 5 members annual expenditure of Rs. 9401 – 11400, 3 members who spend annually of Rs.13401 and 2 members whose annual expenditure of Rs. 11401 – 13400. Towards clothing and footwear the majority of 27 household members who spends annually of Rs. 1401 – 3400 followed by 21 members who spends annually of Rs. 401 – 1400 and 2 members who spends annually of Rs. 3401 – 5400. The majority of 31 household members who spend annually of Rs. 401 – 1400 towards health followed by 16 members whose annual expenditure of Rs. up to 400/=, members spend annually of Rs. 1401 – 3400 and 1 member who spend annually of Rs. 3401 –5400. Next towards education the majority of 16 households who spend annually of Rs. 401 – 1400 followed by 8 members who spend up to of Rs. 400/=, 5 members whose annual expenditure of Rs. 1401 – 3400 and each 1 member who spend annually of Rs. 3401 – 5400 and Rs. 5401 – 7400. For housing, the majority of 45 household members whose annual expenditure of Rs. 401 – 1400 followed by 4 who spend annually of Rs. 1401 – 3400 and only one member who spend annually of Rs. up to 400/=. The 6 household members who spend annually of Rs. 401 – 1400 towards rituals and 4 members who spend annually of Rs. up to 400/=. For social functions the majority of 28 household members whose annual expenditure of Rs. 401 – 1400 followed by 17 members who spend annually of Rs. up to 400/= and only 5 members who spends annually of Rs. 1401 – 3400. Towards fuel and lighting the majority of 48 household members whose annual expenditure of Rs. 401 – 1400 followed by each one who spend annually of Rs. up to 400/= and Rs. 1401 – 3400. Lastly, for smoking and alcohol the 17 household members who spend annually of Rs. Up to 400/= followed by 9 members who spend annually of Rs. 401- 1400 and 1 member spend annually of Rs. 1401 – 3400.

Table 4.3.8B gives detail about distribution pattern of household expenditure of the sample households. Community wise in the case of scheduled tribe community out of 50 surveyed households the majority of 22 household members whose annual expenditure range of Rs. 13401 and above followed by each 10 members who spend annually of Rs. 9401 – 11400 and Rs. 11401 – 13400. 5 members who spend annually of Rs. 7401 – 9400 and 3 members whose annual expenditure of Rs. 5401 – 7400. Next in the case of non-scheduled tribe community out of 50 surveyed households the majority of 22 household members whose annual expenditure of Rs. 13401 and above followed by each 10 members who spend annually of Rs. 9401 – 11400 and Rs. 11401 – 13400 and 8 members who spend annually of Rs. 7401 – 9400.

Table 4.3.9A deals with the pattern of expenditure annually on agricultural pursuits of the sample households. Community wise in the case of scheduled tribe communities towards agricultural implements no body is found to spend annually. Towards ploughing the majority of 27 household members who spend annually of Rs. below 500/= followed by 5 members who spend annually of Rs. 501 – 1000 and 4 members who spend annually of Rs. 1001 – 1500. Towards purchasing of seeds the 36

Table—4.3.8.B. Distribution Pattern of Household Expenditure (Annually) of the Sample Households of Gosaba Block in the District of South 24-Parganas

Community	Amount of Total Expenditure (In Rs.)						Total no. of Household
	Upto 5400	5401-7400	7401-9400	9401-11400	11401-13400	13401 +	
Scheduled Tribes	-	03	05	10	10	22	50
Non- Scheduled Tribes	-	-	08	10	10	22	50
Total	-	**03**	**13**	**20**	**20**	**44**	**100**

Table—4.3.9.A. Pattern of Expenditure (Annually) on Argicultural Pursuit of the Sample Households of Gosaba Block in the District of South 24-Parganas

Item of the Expenditure	Community															
	Scheduled Tribes								Non- Scheduled Tribes							
	<500	501-1000	1001-1500	1501-2000	2001-2500	2501-3000	3001-3500	3501+	<500	501-1000	1001-1500	1501-2000	2001-2500	2501-3000	3001-3500	3501+
Agricultural Implements	-	-	-	-	-	-	-	-	-	-	-	-	-	-	-	-
Ploughing	27	05	04	-	-	-	-	-	28	09	02	-	-	-	-	-
Purchasing of Seeds	36	-	-	-	-	-	-	-	32	-	-	-	-	-	-	-
Sowing	36	-	-	-	-	-	-	-	25	08	-	01	-	-	-	-
Weeding	34	-	-	-	-	-	-	-	13	01	-	-	-	-	-	-
Fertilizers & pesticides	20	-	-	-	-	-	-	-	29	03	01	01	-	-	-	-
Irrigation	11	-	-	-	-	-	-	-	08	02	-	-	-	-	-	-
Harvesting	29	05	01	01	-	-	-	-	23	11	03	01	01	-	-	-

houses hold members who spends annually of Rs. below 500/=. For sowing too the majority of 36 household members who spend annually of Rs. below 500/=. For weeding the 34 household members whose annual expenditure of Rs. below 500/=. Towards fertilizers and pesticides the 20 household members who spends annually of Rs. below 500/=. For irrigation the altogether 11 household members who also spend annually of Rs. below 500/=. Lastly towards harvesting the majority of 23 household members who spend annually of Rs. blow 500/= followed by 5 members who spend annually of Rs. 501 – 1000 and each 1 member whose annual expenditure of Rs. 1501 – 2000 and Rs. 2001 – 2500.

Table 4.3.9B gives detail about the pattern of distribution of expenditure annually on agricultural pursuits of the sample households. Community wise in the case of scheduled tribe communities out of total 36 households the majority of 11 members who spends annually of Rs. 501 – 1000 followed by 9 members whose annual expenditure range of Rs. 1001 – 1500, 5 members annual expenditure of Rs. below 500/=, 4 members annual expenditure of Rs. 1501 – 200, each 3 members annual expenditure of Rs. 2501 – 3000 and Rs. 3501 and above, and 1 member who spend annually of Rs. 2001-2500. In the case of non-scheduled tribe community out of total 39 households the majority of 12 members whose annual expenditure of Rs. 501 – 1000 followed by each 7 members who spend annually of Rs. 1001 – 1500 and Rs. 3501 and above, each 3 members whose annual expenditure of Rs. below 500/= and Rs. 2001 – 3500 and each 2 members whose annual expenditure of Rs. 1501 – 2000 and Rs. 2501 – 3000.

Table 4.3.10 gives detail about the nature of indebtedness among the sample households. Community wise in the case of scheduled tribe community there are altogether 32 respondents who took the loan from various sources. Out of 32 one person who took the loan amount of Rs. up to 1000/= from neighbours for purchasing of food materials and did not pay the loan amount and mortgaged his land as security followed by 6 persons whose loan amount is Rs. 1001 – 2000. Out of 6 persons 5 persons took the loan from neighbours and one took from local traders. Three persons used the loan amount for purchasing of food materials, 2 persons used the loan amount for other purpose and only one person used the loan amount for medical purpose. Out of 6 persons 5 persons did not pay the loan amount and one person paid the amount partially and 3 persons

Table—4.3.9.B. Pattern of Distribution Expenditure (Annually) on Argicultural Pursuit of the Sample Households of Gosaba Block in the District of South 24-Parganas

Community	Amount of Total Expenditure (in Rs.)								Total Households
	<500	501-1000	1001-1500	1501-2000	2001-2500	2501-3000	3001-3500	3501+	
Scheduled Tribe	05	11	09	04	01	03	-	03	36
Non- Scheduled Tribe	03	12	·07	02	03	02	03	07	39
Total	08	23	16	06	04	05	03	10	75

Table—4.3.10. Nature of Indebtedness among the Sample Households of Gosaba Block in the District of South 24-Parganas

		Source of borrowing			Purpose of borrowing					Repayment Status		Security			Debt	
Community	Amount of borrowing	Neighbours	Local Traders	Friends & Relatives	Purchasing of food materials	Life cycle ceremonies	To pay bride price	Medical treatment	Others *	Due fully	Due partially	Land	Ornaments	Others	Ancestor	Respondent
	Up to 1000	01	-	-	01	-	-	-	-	01	-	01	-	-	-	01
	1001 - 2000	05	01	-	03	-	-	01	02	05	01	03	-	-	-	06
	2001 - 3000	03	-	-	-	03	-	-	-	03	-	02	-	-	-	03
Scheduled Tribes	3001 - 4000	04	-	-	01	02	-	01	-	04	-	04	-	-	-	04
	4001 – 5000	02	-	-	-	01	-	-	01	02	-	02	-	-	-	02
	5001 – 6000	14	01	01	05	03	02	04	02	16	-	15	-	-	-	16
	Sub-total	**29**	**02**	**01**	**10**	**09**	**02**	**06**	**05**	**31**	**01**	**27**	-	-	-	**32**

Comm-unity	Amount of borro-wing	Source of borrowing			Purpose of borrowing					Repayment Status		Security			Debt	
		Neigh-bours	Local Tra-ders	Friends & Rela-tives	Purcha-sing of food mate-rials	Life cycle cere-monies	To pay bride price	Medi-cal treat-ment	Others *	Due fully	Due par-tially	Land	Orna-ments	Others	Ancestor	Resp-ondent
Non-Scheduled Tribes	Up to 1000	03	01	-	02	-	-	02	-	04	-	-	-	-	-	04
	1001 - 2000	02	01	03	02	-	-	01	03	05	01	-	-	-	-	06
	2001 - 3000	01	-	-	-	-	-	-	01	01	-	01	-	-	-	01
	3001 - 4000	03	-	-	-	-	-	01	02	03	-	01	-	-	-	03
	4001 – 5000	02	-	-	01	01	-	-	-	02	-	-	-	-	-	02
	5001 – 6000	10	03	01	02	01	04	01	06	13	01	07	01	-	-	14
	Sub-total	**21**	**05**	**04**	**07**	**02**	**04**	**05**	**12**	**28**	**02**	**09**	**01**	-	-	**30**
Total		**50**	**07**	**05**	**17**	**11**	**06**	**11**	**17**	**59**	**03**	**36**	**01**	-	-	**62**

Other includes: Purchasing of boat and net, boat repairing, business, digging pond, agriculture and housing.

mortgaged their land as security. Next 3 persons took the loan amount of Rs. 2001 – 3000. All the three persons took the loan amount from neighbours for life cycle ceremony purpose. Regarding repayment all the three did not pay the amount and 2 persons mortgaged their land as security. Four persons whose loan amount is found to be of Rs. 3001 – 4000 and all the persons took the loan from neighbours only. Out of four 2 persons used the loan amount for life cycle ceremony purpose and each one who used the loan amount for purchasing of food material and medical purpose. All the four did not pay the loan amount and found to be mortgaged their land as security. Two persons who took the loan amount of Rs. 4001 – 5000 from neighbour only. Out of 2 each one used the loan amount for the purpose like life cycle ceremony and other purposes. All the 2 persons did not pay the loan amount and found to be mortgaged their land as security. Lastly the majority of 16 respondents took the loan amount of Rs. 5001 – 6000. Out of 16 the majority of 14 persons who took the loan amount from neighbours and each one who took the loan amount from local traders, friends and relatives. Out of those the majority of 5 persons who used the loan amount for purchasing of food materials followed by 4 persons who used the loan amount for medical purpose, 3 persons used the loan amount for the purpose like life cycle ceremony and each 2 persons who used the loan amount for bride price and other purposes. All the 16 persons did not pay the loan amount and 15 persons mortgaged their land as security. With reference to non-scheduled tribe community altogether 30 persons are found to take loan. Out of 30 the 4 nos. of persons who took the loan amount of Rs. up to 1000/=. Out of 4, three persons took the loan amount from neighbour and one person took the loan from local traders. Each 2 persons used the loan amount for purchasing of food materials and medical purpose. Regarding repayment all the four did not pay the loan amount. The 6 persons took the loan amount of Rs. 1001 – 2000. Out of 6 the majority of 3 persons took the loan from friends and relatives followed by 2 persons who took the loan amount from neighbours and only one person took the amount from local traders. Out of 6 there are 3 persons who are found to be used the loan amount for other purposes followed by 2 persons who used the loan amount for purchasing of food material. Regarding repayment the majority of 5 persons who did not pay the loan amount followed by one who paid partially. One person who took the loan amount of Rs. 2001 – 3000 from neighbours only. He used the loan amount for other purposes. Regarding repayment it has been observed that the concerned person did not pay the loan amount and mortgaged his land as security. Next the total 3 persons who took the loan amount of Rs. 3001 – 4000 from the source like neighbour only. Out of those family 2 persons used the loan amount for other purposes and one person who used the loan amount for medical purpose. Regarding repayment all the 3 persons did not pay the loan amount and out of 3, one person mortgaged his land as security. Next 2 persons who took the loan amount of Rs. 4001 – 5000 from neighbour only. Each one found to be used the loan amount for purchasing of food materials and life cycle ceremony. Regarding repayment all are not founds to be paid the loan amount. Lastly, the majority of 14 persons took the maximum loan amount of Rs. 5001 – 6000. Out of those the majority of 10 persons who took the loan from neighbour followed by 3 persons who took the loan from local traders and one person took the loan from friends and relatives. The majority of 6 persons who used the loan amount for other purpose followed by 4 who used the loan amount to pay bride price. 2 persons used the loan amount for purchasing of food materials and each one is found to be used the loan amount for life cycle ceremony and medical purpose. Regarding repayment out of 14 the majority of 13 persons did not pay the loan amount. Only one person paid the loan amount partially. Out of 14 persons, 7 persons mortgaged their land as security and one person took the loan against ornaments.

Table 4.3.11 gives detail about the loan received by the sample households from various credit institution for development purposes. Community wise in the case of scheduled tribe community total 3 respondents are found to be received loan. Out of 3 for agricultural purpose 2 persons took the loan amount of Rs. 3001 – 6000. Regarding repayment one person paid the amount partially and other did not pay the amount. Lastly one person took the loan amount of Rs. 6001 –9000 for business purpose. Regarding repayment he did not pay the loan amount. In the case of non-schedule tribe community total 8 persons are found to be received loan for various purposes. Out of 8 persons 2 persons who received the loan amount. Out of 2 each one is found to be received loan of Rs. 3001 – 6000 and Rs. 9001 and above. Both of them took the loan for agricultural purpose. Regarding repayment one paid the amount partially and the other did not pay the loan amount and one person mortgaged his land as security. The six persons took the loan amount, for business purpose. Out of 6

Table—4.3.11. Loand Received by the Sample Households of Gosaba Block in the District of South 24-Parganas

Type of Loan	Community																					
	Scheduled Tribe											Non - Scheduled Tribe										
	Loan Amount				Loan Repayment			Security		Loan taken by		Loan Amount				Loan Repayment			Security		Loan taken by	
	upto 3000	3001 - 6000	6001 - 9000	9001 +	Paid fully	Paid partially	Due totally	Land	Ornaments	Respondent	Ancestor	upto 3000	3001 - 6000	6001 – 9000	9001 +	Paid fully	Paid partially	Due totally	Land	Ornaments	Respondent	Ancestor
Agri-culture	-	02	-	-	01	-	01	-	-	02	-	-	01	-	01	-	01	01	01	-	02	-
Busi-ness	-	-	01	-	-	-	01	-	-	01	-	05	01	-	-	-	03	03	-	-	06	-
Animal Hus-bandry	-	-	-	-	-	-	-	-	-	-	-	-	-	-	-	-	-	-	-	-	-	-
Total	-	**02**	**01**	-	**01**	-	**02**	-	-	**03**	-	**05**	**02**	-	**01**	-	**04**	**04**	**01**	-	**08**	-

* Source of Loan : Generally the households take loan from any Nationalised Bank, Gramin Bank and Co-operative Societies.

persons the individual loan amount of 5 persons are of Rs. up to 3000/= and one person who took the loan amount of Rs. 3001-6000. Out of six 3 persons paid partially and other 3 who did not pay the amount.

IV

Three Districts Together

The Table 4.4.1 gives details about the Age-Sex Composition of the population of the sample households of the three studied districts in the state of West Bengal. Among the surveyed Scheduled Tribe Community there are 741 persons of which 376 persons are male and the rest 365 are female. Maximum number of male (171) and female (180) persons belongs to the age-group of 15-44 followed by 105 male and 93 female in the 6-14 age-group. Minimum number of persons belongs to the 60+ age-group. Among the Non-Scheduled Tribe Community there are altogether 779 persons of whom 407 persons are male and 372 female. Maximum number of population belong to the age-group of 15-44 and it numbers 193 male and 185 female followed by 104 male and 83 female in the age-group of 5-14. Lowest number of population belongs to the age-group of 60+. Similarly, out of total population of 1520 of S.T and Non- S.T communities male out-numbered female by 783 to 737. But in the age-group of 15-44 the male-female difference is lowest where 364 persons are male and 365 persons are female. It is interesting to note that in the age-group of 0-5 both in case of S.T. and Non-S.T community female persons outnumbered male persons. In case of both S.T. and Non-S.T community the figures are 67 (8.55%) and 77 (10.45%). Only 6.54% male persons and 5.97% females belong to the age-group of 60+.

The Table 4.4.2 gives details about the Level of Education of the population of the sample households of the three studied districts in the state of West Bengal. Community-wise break-up shows that among the S.T. community out of 329 male and 321 female persons 112 male and 209 female persons are illiterate respectively. The number of functional literate male is 20 whereas it is only 9 in case of female persons. Regarding formal education, it is found that 94 male and 68 female folks are in the standard of I-IV followed by 72 male and 31 female folks in the V-VIII standard. Only 24 male and 3 female persons are in the standard of IX-X group. Four male folks are in the Graduation level and there is no female folk I this group. In

4.4.1 Age Sex composition of the sample householdof the three district in the state of West Bangal

Community (No. of surveyed household)	Age Group (yrs.) 0-4		5-14		15-44		45-59		60+		Total Population Population		
	M	F	M	F	M	F	M	F	M	F	M	F	Total (%)
Scheduled Tribes (150)	36	38	105	93	171	180	44	36	20	18	376	365	741 (48.75)
Non-Scheduled Tribes (150)	31	39	104	83	193	185	47	39	32	26	407	372	779 (51.25)
Total (%)	67 (08.55)	77 (10.45)	209 (26.69)	176 (23.88)	364 (46.49)	365 (49.52)	91 (11.62)	75 (10.18)	52 (06.64)	44 (05.97)	783 (99.99)	737 (100.00)	1520 (100.00)

Table : 4.4.2 Level of Education of the sample Households of the three Districts in the state of the West Bengal

Comm-unity (No. of surveyed house-holds)	Illiterate		Functional Literate		Formal Education								Graduate or Others		Population (above 6 yrs.)	
					I - IV		V - VIII		IX - X		XI - XII					
	M	F	M	F	M	F	M	F	M	F	M	F	M	F	M	F
Scheduled Tribes (150)	112	209	20	09	94	68	72	31	24	03	03	01	04	-	329	321
Non-scheduled Tribes (150)	82	125	18	17	118	87	120	79	41	17	09	02	06	03	394	330
Total (% to the total population of above 6 yrs. age)	194 (26.83)	334 (51.30)	38 (05.25)	26 (03.99)	212 (29.33)	155 (23.81)	192 (26.55)	110 (16.90)	65 (08.99)	20 (03.07)	12 (01.66)	03 (0.46)	10 (01.38)	03 (0.46)	723 (99.99)	651 (99.99)

case of Non-S.T. community out of 394 male and 330 female persons 82 male and 125 female persons are illiterate. The number of functional literate is 18 male and 17 female respectively. In the I-IV standard there are 118 male and 87 female persons followed by 120 male and 79 female persons respectively in the standard of V-VIII. Only 41 male and 17 female persons belong to the IX-X standard. In case of XI -XII, it is 9 male and 2 female respectively. There are 6 and 3 male and female persons respectively belong to the standard Graduation and above. The combined figures shows that out of 723 male and 651 female persons 194 (26.83%) male and 334 (51.30%) female persons are illiterate respectively. 212 male and 155 female persons are studying/studied in the I-IV standard. In case of V-VIII level the respective figures of both male and female are 192 and 110 respectively. Only 65 male and 20 female studied /studying in the level of IX-X followed by 12 male and 3 female folks in the X-XII standard. Only 10 male and 3 female persons studied/studying in the graduation level.

The combined data of both S.T. and Non-S.T. community shows that women are lagging far behind in educational achievement. The number of illiterates is also high among the female population. Male-female differences are also alarming. It is 51.30% in case of female persons whereas the percentage of male illiteracy is only 26.83%. The percentage of enrolment in schools also high among the male persons. The percentage of female persons studying decreases as one moves from I-IV standard to XI-XII level.

The Table 4.4.3 gives details about the Age-group wise Marital Status of the population of the sample households of the three studied districts in the state of West Bengal. In case of Scheduled Tribe community maximum number of unmarried persons belong to the age-group of 0-14 and the corresponding figures of male and female persons are 140 and 131 respectively. In the age-group of 15-29 there are 46 male and 27 female persons. There are also 3 male and 1 female unmarried person in the age-group of 30-44 and 1 person each in 45-59 age-group. Maximum number of married persons is in the age-group 30-44 followed by 36 male and 69 female persons in the 15-29 age-group. Forty male and 24 female persons are in the age-group of 45-59 and 18 male 6 female in the 60+ age-group. Maximum number of widows (12) belong to the age-group 45-59and 60+ followed by 8 in the 30-44 age-group and 2 in the age-group of 15-29. Widowers (6) belong to the age-group of 30 and above. In case of Non-

Table : 4.4.3 Martial Staus of the Sample Household of the Three Districts in the State of West Bengal

Community (No. of surveyed household)	Age- group (In years)	Marital Status								Total	
		Unmarried		Married		Widower/Widow		Separated			
		Male	Female	Male	Female	Male	Female	Male	Female	Male	Female
Scheduled Tribe (150)	Up to 14	140	131	-	-	-	-	-	-	140	131
	15 – 29	46	27	36	69	-	02	-	-	82	98
	30 – 44	.03	01	84	74	01	08	-	-	88	83
	45 – 59	01	01	40	24	03	12	-	-	44	37
	60 +	-	-	18	06	02	12	01	-	21	18
	Sub-total	**190**	**160**	**178**	**173**	**06**	**34**	**01**	-	**375**	**367**
Non – Scheduled Tribe (150)	Up to 14	133	125	-	-	-	-	-	-	133	125
	15 – 29	73	33	32	71	-	-	-	-	105	104
	30 – 44	04	-	81	80	01	02	-	-	86	82
	45 – 59	01	-	45	28	01	10	-	01	47	39
	60 +	-	-	27	12	03	15	01	-	31	27
	Sub-total	**211**	**157**	**185**	**191**	**05**	**27**	**01**	**01**	**402**	**377**
TOTAL		**401**	**317**	**363**	**364**	**11**	**61**	**02**	**01**	**777**	**744**

Scheduled Tribe community also maximum number of unmarried persons (133 male and 125 female) belong to the age-group of 0-14 followed by 73 male and 33 female in the 15-29 age-group. Maximum number of married persons are in the age-group of 30-44 followed by 32 male and 71 female in the 15-29 age-group and 45 male and 28 female in the age-group of 45-59 and 27 male and 12 female in the age-group of 60+. Number of widow/ widower is highest in the 60+ age-group and the corresponding figures are 15 and 3 respectively.

The Table 4.4.4 gives details about the Occupational Distribution of the population of the sample households of the three studied districts in the state of West Bengal. Community-wise data show that in case of Scheduled Tribe community most of the people (85 male and 106 female) are engaged in cultivation out of a total working force of 219 male and 211 female population followed by agriculture (36 male and 38 female) and non-agricultural labour (57 male 17 female) jointly. Only 6 and 1 female folk subsist on petty business and 14 female on animal husbandry. Among the S.T. community only 8 male folks are service-holders. Seven male and 24 female engaged in the collection of forest produces and 19 male and 11 female folks are engaged in 'others' activities like masonry, carpentry and maid servant. In case of Non-S.T community the same trend is also witnessed where most of the people (106 male and 136 female) are engaged in cultivation out of a total working force of 244 male and 226 female followed by 'others' (29 male and 24 female), fishing (23 male and 21 female), agricultural labour (30 male and 5 female), petty business (25 male and 1 female) and animal husbandry (8 female) and service (8 male) jointly. The combined figures of the two communities also show that 41.25% male and 55.38% female persons are engaged in cultivation, followed by agricultural labour (11.88% male 12.81% female), non-agricultural labour (18.80% male and 5.30% female), collection of forest produce (2.37% male and 8.47% female) respectively.

The Table 4.4.5 gives details about the Occupational Mobility over Generations of the population of the sample households of the three studied districts in the state of West Bengal. Among the Scheduled Tribes, it is seen that from the table that out of 69 respondents engaged in cultivation, 65 respondents' fathers were cultivator and 2 agricultural labourers and 1 non-agricultural labour and others. Regarding occupation of the son of the respondent it has been found that there is a tendency

Table– 4.4.4. Occupational Distribution of the Sample Household of the Three District in the State of the West Bengal

Community (No. of surveyed household)	Type of Occupation *																			
	Agril. Labour		Non-agril. Labour		Cultivation		Petty Business		Animal Husbandr y		Service		Fishing or Aqua-culture		MFP/NTF/ TFP Collection		Others**		Total Working Population	
	M	F	M	F	M	F	M	F	M	F	M	F	M	F	M	F	M	F	M	F
Scheduled Tribe (150)	36	38	57	17	85	106	06	01	-	14	08	-	01	-	07	24	19	11	219	211
Non-Scheduled Tribes (150)	19	18	30	05	106	136	25	01	-	08	08	-	23	21	04	13	29	24	244	226
Total (300)	55	56	87	22	191	242	31	2	-	22	16	-	24	21	11	37	48	35	463	437
(%)	11.88	12.81	18.80	05.03	41.25	55.38	06.69	0.46	-	05.03	03.45	-	05.18	04.80	02.37	08.47	10.37	08.01	99.99	99.99

Table 4.4.5 Occupational Mobility of the Sample Households oF the Three Districts in the State of the West Bengal.

Occupation of the Respondent		*Occupation of the Respondent's Father*									*Occupation of the Respondent's Son*								
		I	*II*	*III*	*IV*	*V*	*VI*	*VII*	*VIII*	*IX*	*I*	*II*	*III*	*IV*	*V*	*VI*	*VII*	*VIII*	*IX*
Non - Scheduled Tribe																			
I. Cultivation	68	62	01	01	01	-	01	01	-	01	08	03	05	02	-	02	04	-	01
II. Agril. Labour	11	03	08	-	-	-	-	-	-	-	-	-	-	-	-	-	-	-	-
III. Non- Agril. Labour	10	06	03	01	-	-	-	-	-	-	01	-	01	-	-	-	-	-	-
IV. Petty Business	17	07	07	01	02	-	-	-	-	-	-	-	01	01	-	-	-	-	-
V. Animal Husbandry	-	-	-	-	-	-	-	-	-	-	-	-	-	-	-	-	-	-	-
VI. Service	04	03	-	-	-	-	-	-	-	01	02	-	-	-	-	-	-	-	-
VII. Fishing or Aquaculture	15	07	06	-	-	-	-	02	-	-	-	-	-	-	-	-	01	-	-
VIII. MFP /NTFP/ TFP collection	-	-	-	-	-	-	-	-	-	-	-	-	-	-	-	-	-	-	-
IX. Others*	24	04	03	01	-	-	01	-	02	13	03	02	04	-	-	-	-	-	03

Occupation of the Respondent		Occupation of the Respondent's Father									Occupation of the Respondent's Son								
		I	II	III	IV	V	VI	VII	VIII	IX	I	II	III	IV	V	VI	VII	VIII	IX
Non - Scheduled Tribe																			
I. Cultivation	68	62	01	01	01	-	01	01	-	01	08	03	05	02	-	02	04	-	01
II. Agril. Labour	11	03	08	-	-	-	-	-	-	-	-	-	-	-	-	-	-	-	-
III. Non- Agril. Labour	10	06	03	01	-	-	-	-	-	-	01	-	01	-	-	-	-	-	-
IV. Petty Business	17	07	07	01	02	-	-	-	-	-	-	-	01	01	-	-	-	-	-
V. Animal Husbandry	-	-	-	-	-	-	-	-	-	-	-	-	-	-	-	-	-	-	-
VI. Service	04	03	-	-	-	-	-	-	-	01	02	-	-	-	-	-	-	-	-
VII. Fishing or Aquaculture	15	07	06	-	-	-	-	02	-	-	-	-	-	-	-	-	01	-	-
VIII. MFP /NTFP/ TFP collection	-	-	-	-	-	-	-	-	-	-	-	-	-	-	-	-	-	-	-
IX. Others*	24	04	03	01	-	-	01	-	02	13	03	02	04	-	-	-	-	-	03

among them to continue their traditional/family occupation among them. Twenty-four respondents working as agricultural labour, recollect that 14 of their fathers' occupation were agricultural labour and 10 as non-agricultural labour. Among the sons of the respondents they are also continuing their father's occupation. Thirty-eight respondents subsist on non-agricultural labour, of which 16 respondents' fathers each were cultivator and non-agricultural labour respectively. Regarding petty business, 4 respondents following their father's occupation of business. Same thing is also noticed in case of animal husbandry (2) and collection of forest produces. Three respondents engaged in govt. service, responded that among their fathers 2 were also in govt. service and 1 in non-agricultural labour. Those 9 persons are engaged 'others' category of occupation recollect their fathers' occupation were cultivation (3) and agricultural labour (6).

In case of Non-S.T community respondents and respondents' fathers are in the same occupational category in case of 68 cultivators. But their sons are in diverse occupation. Same profession is also followed by the 11 agricultural labourers, where 3 respondents' fathers were cultivator and 8 agricultural labourers. And this is also same in case of non-agricultural labourers where 6 respondents' father were cultivators and 3 agricultural labourers and 1 non-agricultural labourer. Regarding petty business of 17 respondents, 7 each respondent's fathers were cultivators and agricultural labourers, 1 non-agricultural labourer and 2 petty business respectively. Those who are engaged in fishing or aquaculture, their father's occupation were cultivation (7), agricultural labourers (6) and 2 fishing respectively. 'Others' occupation (24) of the respondents' fathers were mainly 'others' (13). Among the sons of the respondents most of them are following their father's / respondents' occupation.

The Table 4.4.6 gives details about the size of land holding of the sample households of the three studied districts in the state of West Bengal. Size of land holding of the S.T. community varies from landless to 4.01+ acres of land. Community-wise break-up shows that among the S.T. (150), 22 households are landless, 34 households possess land between 1.01 – 1.50 acres followed by 30 households possess upto 0.49 acres of land. Between 2.51 acres above there are 20 households. In case of Non-S.T community also the size of land holding varies from landless to 4.01+ acres. Maximum number of households are landless (31) followed by 29

Table–4.4.6–Size of Land Holding of the Sample Households of the Three District in the State of West Bengal

Community (Total No. of surveyed household)	*Size of Land (in Acres)*										Total no of surveyed households
	Landless*	Up to 0.49	0.50-1.00	1.01-1.50	1.51-2.00	2.01-2.50	2.51-3.00	3.01-3.50	3.51-4.00	4.01 +	
Scheduled Tribes (150)	22	30	22	34	08	14	07	03	03	07	150
Non-scheduled Tribes (150)	31	20	23	29	07	17	05	05	02	11	150
Total (300)	53	50	45	63	15	31	12	08	05	18	300

households possess land between 1.01 – 1.50 acres, 23 households 0.50 – 1.00 acre, 20 households possess land upto 0.49 acre. There are 11 households who possess land more than 4.01+ acres. The combined figures show that out of 300 households 53 households are landless and maximum number of households possess land between 1.01 – 1.50 acre followed by 50 households upto 0.49 acres, 45 households 0.50 – 1.00 acre and 18 households possess more than 4.01 acres of land.

The Table 4.4.7A gives details about the source of income of the population of the sample households of the three studied districts in the state of West Bengal. Community-wise break-up shows that among the Scheduled Tribe community out of 150 households 114 households' main source of income comes from agriculture followed by agricultural labour (95), non-agricultural labour (95) and collection of forest produce (95). Animal husbandry also plays a vital role here. Sixty-two (62) households' income comes from animal husbandry. Only 28 households depend on 'others' sources of income. In case of Non-S.T community maximum number of households' (134) main source of income comes from collection of forest produce. Agriculture forms the second major source of income for the 119 households followed by animal husbandry for 60 households, agriculture for 58 households and non-agricultural labour for 37 households. Fishery also plays a major source of income for the 26 households. Only 32 households depend on 'other' sources of income. The combined figures show that the maximum number of households' main source of income comes from agriculture (233) followed by collection of forest produce (229) out of 300 households.

The Table 4.4.7B gives details about the annual distribution of income pattern of the sample households of the three studied districts in the state of West Bengal. In case of S.T community the maximum households' income pattern ranges between Rs. 14401-17400 followed by 38 households' income pattern ranges between Rs. 11401-14400. Out of 150 households only 18 households are lying below poverty line (BPL). In case of Non-S.T community maximum number of households' (38) income pattern ranges between Rs. 17401-21400 followed by Rs. 8401-11400 for 28 households, Rs. 11401-14400 for 26 households and 33 households' income pattern ranges more than Rs. 21400. The number of householdsstands below poverty line is 37 only. The combined figures for both the communities show that maximum number of households' income pattern

Table–4.4.7.A. Sources of Income (Annual) of the Sample Households of the Three Districts in the State of West Bengal.

Source of Income	Community																	
	Scheduled Tribes (150) Amount of Income (annually in Rs.)									Non-Scheduled Tribes (150) Amount of Income (annually in Rs.)								
	Upto 2400	2401-5400	5401-8400	8401-11400	11401-14400	14401-17400	17401-21400	21401+	Total house-holds	Upto 2400	2401-5400	5401-8400	8401-11400	11401-14400	14401-17400	17401-21400	21401+	Total house-holds
Agri-culture	26	29	27	12	12	03	03	02	114	15	31	27	20	10	07	03	06	119
Agri-labour	20	39	17	10	09	-	-	-	95	19	28	09	-	01	-	-	01	58
Non-agril.labour	27	22	25	13	04	01	03	-	95	06	17	09	02	03	-	-	-	37
Service	-	-	-	02	01	-	-	04	07	-	-	-	-	-	-	01	07	08
Busi-ness	-	02	02	01	01	-	-	-	06	02	04	04	02	06	01	02	02	23
A. Husban-dry	40	17	02	02	-	-	01	-	62	50	07	03	-	-	-	-	-	60
Fishery	01	03	-	-	-	-	-	-	04	04	06	10	04	-	01	01	-	26
Colle-ction of F. produce	27	63	04	-	-	01	-	-	95	101	27	05	01	-	-	-	-	134
Others*	07	13	05	02	-	-	01	-	28	03	14	09	03	-	01	01	01	32

Table–4.4.7.B. Distribution of Income Pattern of the Sample Households of the Three Districts in the State of West Bengal

Community	Amount of Total Income (In Rs.)							
	Upto 5400	5401-8400	8401-11400	11401-14400	14401-17400	17401-21400	21401+	Total no. of Household
Scheduled Tribes	-	03	15	38	41	33	20	150
Non- Scheduled Tribes	-	09	28	26	16	38	33	150
Total	-	12	43	64	57	71	53	300

ranges between Rs. 17401-21400 followed by Rs. 11401-14400 for the 64 households, Rs. 14401-17400 for 57 households and 53 households' annual income ranges more than Rs. 21400. Out of 300 households 55 households live below poverty line.

The Table 4.4.8A reveals the annual expenditure pattern of the sample households of the three studied districts in the state of West Bengal. In case of S.T community the households spend their maximum income on food items followed by clothing & footwear, health, fuel and lighting, and others. Out of 150 households, maximum number of households' (47) expenditure on food ranges between Rs. 5401-7400 followed by Rs. 7401-9400 for the 33 households and Rs. 9401-11400 and Rs. 3401-5400 for 21 households each. Regarding clothing & footwear 101 households' expenditure ranges between Rs. 401-1400, 38 households' for Rs. 1404-3400 and Rs. upto 400 for 8 households and 3 households in the range between Rs. 3401-5400. In case of health, 115 households' expenditure ranges between Rs.401-1400 followed by Rs. upto 400 for the 22 households. Thirty-six households' expenditure on education ranges between Rs. 401-1400 and Rs. upto 400 for 31 households. Most of the households' (89) expenditure on housing purposes fall in the range Rs. upto 400 followed by 52 households in the range of Rs. 401-1400. Only one households' expenditure is more than Rs. 13401. Out of 150 households, only 24 households spend money on rituals and it ranges between Rs. upto 400 to Rs. 401-1400 only. Expenditure on social functions by 124 households fall in the range Rs. 401-1400 followed by 21 households in Rs. upto 400range. Most of the households (64) spend money on fuel & lighting in the range between Rs. 401-1400 followed by 41 households in the range Rs. upto 400, 33 households in the Rs. 1401-3400 range and 12 households on Rs. 3401-5400 range. Out of 150 households, 128 households spend money on smoking and drinking and it ranges between Rs. upto 400 to Rs. 401-1401. In case of Non-S.T community out of 150 households, 44 households' expenditure fall on the range between Rs. 5401-7400 followed by 37 households' on Rs. 7401-9400 and 16 households' expenditure is on the Rs. 13401+ range. Regarding clothing & footwear 62 households' expenditure ranges between Rs. 401-1400 followed by 58 households fall in the Rs. 1401-3400. Ninety-four households' expenditure on health ranges between Rs. 401-1400. Expenditure on education of 43 households fall in the range Rs. 401-1400 followed by 16 households in the Rs. 1401-3400

Table–4.4.8.A. Pattern of Household Expenditure (Annually) of the Sample Households of the Three Districts in the State of West Bengal

Item of the Expend-iture	Community																	
	Scheduled Tribes									Non-Scheduled Tribe								
	Upto 400	401 - 1400	1401- 3400	3401- 5400	5401- 7400	7401- 9400	9401- 11400	11401- 13400	13401+	Upto 400	401- 1400	1401- 3400	3401- 5400	5401- 7400	7401- 9400	9401- 11400	11401- 13400	13401+
Food	-	-	05	21	47	33	21	11	12	-	-	-	15	44	37	28	10	16
Clothing & Footwear	08	101	38	03	-	-	-	-	-	25	62	58	05	-	-	-	-	-
Health	22	115	02	-	01	-	01	01	-	43	94	10	02	-	-	-	01	-
Education	31	36	07	03	-	-	-	01	-	23	43	16	06	02	-	-	-	01
Housing	89	52	04	01	-	-	-	-	01	28	102	20	-	-	-	-	-	-
Rituals	14	10	-	-	-	-	-	-	-	27	29	-	-	-	-	-	-	-
Social Functions	21	124	05	-	-	-	-	-	-	40	90	19	01	-	-	-	-	-
Fuel & Lighting	41	64	33	12	-	-	-	-	-	07	117	17	08	01	-	-	-	-
Smoking & Alcohol	74	54	-	-	-	-	-	-	-	25	71	05	01	-	-	-	-	-

range. Regarding expenditure on housing 102 households spend money in the range between Rs. 401-1400. Only 29 households spend some money, which ranges between Rs. 401-1400 and in social functions 90 households in the Rs. 401-1400 range. Expenditure on fuel and lighting of the 117 households fall in the range Rs. 401-1400 range and 102 households' expenditure on smoking & drinking ranges between Rs. upto 400 to Rs. 3401-5400.

The Table 4.4.8B gives detail about the annual distribution of households expenditure of the sample households of the three studied districts in the state of West Bengal. Pattern of households expenditure of the S.T community shows that maximum number of households (86) spend money in the range Rs. 13400 and above followed by 26 households in the Rs. 11401-13400 range. In case of Non-S.T. community most of the households' (84) expenditure fall in the range Rs. 13401 and above followed by 27 households in the Rs. 9401-1400 and 20 households in the Rs. 11401-13400 range. The combined figure also shows the same trend where 170 households, out of 300 spend money in the range Rs. 13401+ followed by 46 households in the range Rs. 11401-13400 and 45 households in Rs. 9401-11400 range.

The Table 4.4.9A depicts the annual households expenditure pattern on agricultural pursuit of the sample households of the three studied districts in the state of West Bengal. In case of Scheduled Tribe community only 2 households spend money in purchasing of agricultural inputs. Out of 150 households, 117 households spend money in any way. But 79 households' expenditure ranges between Rs. upto 500 followed by 27 households' expenditure in Rs. 501-1000 range. Only 112 households purchased seed for agricultural pursuit and it ranges between Rs. upto 500 to Rs. 1001-1500. In case of sowing 101 households' expenditure fall in the range of Rs. upto 500 followed by 12 households' in the range Rs. 501-1000 and 4 households' in Rs. 1001-1500. Only 102 households spend money on weeding and it ranges Rs. upto 500 to Rs. 501-1000 category. In fertilizer & pesticides purposes only 61 households spent money, which fall in the 1st category, i.e., Rs. upto 500. Irrigation facilities by deep tube well, shallow, etc. is not available in all the studied areas. As a result, only16 households spared some money on this purpose, which is also in the range of Rs. upto 500. All the 117 households spend money on harvesting. In case of Non-S.T community no households spent money in

Table–4.4.8.B. Distribution of Household Expenditure (Annually) of the Sample Households of the Three Districts in the State of West Bengal.

Community	Amount of Total Expenditure (In Rs.)						
	Upto 5400	5401-7400	7401-9400	9401-11400	11401-13400	13401 +	Total no. of Household
Scheduled Tribes	-	05	15	18	26	86	150
Non- Scheduled Tribes	-	04	15	27	20	84	150
Total	-	**09**	**30**	**45**	**46**	**170**	**300**

Table–4.4.9.A. Pattern of Expenditure (Annually) on Agricultural Pursuit of the Sample Households of the Three Districts in the State of West Bengal.

Item of the Expenditure	Community															
	Scheduled Tribes (150)								Non- Scheduled Tribes (150)							
	Upto 500	501-1000	1001-1500	1501-2000	2001-2500	2501-3000	3001-3500	3501+	Upto 500	501-1000	1001-1500	1501-2000	2001-2500	2501-3000	3001-3500	3501+
Agricultural Implements	02	-	-	-	-	-	-	-	-	-	-	-	-	-	-	01
Ploughing	79	27	10	01	-	-	-	-	73	31	08	03	03	01	-	-
Purchasing of Seeds	108	03	01	-	-	-	-	-	107	04	-	-	-	-	-	-
Sowing	101	12	04	-	-	-	-	-	75	26	05	04	01	03	-	-
Weeding	100	02	-	--	-	-	-	-	75	03	-	-	-	-	-	-
Fertilizers & pesticides	55	06	-	-	-	-	-	-	71	17	07	02	-	-	-	-
Irrigation	16	-	-	-	-	-	-	-	23	03	-	-	-	-	-	-
Harvesting	75	26	13	03	-	-	-	-	63	31	14	06	02	01	01	01

purchasing of agricultural implements. But in ploughing, 119 households' expenditure ranges between upto Rs. 500 to Rs. 2501-3000 category. Seed was purchased by all the 111 households and it ranges Rs. upto 500. Regarding sowing 75 households' expenditure in the range between Rs. upto 500 followed by 26 households' in Rs. 501-1000 and the rest households' expenditure ranges between Rs. 1001-1500 to Rs. 2501-3000. In case of weeding out of 78 households, 75 households spent money in the range Rs. upto 500 and 3 in the Rs. 501-1000. Use of fertilizer & pesticides was done by the 97 households and it ranges between Rs. upto 500 to Rs. 1501-2000. Irrigation facilities were availed by only 26 households and spent money in the ranges between Rs. upto 500 to Rs. 501-1000. All the 119 households' expenditure on harvesting fall in the ranges between Rs. upto 500 to Rs. 3501+ category and maximum number of households fall in the Rs. upto 500 ranges.

The Table 4.4.9B reveals the distribution of annual expenditure of households on agricultural pursuit of the sample households of the three studied districts in the state of West Bengal. Community-wise break up shows of the Scheduled Tribe shows that out of 117 households practicing agriculture, 29 households spent money in the range between Rs. 501-1000 followed by 22 households in the Rs. 1001-1500 category and rest of the households are in different categories of expenditure. In case of Non-S.T community 33 households' expenditure fall in the category Rs. 3501 and above followed by 29 households whose expenditure ranges between Rs. 501-1000, 21 households in the Rs. 1001-1500 range. The combined data for both the communities show that out of 236 households, 58 households' expenditure fall in the expenditure category of Rs. 501-1000 followed by 46 households in the Rs. 3500+ category and 43 households in the Rs. 1001-1500 range. Other households' expenditure ranges between Rs. upto 500 to Rs. 3501+.

The Table 4.4.10 states the nature of indebtedness among the sample households of the three studied districts in the state of West Bengal. Community-wise break up shows that among the Scheduled Tribe community (150) debts are borrowed mainly from neighbours, traders and friends & relatives for the purposes of purchasing of food materials, life cycle ceremonies, to pay bride price, medical treatment and others. Twenty persons borrowed debt upto Rs. 1000 of which 10 from neighbours and others 8 from friends & relatives to meet the medical treatment and 'others'

Table–4.4.9.B. Distribution of Expenditure (Annually) on Agricultural Pursuit of the Sample Households of the Three Districts in the State of West Bengal

Community	Amount of Total Expenditure (in Rs.)								Total Households
	Upto 500	501-1000	1001-1500	1501-2000	2001-2500	2501-3000	3001-3500	3501+	
Scheduled Tribe	21	29	22	17	04	06	05	13	117
Non- Scheduled Tribe	06	29	21	08	11	08	03	33	119
Total	27	58	43	25	15	14	08	46	236

Table–4.4.10. Nature of Indebteness among the Sample Households of the Three Districts in the State of West Bengal

Community (No. of surveyed households)	Amount of borrowing	Source of borrowing			Purpose of borrowing					Repayment Status		Security			Debt	
		Neighbours	Local Traders	Friends & Relatives	Purchasing of food materials	Life cycle ceremonies	To pay bride price	Medical treatment	Others *	Due – fully	Due – partially	Land	Ornaments	Others	Ancestor	Respondent
Scheduled Tribes (150)	Up to 1000	10	02	08	06	-	-	07	07	18	02	03	-	-	-	20
	1001 - 2000	08	01	-	04	-	-	01	04	07	02	03	-	-	-	09
	2001 - 3000	03	-	-	-	03	-	-	-	03	-	02	-	-	-	03
	3001 - 4000	06	01	-	01	02	-	01	03	07	-	05	-	-	-	07
	4001 – 5000	02	-	-	-	01	-	-	01	02	-	02	-	-	-	02
	5001 – 6000	14	02	01	05	03	02	04	03	17	-	16	-	-	01	16
	Sub-total	**43**	**06**	**09**	**16**	**09**	**02**	**13**	**18**	**54**	**04**	**31**	-	-	**01**	**57**

Community (No. of surveyed households)	Amount of borrowing	Source of borrowing			Purpose of borrowing					Repayment Status		Security			Debt	
		Neighbours	Local Traders	Friends & Relatives	Purchasing of food materials	Life cycle ceremonies	To pay bride price	Medical treatment	Others *	Due – fully	Due – partially	Land	Ornaments	Others	Ancestor	Respondent
Non-Scheduled Tribes (150)	Up to 1000	05	04	02	04	01	-	04	03	12	-	-	-	-	-	12
	1001 - 2000	06	03	05	06	-	01	03	04	13	01	02	-	-	01	13
	2001 - 3000	02	01	01	01	01	-	01	01	04	-	02	-	-	-	04
	3001 - 4000	03	-	-	-	-	-	01	02	03	-	01	-	-	-	03
	4001 – 5000	03	-	-	01	01	-	-	01	02	01	-	-	-	-	03
	5001 – 6000	12	03	01	02	01	05	01	07	14	02	07	01	-	-	16
	Sub-total	**31**	**11**	**09**	**13**	**04**	**06**	**10**	**17**	**48**	**04**	**13**	**01**	-	**01**	**48**
Total (300)		**74**	**17**	**18**	**29**	**13**	**08**	**23**	**35**	**102**	**08**	**44**	**01**	-	**02**	**105**

7 cases each. Regarding repayment 18 persons did not repay the amount and only 2 persons repaid partially. In the Rs. 1001-2000 range 9 persons borrowed debts from neighbours (68) and from traders (1) for purchasing of food materials and 'others' of which 3 persons mortgaged their land as security. But none of them repaid the debt. in the Rs. 2001-3000 category only 3 persons took debt from neighbours to meet the life cycle ceremonies of which 2 have mortgaged their land and did not repay at all. In the Rs. 3001-4000 category the number of indebted persons is 7 of which 6 has taken money neighbours by mortgaging their agricultural land to meet the 'others' and did not repay any amount of debt. Most of the persons (17) borrowed debts belong to the group of Rs. 5001-6000 of which 14 from neighbours for purchasing of food materials, life cycle ceremonies, medical treatment (4) and 'others' (3). None of them repaid the debt amount. Most of them (16) have also mortgaged their agricultural land as security. Fifty-eight households borrowed debt of which 43 households received it from neighbours, 9 from friends & relatives and 6 from traders for purchasing of food materials (16), 'others' (18), medical care (18), life cycle ceremonies (9) and to pay bride price (2). None of them repaid the dues and have also mortgaged the land (31) as security.

In case of Scheduled Tribe community (150) out of 48 most of the debts are taken from neighbours (31), traders (11) and friends & relatives (9). Purpose o borrowing was for 'others' (17), purchasing of food materials (13), medical treatment (10), to pay bride price (6) and for life cycle ceremonies (4). Regarding repayment nobody repaid the debt amount fully of which 13 households mortgaged his or her land and one household ornaments. Most of the cases of debts occurred in the range between Rs. upto 1000 to Rs. 2000-3000 and then in the range between Rs. 5001-6000. The combined data show that out of 107 cases of debts, 74 persons took it from neighbours, 18 from friends & relatives and 17 from traders for the purposes of 'others' (35), purchasing of food materials (29), medical treatment (23), life cycle ceremonies (13) and to pay bride price (8). Regarding status of repayment, 102 persons did not repay and only 8 persons repaid partially. Out of 107 persons took debt, 44 persons mortgaged their land and one ornaments as security. Most of the debts (105) were taken by the head of the households and only in 2 cases by fathers of the respondents.

The Table 4.4.11 gives detail about the loan received by the sample households from various sources of the three studied districts in the state

Table–4.4.11. Loan Received by the Sample Households from Various Sources of the Three Districts in the State of West Bengal

Type of Loan	Community: Scheduled Tribe: Loan Amount				Scheduled Tribe: Loan Repayment			Scheduled Tribe: Security		Scheduled Tribe: Loan taken by		Non - Scheduled Tribe: Loan Amount				Non - Scheduled Tribe: Loan Repayment			Non - Scheduled Tribe: Security		Non - Scheduled Tribe: Loan taken by	
	upto 3000	3001 - 6000	6001 - 9000	9001 +	Paid fully	Paid partially	Due totally	Land	Ornaments	Respondent	Ancestor	upto 3000	3001 - 6000	6001 – 9000	9001 +	Paid fully	Paid partially	Due totally	Land	Ornaments	Respondent	Ancestor
Agri-culture	02	04	-	-	01	-	05	-	-	05	01	-	04	-	01	01	03	01	01	-	05	-
Busi-ness	02	02	01	-	-	01	04	-	-	05	-	12	06	03	02	02	07	14	01	-	23	-
Animal Hus-bandry	06	01	-	-	-	-	07	-	-	06	01	02	03	-	01	04	02	-	-	-	05	01
Total	**10**	**07**	**01**	-	**01**	**01**	**16**	-	-	**16**	**02**	**14**	**13**	**03**	**04**	**07**	**12**	**15**	**02**	-	**33**	**01**

* Source of Loan : Generally the households take loan from any Nationalised Bank, Gramin Bank and Co-operative Society.

of West Bengal. Loans were given mainly in three sectors : agriculture, business and animal husbandry. The Scheduled Tribe community received 6 number of agricultural loan and nobody repaid the loan fully. Their loan amount varies from Rs. upto 3000 to Rs. 3001-6000. In case of business 5 nos. of loans were disbursed and the loan amount varies from Rs. upto 3000 to Rs. 6001-9000. Regarding status of repayment none repaid the loan amount. In all cases loans were taken by the respondents himself/herself. In case of animal husbandry, 7 nos. of loans were disbursed and its amount varies from Rs. upto 3000 to Rs. 3001-6000. Loan recovery was nil. In case of Non-S.T community total number of loans was disbursed is 34. In agriculture sector only 5 households receives loan whose loan amount varies from Rs. 3001-6000 to Rs. 9001+. Only one loanee repaid the loan amount fully. Maximum number of loans (23) was disbursed in the petty business sector and their loan amount varies from Rs. upto 3000 to Rs. 9001+. Regarding status of repayment, only 2 loanee repaid the loan amount fully. In the animal husbandry sector 6 loans were disbursed and out of them 4 loanee have repaid the loan amount fully and the rest 2 loanee repaid partially the loan amount. The combined figures show that though number of loans disbursed are not sufficient but the poor recovery of loan amount have made the concerned authority not to disburse the loan to non-potential beneficiaries.

5

Concept of Sustainable Development

I

Theories and Conceptual Framework

In the next twenty years, the issue of sustainability can be expected to significantly alter the parameters of doing business. Sustainable development has become the buzzword of the 1990's. Weekly new legislation and regulations are being promulgated, restricting and codifying economic activity with the objective of sustainability. In this chapter an attempt will be made to discuss the concept of sustainable development, how it has arisen, the state of the debate and its application.

The concept of sustainable development advanced by the Brundtland Report was defined as "development that meets the needs of the present without compromising the ability of future generations to meet their needs" (Brundtland 1987). In a static world, it should be possible to forgo some economic growth to reduce pollution or to conserve non-renewable resources. However, with rapid population growth imposing increasing demands on land, resources and the "global commons", the opportunity costs of reducing pollution and resource depletion can become significant.

However, slower economic growth brings its own environmental problems through lowered efficiencies (Beekerman 1992). Yet environmental degradation and rapid depletion of natural resources will hamper future growth. In this sense the environment and economic growth are joint products. There are major problems with accepted definition of sustainable development. Notwithstanding the inclusion of inter-generational equity in the definition (which raises philosophical issues about distributive justice), the Brundtland Report does not recognise the dynamics of technological progress and substitution.

Once ecological sustainability is introduced, the notion of a fixed quantum and composition of environmental resources as well as commitment to traditional patterns of land use can affect potential economic growth. This is much more conservative view of sustainability than usually adopted by economists and it makes no allowance for trade offs among alternative objectives (Tisdell 1988).

The extent to which natural resources can be converted into human or physical capital or new technology to support sustainable development has become major issue in the environmental debate. This brings into question also the definition of non-renewable resources. Most natural resources are renewable, given sufficient time (Dasgupta and Maler, 1990). Even the life of known mineral stocks can be extended as technology improves extraction techniques and reduces costs.

Many definitions of "sustainable development" become distorted because they neglect the effect of price changes on investment and technology, on conservation decisions and on the adoption of substitutes. The concept of sustainable development adopted by the Brundt – land report embodies many of the same weaknesses as the club of Rome Report (meadows et al 1972), which was criticised because it failed to allow for economic feed back meelanisms (Beekerman 1974 and 1952)

Pezzey (1989) identified 62 different definitions of sustainable development. The attention given to sustainable development during last several years has done little to make definitions operational. Discussion returns to the Brundt land Reports definition. The concept of inter-generational equity provides the core ethic for sustainable development. Yet each generations already seems to achieve higher levels of real income (utility) than earlier generations. In developing countries sustainable development must benefit both present and future generations. That means economic growth to alleviate poverty, reduce fertility rates, substitute human and physical capital for natural resources, protect the environment and promote supply responses in other words, improve economic efficiency.

Sustainability from a social viewpoint is generally recognised as requiring equity in distribution, income, wealth, access to power, inter and intra generational equity, a sociologically compatible style of production and consumption and community consultation.

Sustainable development theory links models of long term biological and economic maximisation. It extends cost benefit analysis and bio-economics and combines it with ideas of economic welfare first expressed by J.S. Mill in the nineteenth century. Sustainable development received its first exposure in 1980 with publication of world conservation strategy.

Intergenerational equity implies providing a wealth or capital inheritance for future generations equal to that which we ourselves received. Distinction may be drawn between human, man-made and natural capital such as minerals and fossil fuels, tropical rainforests, fertile topsoil, and animal and plant species once lost cannot be replaced, though substitutes may be found. In fact, most economists would argue that man-made capital and technical know-how can substitute to some extent for natural capital and that consuming some natural resources at present can make both current and future generations better off.

According to this view, sustainable development could include such things as limiting extraction of biological resources to renewal rates; control our degradation of soil and water resources; maintenance of biological diversity, ecosystem and wild life habitat; prevention of species extinctions in terms of flora and fauna, restrained use of non-renewable resources and recycling to the maximum extent viable on cost grounds, and avoiding exceeding the capacity of the environment to absorb waste products.

In a narrow sense, "locking up" resources could achieve ecological sustainability, but there is an over whelming case for economic growth and development, to provide goods and serving (including basic necessities) and to create employment for increasing population numbers. Any of the myriad forms of development from small management changes to mega – projects will use up some resources (including non-renewable resources) and create some waste products, which must be absorbed by the environment.

From an anthropocentric perspective ecological sustainability is not necessarily a good in its own right, unless degradation of ecosystems leads to reduced welfare of mankind. In this regard it has been suggested that attention should be paid to protection of three systems, viz. ecological, economic and social.

Since it would be unrealistic to think that land, water and vegetation could ever be managed such that no loss of resource quality takes place, our definition will include capacity of socio-economic systems to accommodate ecological change. Development can still be ecological change. Development can still be ecologically sustainable where change in the condition of resources takes place, as long as individuals and communities depending on those resources can continue to function in and adequate fashion. This is a weaker requirement than preservation of an ecological system in a steady state.

Finally, it must be recognized that sustainability is not a static concept. What is regarded as sustainable may change over time as community values change. As well, in the case of some pollutants (e.g. insecticides in rivers), community expectations as to acceptable levels tend to be set by limits of defection, which are continually improving.

In the light of the series of integrative foci of the past decades, "sustainable development" can be considered humanities last and latest effort to reconceptualize "the good, the true and the beautiful" for the international community. Given the responses to past efforts, notably Brundt Commission, it is fruitful to ask how sustainable over time is the concept of "sustainable development" Already there is evidence of multiple interpretations (Pezzey, 1989), some of them quite incompatible, just as has been the case with "development" alone.

The challenge is to identify how the development of any such insight can be sustained, especially in a policy forum. The difficulty lies in assumptions made by those actively involved in promoting or clarifying such an insight. These include:

(a) a tendency to consider it the only valid integrative concept that has ever been formulated. This ignores the history of previous concepts, which have created the context for the emergence of this latest one. It also ignores what happened to the previous ones and the nature of the relationships they established.

(b) a tendency to consider that no further valid integrative concepts will emerge to replace the current one. This structures reflection on the concept to preclude the future emergence of more appropriate concepts. It engenders dogmatism and identification of heresies.

(c) a tendency to believe that the concept is inherently credible and desirable to those who have not been involved in its formulation. The step beyond this is to assume that they ought to be persuaded to that conviction if they do not hold it.

(d) a tendency to believe that policy insights of requistic variety can be adequately embodied within in a single policy framework.

(e) A tendency to fail to recognize that groups are sensitive to quite different forms of information in relation to any issue and frequently consider other forms as having marginal significance, if any.

As more people and groups are touched by the insight, they reinterpret it to better reflect their own understanding. This leads to factionalism and multiple interpretations which may be highly critical of each other, even to the point of subverting each others initiatives in competition of resources "Sustainable development" has to survive in this environment.

Finally, it can be said that the world commission on Environment and Development drew attention to the common challenges of population growth, the need for strategies for sustaining food security and the need to conserve natural resources. Agenda 21, the plan of action for implementing sustainable development elaborated further. It states

"Major adjustments are needed in agricultural, environmental and macroeconomic policy at both national and international levels, in developed as well as developing countries, to create the conditions for sustainable agriculture and rural development. The major objective of sustainable agriculture and rural development is to increase food production in a sustainable way and enhance food security. This will involve education initiatives, utilization of economic incentives and the development of appropriate and new technologies, thus ensuring stable supplies of nutritionally adequate food, access to those sappies by vulnerable groups, and production for markets; employment and income generation to alleviate poverty and natural resource management and environmental protection". (Agenda 21, 1992)

Definitions of sustainable agriculture are generally concerned with the need for agricultural practices to be economically viable to meet human needs for food, to be environmentally positive and to be concerned with quality of life. Since these objectives can be achieved in a number of different ways, sustainable agriculture is not linked to any particular technological practice. Nor is sustainable agriculture the exclusive domain of organic farming. Rather, sustainable agriculture is thought of in terms of its adaptability and flexibility over time to respond to the demands for food and fiber (both high and low), its demands on natural resources for production, and its ability to protect the soil and the resources. This goal requires an efficient use of technology in a manner conducive to sustainability.

The International Agriculture Research (CGIAR) points out, "Sustainable agriculture is the successful management of resources to satisfy the changing human needs, while maintaining or enhancing the quality of environment and conserving natural resources". The ultimate goal or the ends of sustainable agriculture is to develop farming systems that are productive and profitable, conserve the natural resource base, protect the environment and enhance health and safety and do so over the long term. The means of achieving this is low input methods and skilled management, which seek to optimise the management and the use of internal production inputs (i.e. on farm resources) in ways that provide acceptable levels of sustainable crop yields and livestock production and result in economically profitable returns. This approach emphasises such cultural and management practices as crop rotations, recycling of animal manure and conservation tillage to control soil erosion and nutrient losses and to maintain or enhance soil productivity. Low input farming systems seek to minimise the use of external production inputs such as purchased fertilizer and pesticides, where ever and whenever feasible and practicable; to lower production costs to avoid pollution of surface and group water, to reduce pesticide residues in food, to reduce a farmer's overall risk and to increase both short and long term farm profitability.

6

Facets of Bio-Diversity and Its Utilization

I

Meaning of Biodiversity

The term 'Biodiversity' encompasses the variety of all life on Earth. It is defined as the variability among living organisms and the ecological complexes of which they are part, including diversity within and between species and eco-systems. Biodiversity manifests at species, genetic and eco-system levels.

Biological diversity has direct consumptive value in food, agriculture, medicine, industry, etc. It also has aesthetic and recreational value. Biodiversity maintains ecological balance and continues evolutionary processes. The indirect ecosystem services provided through biodiversity are photosynthesis, pollination, transpiration, chemical cycling, nutrient cycling, soil maintenance, climate regulation, air, water system management, waste treatment and pest control.

All species in a community provide a better basis for understanding the causative factors for the presence of a species. Further, the presence of certain species in a community may not be of much significance because it indicates the potentiality of the species for a wide range of tolerance and therefore, in such situations, other criteria may be more meaningful in establishing correlations between the presence or absence of a species. According to Williams (1964) the low generic and species diversity indicate the high probability of extinction of the living organisms of the genera and species of the complex.

II

Value of Environment

Although valuing the environment is an essential prerequisite for biodiversity conservation and sustainable development there is no simple and easily acceptable way of evaluating the floral and faunal components of environment. Any evaluation of the biota will invariably involve the calculation of its financial price. We are accustomed to accepting financial indicators as guides to the state of national economics. Thus, there are indices of monetary supply, inflation rate, bank rate, gross domestic product, share indices and a host of other economic calculations with which to judge the health and wealth of national economics.

No such indices exist currently either on what should be the parameter to indicate the value of forests – should it be productivity, quality, calorific value, genetic purity, or genetic adaptability.

Many conservationists abhor the placing of financial values or abiotic resources preferring instead to use an aesthetic and scientific value. Unfortunately industrialists, economists and politicians cannot equate this type of non-financial valuation with a traditional fiscal balance sheet in which income and expenditure can be translated into neat columns of profit and loss. When it comes to flower scent, colouration, wildlife and avifaunal aesthetics, melody and nature's trend in ontogeny and phylogeny evaluation, it becomes a trying job.

Valuation is not everything on the agenda of sustainable development but (i) it measures the rate at which environmental resources are being utilised, and signals the growing scarcity of their uses; (ii) it provides a truer indication of economic performance; (iii) it helps to redress the balance between quantifiable and non-quantifiable effects in cost – benefit analysis of between monetary or non-monetary values; (iv) it requires a great deal of technical and economic data; (v) trying to put economic values in environmental effects which are inherently non-quantifiable merely devalues the debate. Certain things do have an absolute value, which makes them essentially non-quantifiable – life itself, beauty, the diversity of species are some examples. However, there are many instances of apparent, non-quantifiable value to which the economic rod is already being partially applied, e.g., health, an obstructed view, water quality, etc.

III

Field Observation

While doing the biodiversity study in different plots of Ranibandh Range (Bankura District), Moraghat Range (Jalpaiguri District) and Sajnekhali Wildlife Sanctuary (South 24 Parganas District) in West Bengal various types of faunas and floras were encountered. The faunas included mammals, birds, reptiles, etc. The floras included the tree species, shrubs, herbs, climber, etc. Most of the plant species are important from the point of view of their use as timber, food, fodder, medicine, NWFPs and decorative materials. The following are the detailed description of the species occurring in the localities mentioned above.

Ranibandh Range (Bankura District)

Climate, soil, topography and biotic factors usually determine the nature of forest and their distribution. In Bankura, however, the effects of biotic factors are so pronounced and the results so far reaching that these are almost the determining factors and the forest types may be called biotic climax. Nowhere in West Bengal, has so vast a tract as Bankura district, with so rich a forest cover, suffered so much and their cattle's in so short a time. The elders recall with nostalgia rich sylvan traditions of their district, which is amply borne out by old name of the district as "*JUNGLE MAHAL*".

Wherever the natural crop exists, the characteristic species are gregarious *Sal* (*Shorea robusta*) with associates like *Asan* (*Terminali tomentosa*), *Bahera* (*Terminali bellerica*), *Piasal* (*Peterocarpus marsupium*), *Kend* (*Diospyros melanoxylon*), *Palash* (*Butea monosperma*), *Parasi* (*Cleistanthus collenius*), *Panjon* (*Ongeria dalbergiodes*), *Dhaw* (*Anogeissus latitolia*), etc.

The Sal forests are typical of the district and its status ranges from natural Sal forests through coppice Sal to degraded Sal forest. The barren areas have been taken under plantations, with a combination of quick growing species mainly, Eucalyptus sps. And *Acacia auricoliformis* (*Akashmani*) and indigenous species like Sisoo, Gamar, Chhatim, Neem, Harra, Bahera, Amloki, Siris, etc.

The forest of Bankura is "Treasure house of Non-Timber Forest Produces (NTFPs)". The major NTFPs collected from forests are medicinal plants like Bhui-kumra, Satamuli, Kalmegh, Anantamul, Kantikari, Lal Palash, Ban Piaz, Kurchi, etc. Oil seeds Mohul, Sal, Karanj, Neem, Kusum, etc, are plenty available in the forest. Kendu leaves, Mohua flowers,

Mushroom, Sal leaves, decorative herbs, are also available in the forest. A part of the livelihood of the fringe area dwellers or the 'Eco-system People' is made from NTFPs collection in many areas. Due to resuscitation of Sal forest abundance of NTFPs has increased and contribute sustainability to success Joint Forest Management (JFM) practiced in South West Bengal. It has been estimated that roughly about 90 lakhs rupees worth NTFPs are collected from forest area of Bankura district either for self-consumption or for sale in the local market.

Apart from the receiving 25% share of net sale proceed of final felling the FPC members are also allowed to enjoy the benefit of collection of minor forest produces (MFPs) like, flowers, seeds (except Kaju and Sal), leaves, dry twigs and fallen leaves for their own consumption free of cost. They also enjoy the benefit to receive the share of 25% of produce obtained by different tending operation in Sal forest like coppicing, m.s.cutting, and thinning. In addition the wage component earmarked for different forestry activities like, Aforestation, Soil Conservation Work, Harvesting, Wild Life Management, and other development activities directly goes to the FPC members.

Forest area covering about 22,000 hac. is the home of various wild lives. Roughly these areas are Ranibandh, Jhilimili, Chandapathar, Joypur, Susunia and Badrinath Forests. Major species found are Wild Boar, Spotted Deer, Pangolin, Python, Viper, Peacock, Langoor, Porcupine, Leopard, Wolf, Jackal, Hyena, Fox, Hare, Migratory birds and migratory as well as resident Elephant. Due to protection afforded through JFM (about 90% of the total areas in under JFM) the abundance of each and every species has increased over the years. Recently spotted deer has been released in the wild in Sutan and Joypore forests. This introduction of deer has already proved to be a success and the population is increasing.

Moraghat Range (Jalpaiguri District)

Jalpaiguri has a very rich and varied heritage of biodiversity, encompassing a wide spectrum of floras and faunas. Other than Bankura district in West Bengal, Jalpaiguri district has the highest varieties of floras and faunas in the biodiversity map. The nature of forest and its distribution is normally determined by climate, soil, topography and biotic factors.

Wherever the natural flora exists, the characteristic species are *Sal* with associates like *Gamar, Sisoo, Arjun, Mahagony, Chiluni, Hollong, Panchpate, Garjan, Lasaune, Gante, Kapak, Karanj, etc.* The *Sal* forests are typical of the district and its status ranges from natural *Sal* forests to degraded *Sal* forest. The major NTFPs collected from forests are medicinal plants like *Satamuli, Kalmegh, Anantamul, Ishwarmul, Bahera, Haritaki, Amloki,* etc. A part of the livelihood of the 'Eco-system People' is made from NTFPs collection in many areas.

Forest area of Jalpaiguri district is the home of various wild lives. Major species found are Wild Boar, Spotted Deer, Pangolin, Python, Viper, Peacock, Langoor, Porcupine, Leopard, Wolf, Jackal, Hyena, Fox, Hare, Migratory birds and migratory as well as resident Elephant.

Sajnekhali Wildlife Sanctuary Range (District - South 24 Parganas)

Sundarban is representative of an area of very rich biodiversity of mangrove flora and fauna in Asian province where environmental adaptation limits are significantly stretched. The mangrove tract in Sundarban signifies the special ecological effect due to tidal ingress of sea undeterred by upstream flow and plant community manifests abnormal adaptation like development of *pneumatophores* (breathing roots), stilt roots, and viviparous germination for survival in partly saline and partly submerged coastal eco-systems. The existence of mangrove eco-system and its diverse animal and plant community in the area depends on their symbiotic relationship. The number of mangrove species here are 64 whereas other geographic provinces do not bear more than 20 species. Naturally, Sundarban is the unique being the only mangrove tiger land on globe where tiger occupies the pinnacle of both aquatic as well as terrestrial food-web. There are also Cheetal, Wild Boar, Rhesus macaque, Fishing cat, etc. The aquatic fauna includes Gangetic Dolphin, River Terrapin (Batagur Baska), Olive Ridley Turtle, Green Turtle, Hawk's Turtle, and different species of crabs, prawns, lobsters and fishes. Aquatic animals like the crabs and other fish appears in the list of feeds of tiger, monkey, etc. In the month of May to June when salinity of water increases, the availability of fish declines. The crocodile, the only surviving member of Jurassic time, which feeds on aquatic animals and predator fish in turn help to increase the population of edible fish. To add colour and melody there are birds like Rose ringed Parakeet, Crow Pheasant, Pied Myna, Dronga, Bulbul, Tailor Bird, Magpie, Robin, Brahmini Kite, Spotted Dove, Adjutant Stroke, etc.

Mangroves are woody plants that grow at the inter-tidal zones of sheltered shores, estuaries, tidal creeks, backwaters, lagoons, marshes and mud flats in the tropical and sub-tropical regions of the world. These plants exist under very hostile and inhospitable conditions. They have to encounter higher salinity, tidal extremes, heavy winds, high temperature and anaerobic soil substrates there by developing peculiar adoptive morphological features and physiological mechanisms such as supporting and breathing roots, viviparous germination, salt excreting leaves etc. Mangroves and their associates together constitute a fragile coastal ecosystem supporting rich microbial, floral and faunal components. These constitute important ecological asset and economic resource in the coastal marine environment. Mangrove forests are among the most productive ecosystems and play an important role in protection of the coastal areas, fertilisation of the sea and serve as the breeding and feeding grounds for prawns and fishes.

The mangrove eco-system is however, so fragile that any interference may lead to extinction of various components and also the eco-system as a whole. People living in the area are poor; subsist on single-crop agriculture, fishing, honey and wood collection from the forests. In absence of any alternative employment, they depend on traditional skills to earn their livelihood and depend largely on forest resources like firewood, timber wood, honey, bee wax, golpata and tend to resort to illegal practices like poaching and felling. They collect Tiger Prawn seeds in great numbers causing damage to juvenile fish stock, mangrove plantation and earthen dams and dykes. Continuous hack on the trees due to pressure on population, pollution in the habitat due to exhaust oil from watercraft, destruction of seeds of various fish in the process of catching tiger prawn seeds will have adverse effect in maintenance of ecological balance in the area on account of elimination of different species of flora and fauna. In case of faunal species the smaller animals feel the initial impact and in turn the bigger animals are also affected. Construction irrigation *bundhs* to protect reclaimed area, has affected the flow of tidal water. The sewerage wastes of metropolis of Kolkata are dumped into the area, which acts as a natural biological detoxifier, but the metallic pollutants remain intact in the system. Due to increase in siltation and also neo-tectonic tilt to Gangetic basin, which occurred during early years, the fresh water inflow has greatly diminished and stopped at major places. As a result of which, the fresh water-tidal saline water interface has been restricted causing detrimental effects to the eco-system. This adverse effect may be very serious and far-reaching, rendering certain plant and animal species totally extinct. Nearness to urban metropolis of Kolkata has increased the demand for forest and marine resources, which has resulted in possible excess harvest of resources causing threat to eco-system. The lost lot who did not get a chance to survive due to indiscriminate human interference are Javan Rhino, Wild Buffalo, Swamp Deer, Bark Deer and many other important animal species.

Table–6.1.1. List of Floras Exist and Their Utilisation in Ranibandh Range Under Ranibandh Block in the District of Bankura, West Bengal

Sl. No.	*Scientific Name*	*Local Name*	*Utilisation*	*Household Consumption / Commercial*
1.	*Abrus precatorius*	Kunch	Seeds and roots are medicinal	Household Consumption
2.	*Acacia auriculiformis*	Sonajhuri	Leaves – fodder, Poles – useful, Timber – furniture, Pods – detergent quality.	Household Consumption/ Commercial
3.	*Acacia pinnata*	Akashmani	Leaves – fodder, Poles – useful, Timber – furniture, Pods – detergent quality.	Household Consumption/ Commercial
4.	*Achyranthes aspera*	Apang	Entire plants and seeds are medicinal.	Household Consumption
5.	*Adhatoda zeylanica*	Vasaka	The fresh dried leaves contain an alkaloid vasicine, and an essential oil and used as an expectorant.	Household Consumption
6.	*Aegle marmelos*	Bel	Fresh, ripe or half ripe fruits of the tree are valuable for its mucilage and pectin; it is very useful in chronic diarrhoea dysentery, particularly for patients having diarrhoea alternating with spells of constipation. The unripe or half ripe fruits improve appetite and digestion.	Household Consumption/ Commercial
7.	*Albizzia lebbeck*	Siris	Bark of root and stem, leaves, flower, seed and wood extract are medicinal. Timber tree.	Household Consumption/ Commercial
8.	*Allium sativum*	Rasun	Used for general debility, worms, anti-T.B., Venereal Disease, Dysentery, and Typhoid.	Household Consumption
9.	*Alocasia indica*	Kochu	Roots edible.	Household Consumption/ Commercial

Sl. No.	Scientific Name	Local Name	Utilisation	Household Consumption Commercial
10.	*Alstomia scolaris*	Chhatim	Dried bark of the tree is considered very efficacious in chronic diarrhoea and dysentery. It is useful in malarial fever. Also useful in skin diseases.	Household Consumption
11.	*Anacardium occidental*	Cashew nut	Nuts edible and extract of seed is used in preparation of oil.	Household Consumption/ Commercial
12.	*Anacardium occidentalis*	Kaju	Nuts edible.	Household Consumption/ Commercial
13.	*Andrographis paniculata*	Kalmegh	All parts of the plant above ground level are used in curing fevers, worms, dysentery, general weakness and excessive gas formation in stomach. It is also reported to be useful for children suffering from liver and digestion complaints.	Household Consumption/ Commercial
14.	*Anogeissus latigokia*	Dhaw	Pulp (news-print), Fuel wood.	Household Consumption/ Commercial
15.	*Anthocephalus cadamba*	Kadam	Matchwood and Plywood species.	Household Consumption/ Commercial
16.	*Aristolochia indica*	Ishwarmul	Dried roots and leaves are useful in curing snake bite, cold and asthma.	Household Consumption
17.	*Asparagus racesoma*	Satamuli	Roots, leaves medicinal. Used in curing blood dysentery, epilepsy, filarial.	Household Consumption/ Commercial
18.	*Azadirachta indica*	Neem	Dried stem bark, leaves and roots are used as medicine. The bark is bitter tonic, astringent and anti-periodic. That is, it is useful in fevers; it breaks the periodic sequence of fevers (like malaria) and is useful in skin diseases. The leaves and roots are used in skin diseases.	Household Consumption/ Commercial

Sl. No.	Scientific Name	Local Name	Utilisation	Household Consumption / Commercial
19.	*Bacopa monnieri*	Brahmi	The whole plant is medicinal. Used for nervous disorders, mental diseases, constipation and to promote urination. Leaf juice is given to infants in bronchitis. Leaf juice, mixed with petroleum, is applied on rheumatism. The plant is considered a blood purifier.	Household Consumption/ Commercial
20.	*Basella alba*	Bon-Pui	Used as plant vegetables.	Household Consumption
21.	*Bombax ceiba*	Simul	Bark of root and stem, flower, seed are medicinal. Fruit produces floss. Match and plywood.	Household Consumption/ Commercial
22.	*Borassus flabellifer*	Tal	Fruit edible and medicinal.	Household Consumption/ Commercial
23.	*Buchanania latifolia*	Pial (Chiranji)	Bark of root, leaves, gum, flower, seed, and seed oil all are medicinal. Used in skin diseases. Fruit yields jam. Wood as timber.	Household Consumption/ Commercial
24.	*Butea monosperma*	Palash	The red coloured gums contain tannins and is valuable for treatment of diarrhoea. The seeds are used as anti-helmintic in treatment of roundworms and tapeworms.	Household Consumption/ Commercial
25.	*Cassia tora*	Chakunda	Medicinal plant.	Household Consumption/ Commercial
26.	*Cleistanthus collinus*	Parashi	Fruits extremely poisonous. Stem used as fuel wood, fencing material, roof structure. Leaf, root, capsule – insecticide, skin disease, arthritis.	Household Consumption/ Commercial

Sl. No.	*Scientific Name*	*Local Name*	*Utilisation*	*Household Consumption / Commercial*
27.	*Cleradendron infortuna*	Bhat/Ghentu	Leaves, flower and root are medicinal.	Household Consumption/ Commercial
28.	*Coccinia Cordifolia*	Bon-Kundri	Bitter tasted is medicinal. Sweet one is used as vegetable.	Household Consumption
29.	*Combretum decondrum*	Atari	Fuel wood. Young shoots used for basket making, fruits decorative.	Household Consumption/ Commercial
30.	*Commuelina benghalensis*	Kansira	Entire plant is medicinal.	Household Consumption
31.	*Croton oblongifolius*	Putla	Fuel wood. Ornamental.	Household Consumption
32.	*Dalbergia sisso*	Sisso	Timber.	Household Consumption/ Commercial
33.	*Dioscorea alata*	Khamalu	Tuber edible.	Household Consumption/ Commercial
34.	*Dioscorea deltoidea*	Pan Alu	Tuber edible.	Household Consumption/ Commercial
35.	*Dioscorea pentaphylla*	Kanta Alu	Raw tuber poisonous but boiled one is food and medicinal.	Household Consumption

Sl. No.	Scientific Name	Local Name	Utilisation	Household Consumption / Commercial
36.	*Diospyrus melanoxylon*	Kend	Wood known as black ebony of N. India, used for carving, cabinet making. Leaves used for wrapping Bidis. Fruits edible, astringent, and not unpleasant to taste.	Household Consumption/ Commercial
37.	*Embelica officinalis*	Amloki	One of the myrobalans. Fruits of Amloki, Haritaki & Bahera are soaked in water at night and used to remove gastric problem, liver trouble, and digestion. Leaves are good fodder. Fruits edible – had high vitamin C content.	Household Consumption/ Commercial
38.	*Eucalyptus camandulensis*	Eucalyptus	Fuel-wood, small timber, pulpwood.	Household Consumption/ Commercial
39.	*Flacourtia catafracta*	Bainchi	Fruit edible, used for making jam.	Household Consumption
40.	*Gardenis gummifera*	Bhurur	Gum medicinal.	Household Consumption
41.	*Gmelina arborea*	Gamar	Timber for furniture. Leaves, bark and fruits are medicinal.	Household Consumption/ Commercial
42.	*Helicteres isora*	Atmora	Bark of stem and root, fruits, leaves are medicinal.	Household Consumption
43.	*Hemidesmus indicus*	Anantamul	The dried root of the plant is useful in curing fever, skin diseases, loss of appetite, syphilis, leucorrhoea and other urinary complaints. It is also used as blood purifier and in rheumatism.	Household Consumption/ Commercial
44.	*Holarrhena antidysenterica*	Kurchi	The dried bark of the plant is used in curing amoebic dysentery.	Household Consumption/ Commercial

Sl. No.	*Scientific Name*	*Local Name*	*Utilisation*	*Household Consumption / Commercial*
45.	*Ichnocarpus frutescdns*	Dudhilata	Bark, root medicinal for blood dysentery.	Household Consumption
46.	*Madhuca indica*	Mahua	Decoction of the bark is applied in curing itch, bleeding gums and ulcers; it is given internally in diabetes. Leaves are astringent, their ash, mixed with butter (ghee), is applied on burns and scalds. Flowers are used in cough and bronchitis, they are cooling and nutritive. Seeds promote formation and flow of milk. Oil from seeds is good on skin diseases and as laxative.	Household Consumption/ Commercial
47.	*Mallotus philippinensis*	Kamala	It is chiefly used for destroying tapeworms. Also used externally in treatment of skin diseases like ringworm and scabies, etc.	Household Consumption
48.	*Mangifera indica*	Mango	Fuel wood, fruit edible.	Household Consumption
49.	*Mimosa pudica*	Lajjabati	Root and entire plant is medicinal.	Household Consumption
50.	*Moringa pterygosperma*	Bon-Sajna	Fruit edible and medicinal.	Household Consumption
51.	*Nyctanthes arbortristis*	Seuli	Leaves and seed are medicinal; leaf extract used in sciatica.	Household Consumption
52.	*Ouguinia oojeinensis*	Panjan	Bark medicinal for blood dysentery, diarrhoea.	Household Consumption
53.	*Phaseolus adenanthus*	Bon Barbati	Roots eaten in times of scarcity. Roots used to stop excessive salivation. Decoction of the plant is used bowel complaint and strictures.	Household Consumption
54.	*Phoenix sylvestris*	Khejur	Fruit edible, juice of the stem used for preparing *gur*.	Household Consumption

Sl. No.	*Scientific Name*	*Local Name*	*Utilisation*	*Household Consumption / Commercial*
55.	*Pogamia glabra*	Karanj	Oil seed plant. Bark of root & stem, carnal and seed oil are medicinal.	Household Consumption/ Commercial
56.	*Pterocarpus marsupiun*	Pia Sal	Timber. Gum, leaves, extract of wood are medicinal.	Household Consumption/ Commercial
57.	*Saraca asoca*	Ashoka	Bark of stem is medicinal, used in gynaecological diseases.	Household Consumption/ Commercial
58.	*Schleichera oleosa*	Kusum	Bark and seed are medicinal. Lac host tree. Yield macassar oil.	Household Consumption/ Commercial
59.	*Schrebera swieenioides*	Bon-Palas (Ghanta Parul)	Root, flower and leaves are medicinal.	Household Consumption
60.	*Semecarpus anacardium*	Bhela (Dhobi-nut)	Seed is medicinal. Mixing with lime, the juice yields indelible ink used by washerman for marking cloth.	Household Consumption
61.	*Shorea robusta*	Sal	A timber tree. Leaves used as fuel and making plates; seeds yield oil; gum incense.	Household Consumption/ Commercial
62.	*Smilax macrophylla*	Ramdatan (Kumarica)	Root medicinal, tonic.	Household Consumption
63.	*Sricinus communis*	Bherenda (Castor, Rerhi)	Yield non-edible oil.	Household Consumption

Sl. No.	Scientific Name	Local Name	Utilisation	Household Consumption / Commercial
19.	*Swertia chirayita*	Chirata	It is well known for its bitter, stomachic, febrifuge and anti-helmintic properties. The whole plant, collected in flowering stage and dried used in fever, diarrhoea, and weakness.	Household Consumption/ Commercial
20.	*Syzygium cumini*	Jam	Fruits edible.	Household Consumption/ Commercial
21.	*Tamarindus indica*	Tentul	Useful parts are leaves, bark, carnel of ripe and unripe fruit, carnal and husk of seed.	Household Consumption/ Commercial
22.	*Tectona grandis*	Segun	Timber.	Household Consumption/ Commercial
23.	*Terminalia arjuna*	Arjun	Barks of stem and root, leaves, fruits are medicinal. Bark has high tannin content.	Household Consumption/ Commercial
24.	*Terminalia belarica*	Bahera	Plywood. One of the myrobalans.	Household Consumption/ Commercial
25.	*Terminalia chebula*	Haritaki	The black myrobalans. Fruits medicinal for wound, burn, skin disease, gall bladder, throat trouble, and asthma.	Household Consumption/ Commercial
26.	*Terminalia tomentosa*	Asan	Bark yield tannin, stem as timber.	Household Consumption
27.	*Vitex negundu*	Nishinda	Dry leaves mosquito repellent. Leaves medicinal (Nerve, brain, stomach, skin, hair, and female disease).	Household Consumption/ Commercial

Table : 6.1.2 List of Faunas exist in Ranibandh Range under Ranibandh Block in the District of Bankura, West Bengal

Mammals—

Sl. No.	*Scientific Name*	*Local Name*
1.	*Axix axix*	The Axix Deer or Chital
2.	*Canis aureus*	The Jackal
3.	*Felis chaus*	The Common Jungle Cat
4.	*Macaca mulatta*	The Rhesus Monkey
5.	*Neophocaena phocaenoides*	The little Indian porpoite
6.	*Petropus giganteus*	The Indian Flying Fox
7.	*Scotophilus kuhli*	The common yellow Bat
8.	*Sus scrofa*	The Indian Wild Boar
9.	*Viverra zibetha*	The Large Indian Civet

Reptiles—

Sl. No.	*Scientific Name*	*Local Name*
1.	*Ahetula nasutus*	Ground Whip Snake
2.	*Batagur baska*	Common Batagur
3.	*Bungurus fasciatus*	Banded Krait
4.	*Naja naja*	Common Cobra
5.	*Ophiophagus Hannah*	King Cobra
6.	*Vipera russelli*	Russell's viper
7.	*Xebicgriogus ouscatir*	Chequered keel back

Birds (Local)—

Sl. No.	*Scientific Name*	*Local Name*
1.	*Alcedo atthis*	Small King fisher
2.	*Ameurornia phoenicurus*	White -breasted Waerhen
3.	*Anastonaus oscitans*	Openbill Stork
4.	*Ardea cinerea*	Grey Heron
7.	*Bulbuleus ibis*	Cattle Egret
8.	*Ceryl rudis*	Lesser pied Kingfisher
9.	*Dendrocygna javanica*	Lesser Whistling Teal
10.	*Egretta garzetta*	Little Egret
11.	*Gelochlidon nilotica*	Gull billed Term
12.	*Metopidius indicus*	Bronzewinged Jacana
13.	*Nycticorax nuycticorax*	Night Heron
14.	*Phalacrocorax niger*	Little cormorant
15.	*Rynchops albicollis*	Indian Skimmer
16.	*Sterna bargii*	Large crested Term

Table–6.2.1. List of Floras Exist and their Utilisation in Moraghat Range Under Dhupguri Block in the District of Jalpaiguri, West Bengal

Sl. No.	*Scientific Name*	*Local Name*	*Utilisation*	*Household Consumption / Commercial*
1.	*Ailanthus grandis*	Gokul	Timber.	Household Consumption/ Commercial
2.	*Albizzia lebbeck*	Siris	Bark of root and stem, leaves, flower, seed and wood extract are medicinal. Timber tree.	Household Consumption/ Commercial
3.	*Allium sativum*	Rasun	Used for general debility, worms, anti-T.B., Venereal Disease, Dysentery, and Typhoid.	Household Consumption/ Commercial
4.	*Amora rohituka*	Lasaune	Timber.	Household Consumption/ Commercial
5.	*Andrographis paniculata*	Kalmegh	All parts of the plant above ground level are used in curing fevers, worms, dysentery, general weakness and excessive gas formation in stomach. It is also reported to be useful for children suffering from liver and digestion complaints.	Household Consumption/ Commercial
6.	*Anogeissus latifolia*	Dhaw	Pulp (news-print), Fuel wood.	Household Consumption/ Commercial
7.	*Anthocephalus candamba*	Kadam	Matchwood and Plywood species.	Household consumption/ Commercial

Sl. No.	Scientific Name	Local Name	Utilisation	Household Consumption/ Commercial
8.	*Aristolocia indica*	Ishwarmul	Dried roots and leaves are useful in curing snake bite, cold and asthma.	Household Consumption/ Commercial
9.	*Asparagus racemosus*	Satmuli	Roots, leaves medicinal. Used in curing blood dysentery, epilepsy, filaria.	Household Consumption/ Commercial
10.	*Baccaurea sapida*	Kusum	Bark and seed are medicinal. Lac host tree. Yield macassar oil.	Household Consumption/ Commercial
11.	*Cedrilatoom sp.*	Toon	Timber.	Household Consumption
12.	*Cephalanthus occidentalis*	Kalikat	Timber.	Household Consumption
13.	*Cibapetendra sp.*	Kapak	Timber.	Household Consumption
14.	*Cinnemomum tamala*	Tejpate	Used as spice.	Household Consumption/ Commercial
15.	*Cynocardia odorata*	Gante	Timber.	Household Consumption/ Commercial
16.	*Dalbergia latifolia*	Seti Sal	Timber.	Household Consumption/ Commercial

Sl. No.	Scientific Name	Local Name	Utilisation	Household Consumption / Commercial
17.	*Dalbergia sisoo*	Sisoo	Timber.	Household Consumption/ Commercial
18.	*Dioscorea alata*	Pan Alu	Root edible.	Household Consumption
19.	*Dioscorea pentaphylla*	Kanta Alu	Root edible.	Household Consumption
20.	*Dipterocapus turbratus*	Garjan	Timber.	Household Consumption/ Commercial
21.	*Dipterocarpus macrocarpus*	Hollong	Timber.	Household Consumption/ Commercial
22.	*Elaeocapu garitrus*	Rudraksha	Religious purposes.	Household Consumption
23.	*Gmelina arborea*	Gamar	Timber for furniture. Leaves, bark and fruits are medicinal.	Household Consumption/ Commercial
24.	*Hernidesmus indicus*	Anantamul	The dried root of the plant is useful in curing fever, skin diseases, loss of appetite, syphilis, leucorrhoea and other urinary complaints. It is also used as blood purifier and in rheumatism.	Household Consumption/ Commercial
25.	*Lagerstroemia hypoleuca*	Benteak	Wood.	Household Consumption/ Commercial

Sl. No.	*Scientific Name*	*Local Name*	*Utilisation*	*Household Consumption / Commercial*
26.	*Magnolia pterocarpa*	Patpate Champ	Timber.	Household consumption/ Commercial
27.	*Mesua ferrea*	Nageshwari	Timber.	Household consumption Commercial
28.	*Michelia cathcathi*	Tite champ	Timber.	Household consumption/ Commercial
29.	*Phoebe attenuata*	Angare	Timber.	Household Consumption/ Commercial
30.	*Phyllanthus emhelica*	Amloki	One of the myrobalans. Fruits of Amloki, Haritaki & Bahera are soaked in water at night and used to remove gastric problem, liver trouble, and digestion. Leaves are good fodder. Fruits edible – had high vitamin C content.	Household Consumption/ Commercial
31.	*Polyalthia simiarum*	Khutikat	Timber.	Household Consumption/ Commercial
32.	*Pongamia pinnata*	Karanj	Oil seed plant. Bark of root & stem, carnal and seed oil are medicinal.	Household Consumption/ Commercial
33.	*Pterocarpus marsupium*	Pia sal	Timber.	Household Consumption/ Commercial
34.	*Schima wallichi*	Chiluni	Timber.	Household Consumption/ Commercial

Sl. No.	*Scientific Name*	*Local Name*	*Utilisation*	*Household Consumption / Commercial*
35.	*Shorea robusta*	Sal	A timber tree. Leaves used as fuel and making plates; seeds yield oil; gum incense.	Household Consumption/ Commercial
36.	*Swietenia mehogini*	Mahagony	Timber.	Household Consumption/ Commercial
37.	*Tarminalia arjuna*	Arjun	Barks of stem and root, leaves, fruits are medicinal. Bark has high tannin content.	Household Consumption/ Commercial
38.	*Tectona grandis*	Segun	Timber.	Household Consumption/ Commercial
39.	*Terminalia bellerica*	Bohera	Plywood. One of the myrobalans.	Household Consumption/ Commercial
40.	*Terminalia chebula*	Haritaki	The black myrobalans. Fruits medicinal for wound, burn, skin disease, gall bladder, throat trouble, and asthma.	Household Consumption/ Commercial
41.	*Vitex heterophylla*	Panchpate	Timber.	Household Consumption/ Commercial

Table : 6.2.2 List of Fauna exist in Moraghat Range under Dhupguri Block in the District of Jalpaiguri, West Bengal

Mammals—

Sl. No.	*Scientific Name*	*Local Name*
1.	*Axix axix*	The Axix Deer or Chital
2.	*Canis aureus*	The Jackal
3.	*Felis chaus*	The Common Jungle Cat
4.	*Herpestes adwardsil*	The Common Mongoose
5.	*Macaca mulatta*	The Rhesus Monkey
6.	*Neophocaena phocaenoides*	The little Indian porpoite
7.	*Petropus giganteus*	The Indian Flying Fox
8.	*Scotophilus kuhli*	The common yellow Bat
9.	*Sus scrofa*	The Indian Wild Boar
10.	*Viverra zibetha*	The Large Indian Civet

Reptile—

Sl. No.	*Scientific Name*	*Local Name*
1.	*Ahetula nasutus*	Ground Whip Snake
2.	*Batagur baska*	Common Batagur
3.	*Bungurus fasciatus*	Banded Krait
4.	*Naja naja*	Common Cobra
5.	*Vipera russelli*	Russell's viper
6.	*Xebicgriogus ouscatir*	Chequered keel back

Birds (Local)—

Sl. No.	*Scientific Name*	*Local Name*
1.	*Alcedo atthis*	Small King fisher
2.	*Ameurornia phoenicurus*	White -breasted Waerhen
3.	*Anastonaus oscitans*	Openbill Stork
4.	*Ardeola grayii*	Pond Heron
5.	*Bulbuleus ibis*	Cattle Egret
6.	*Ceryl rudis*	Lesser pied King fisher
7.	*Dendrocygna javanica*	Lesser Whistling Teal
8.	*Egretta garzetta*	Little Egret
9.	*Gelochlidon nilotica*	Gull billed Term
10.	*Hydrophasianus chirurgus*	Pheasant tailed Jacana
11.	*Phalacrocorax niger*	Little cormorant
12.	*Rynchops albicollis*	Indian Skimmer
13.	*Sterna bargii*	Large crested Term

Table–6.3.1. List of Floras Exist and Their Utilisation in Sajnekhali Wildlife Sanctuary Range Under Gosaba Block in the District of South 24-Parganas, West Bengal

Sl. No.	*Scientific Name*	*Local Name*	*Utilisation*	*Household Consumption / Commercial*
1.	*Acanthus illcifolius*	Harguza	Fruit pulp is used as a blood purifier and leaf is used in rheumatism.	Household Consumption/ Commercial
2.	*Acrostichum aureum*	Hodo	Timber.	Household Consumption/ Commercial
3.	*Aegialitis rotundifolia*	Tora	Timber.	Household Consumption/ Commercial
4.	*Aegiceras carniclatum*	Khalsi	Its flowers are good source for high quality honey and bee-wax, the grass is used for building huts and for fuel.	Household Consumption/ Commercial
5.	*Avicennia alba*	Piara Baen	Over-exploited for fuel wood. Leaves form good resource of fodder and fish – food, flowers are rich in source of honey and bee-wax.	Household Consumption/ Commercial
6.	*Avicennia marina*	Kala Baen	Exploited for fuel wood and fodder. Decomposed leaves constitute fish-food; flowers are source of honey and bee-wax.	Household Consumption
7.	*Avicennia officinalis*	Jat Baen	Used as fuel wood and for building houses and boats. Leaves are used as fodder to increase milk in cattle and the plant is used to cure leprosy. Its bark yields a dye and ash from its wood is used for washing. The flower is a source of honey, kernel of the fruit is edible and the bark resin is considered medicinal.	Household Consumption/ Commercial

Sl. No.	*Scientific Name*	*Local Name*	*Utilisation*	*Household Consumption/ Commercial*
8.	*Bruguiera gymnorhiza*	Kankra	Its hard wood stems are used in building fishing boats, houses, electric poles and for charcoal making extracting tannin. Leaves are used as fodder.	Household Consumption/ Commercial
9.	*Bruguiera parviflora*	Bakul	The species is utilised for its straight-boled stems for poles, fuel, timber and used charcoal making. The fruits are used in making a medicine for eye disease and its knee-bent roots yield a perfume.	Household Consumption/ Commercial
10.	*Ceriops decandra*	Jhamti or Jele Goran	The bark of the species is a source of tannin; wood is used for boat building also as fuel. Flowers make source for honey.	Household Consumption
11.	*Ceriops tagal*	Math Goran	The bark of the species is a source of tannin; wood is used for boat building also as fuel.	Household Consumption/ Commercial
12.	*Excoecaria agallocha*	Genwa	Wood is used in making paper pulp for boards and in tannin.	Household Consumption/ Commercial
13.	*Heritiera fomes*	Sundari	Source of timber, used for boat building, plough making and in viscose rayon industry. Seeds are medicinal in curing piles.	Household Consumption/ Commercial
14.	*Hibiscus tilliaceous*	Bhola	Wood is used for fuel purposes.	Household Consumption/ Commercial
15.	*Kandelia candel*	Garia	It is a potential source of fire wood, charcoal and its leaves are used as fodder.	Household Consumption/ Commercial
16.	*Lumnitzera racemosa*	Kripa	Wood is used for fuel purpose and for extracting tannin.	Household Consumption/ Commercial

Sl. No.	Scientific Name	Local Name	Utilisation	Household Consumption / Commercial
17.	*Mucuna gigantean*	Alshi Lata	Its seeds are considered medicinal and rich in protein.	Household Consumption/ Commercial
18.	*Nypa fruiticans*	Golpata	Leaves are extensively used in thatching roofs of huts and are reported to last for about 10 years. Its sap is extracted for sugar, alcohol and vinegar industries.	Household Consumption/ Commercial
19.	*Phoenix paludosa*	Hental	Leaves are extensively used in thatching mats and wickerwork, forms a good resources in cottage industries.	Household Consumption/ Commercial
20.	*Porterasia coarctata*	Dhanighash	The grass is used as fodder and for paper pulp making and thatching.	Household Consumption/ Commercial
21.	*Rhizophora apiculata*	Garjan	It wood forms a potential source of tannin and finds application in plywood, adhesive, dye bark, cellophane, rayon, ferro – alloy, cellulose acetate industries and as a substitute for petroleum coke for calcium carbide, besides being used as fuel-wood and in medicines; its leaves are used as fodder.	Household Consumption/ Commercial
22.	*Rhizophora stylosa*	Samudra Rai	It wood forms a potential source of tannin and finds application in plywood, adhesive, dye bark, cellophane, rayon, ferro –alloy, cellulose acetate industries and as a substitute for petroleum coke for calcium carbide, besides being used as fuel-wood and in medicines; its leaves are used as fodder.	Household Consumption/ Commercial
23.	*Sonneratia apetala*	Keora	Wood.	Household Consumption

Sl. No.	*Scientific Name*	*Local Name*	*Utilisation*	*Household Consumption / Commercial*
24.	*Suaeda nudiflora*	Gira sak	Used as vegetables.	Household Consumption
25.	*Xylocarpus granatum*	Dhundul	Timber is used for making furniture, agricultural implements and yields tannin, seed oil is used for illumination and grooming hair, seed paste is used for relief of breast tumour.	Household Consumption

Table : 6.3.2 List of Fauna exist in Sajnekhali Wildlife Sanctuary Range under Gosaba Block in the District of South 24 Parganas, West Bengal

Mammals—

Sl. No.	*Scientific Name*	*Local Name*
1.	*Axix axix*	The Axix Deer or Chital
2.	*Canis aureus*	The Jackal
3.	*Felis chaus*	The Common Jungle Cat
4.	*Felis viverina*	The Fishing Cat
5.	*Herpestes adwardsil*	The Common Mongoose
6.	*Macaca mulatta*	The Rhesus Monkey
7.	*Neophocaena phocaenoides*	The little Indian porpoite
8.	*Petropus giganteus*	The Indian Flying Fox
9.	*Platanista gangetica*	The Gangetic Dolphin
10.	*Scotophilus kuhli*	The common yellow Bat
11.	*Sus scrofa*	The Indian Wild Boar
12.	*Viverra zibetha*	The Large Indian Civet

Reptiles—

Sl. No.	*Scientific Name*	*Local Name*
1.	*Ahetula nasutus*	Ground Whip Snake
2.	*Batagur baska*	Common Batagur
3.	*Bungurus fasciatus*	Banded Krait
4.	*Crocodylus porosus*	Estuarine Crocodile
5.	*Lepodochelys olivacea*	Olive Redley turtle
6.	*Naja naja*	Common Cobra
7.	*Ophiophagus Hannah*	King Cobra
8.	*Ptyas nucosus*	Dhamin
9.	*Varanus salavator*	Water monitor
10.	*Vipera russelli*	Russell's viper
11.	*Xebicgriogus ouscatir*	Chequered keel back

Birds (Migratory)—

Sl. No.	*Scientific Name*	*Local Name*
1.	*Actitis hypolencos*	Common Sand piper
2.	*Calidris minutes*	Little stint
3.	*Gallinago gallinars*	Fantail snipe
4.	*Larus brunnicephalus*	Brown Headed Gull
5.	*Larus ridipundus*	Black Headed Gull
6.	*Leptoptoptilos dubius*	Adjuntant stork
7.	*Numonius avagua*	Curlew
8.	*Rostratula benghalensis*	Painted Snipe
9.	*Todorna ferruginea*	Brahmini Duck
10.	*Tringa nebularis*	Green Shank
11.	*Xenorhynchus asiaticus*	Blacknecked stork

Birds (Local)—

Sl. No.	Scientific Name	Local Name
1.	*Alcedo atthis*	Small King fisher
2.	*Ameurornia phoenicurus*	White -breasted Waerhen
3.	*Anastonaus oscitans*	Openbill Stork
4.	*Ardea cinerea*	Grey Heron
5.	*Ardea purpurea*	Purple Heron
6.	*Ardeola grayii*	Pond Heron
7.	*Bulbuleus ibis*	Cattle egret
8.	*Ceryl rudis*	Lesser pied King fisher
9.	*Dendrocygna javanica*	Lesser Whistling Teal
10.	*Egretta alha*	Large Egret
11.	*Egretta garzetta*	Little Egret
12.	*Egretta intermedia*	Smaller Egret

The Table 6.4.1 gives detail about the comparative assessment of forest cover, total vegetative cover, and wastelands degraded/scrub in nine districts of West Bengal between 1988 – 1991-1994. Our studied districts are : Bankura, Jalpaiguri and South 24 Parganas. From the table it has been found that in Bankura district the geographical area of plantations has increased from 29.61 sq. k.m. in 1988 to 168.83 sq. k.m. Same trend is also seen in case of dense forest where the forest coverage have increased slightly from 370.58 sq. k.m. in 1988 to 374.32 sq. k.m. in 1994. But reverse trend is observed when we look at the area of open forest where the area in 1988 was 1296.63 sq. k.m. but increased in the year 1991 (1323.67 sq. k.m.) and decreased to 1280.77 sq. k.m. in the year 1994. Total forest coverage has increased from 1696.82 sq. k.m. to 1823.92 sq. k.m. in 1994, i.e., from 24.66% to 26.50%.

In case of Jalpaiguri, regarding plantation the area has increased from 257.40 sq. k.m. in 1988 to 272.07 sq. k.m. in the year 1994. But the area of dense forest has decreased from 850.24 sq. k.m. in 1988 to 825.48% sq. k.m. in 1994. But the area of open forest has increased from 313.25 sq. k.m. in 1988 to 368.02 sq. k.m. in 1994. Though the area of dense forest has decreased noticeably but the total forest coverage has increased from 1601.73 sq. k.m. (25.72%) in 1988 to 1646.41 sq. k.m. (26.44%) in the year 1994.

In case of South 24 Parganas the area of dense forest has increased from 1466.67 sq. k.m. in 1988 to 1691.01 sq. k.m. in 1994. But the area of open forest has decreased drastically from 683.06 sq. k.m. in 1988 to 535.44 sq. k.m. in the year 1994. But the total forest coverage of the district has increased slightly from 4045.33 sq. k.m. in 1988 to 4122.05 sq. k.m. in 1994, i.e., from 39.82% to 40.58%.

The Table 6.4.2 states that the forest types and other landuse categories of Bankura (South) district. From the table it has been found that though the area of dense *sal* forest has increased from 3.45% in 1988 to 3.84% in 1994 but the area of dense mixed forest has decreased from

Table–6.4.1. Comparative Assessment of Forest Cover, Total Vegetative Cover, Wasteland Degraded/Scrub in Nine Districts of West Bengal Between 1988-91-94 (Area in sq. km.)

Sl. No.	Districts	Geographical Area	Plantations			Dense Forest			Open Forest		
			1988	1991	1994	1988	1991	1994	1988	1991	1994
1.	Midnapore	14081.00		292.63	356.22	501.59	589.61	537.05	1409.26	1348.43	1357.23
2.	Bankura	6882.00	29.61	104.25	168.83	370.58	387.30	374.32	1296.63	1323.67	1280.77
3.	Purulia	6259.00	-	113.16	124.45	243.35	188.22	179.95	870.72	857.18	875.10
4.	Bardhaman	7024.00	-	36.73	36.57	64.93	70.13	69.35	232.19	263.48	260.85
5.	Birbhum	4545.00	36.25	44.55	49.27	22.14	6.62	6.61	113.18	123.50	140.86
6.	24 Parganas (S)	10159.00	-	-	-	1466.67	1669.05	1691.01	683.06	558.76	535.44
7.	Coochbehar	3387.00	-	0.31	-	0.17	0.18	1.39	28.06	34.52	35.70
8.	Jalpaiguri	6227.00	257.40	262.02	272.07	850.24	861.34	825.48	313.25	335.95	368.02
9.	Darjeeling	3149.00	73.90	143.05	152.79	837.95	914.93	932.92	476.46	391.24	371.62
	Total	**61713.00**	**565.22**	**996.70**	**1160.20**	**4357.62**	**4687.38**	**4618.08**	**5422.81**	**5236.73**	**5225.69**
11.	Others*	27039.00	-	-	-	-	-	-	62.00	62.00	62.00
	Grand Total	**8875200**	**565.22**	**966.70**	**1160.20**	**4357.62**	**4687.38**	**4618.08**	**5484.81**	**5298.70**	**5287.69**

Sl. No.	Districts	Wetland	Total Forest Cover			Percentage		
			1988	1991	1994	1988	1991	1994
1.	Midnapore	-	2078.91	2230.67	2250.60	14.76	15.84	15.98
2.	Bankura	-	1696.82	1815.22	1823.92	24.66	26.38	26.50
3.	Purulia	-	1114.07	1158.56	1179.50	17.80	18.51	18.84
4.	Bardhaman	-	297.12	370.34	366.77	4.23	5.27	5.22
5.	Birbhum	-	171.57	174.67	196.74	3.77	3.84	4.33
6.	24 Parganas (S)	1895.60	4045.33	4123.41	4122.05	39.82	40.59	40.58
7.	Coochbehar	6.75	34.98	41.76	43.84	1.03	1.23	1.29
8.	Jalpaiguri	180.84	1601.73	1640.15	1646.41	25.72	26.34	26.44
9.	Darjeeling	221.30	1609.61	1670.52	1678.63	51.11	53.05	53.31
Total		**2304.49**	**12650.14**	**13225.30**	**13308.46**	**20.50**	**21.43**	**21.57**
11.	Others*	-	62.00	62.00	62.00	-	-	-
Grand Total		**2304.49**	**12712.14**	**13287.30**	**13370.46**	**14.32**	**14.97**	**15.06**

Note: * Indicates Malds, North and South Dinajpur, Nadia, Murahidabad, Howrah, Hoogli, 24 Parganas (North), Calcutta.

Surveyed Districts: Bankura, Jaipaipur and South Paraganas.

Source : *"Forest Change Detection Studies and Wetland Mapping in West Bengal through Digital Image Processing of Indian Remote Sensing Satellite Data"*, collaborative Project of Wildlife Wing, Forest Dept., Govt. of West Bengal and Regional Remote Sensing Service Centre. Kharagpur, I.S.R.O., Dept. of Space, Govt. of India, October, 1997.

2.90% in 1988 to 2.57% in the year 1994. Similarly area of open *sal* forest has increased from 13.02% in 1988 to 17.63% in 1994. The area of open mixed forest has increased drastically from 6.85% in 1988 to 3.76% in the year 1994. The area of plantations has increased from 0.48% in 1988 to 2.19% in 1994 and this is due to social forestry programmes.

The Table 6.4.3 reveals the forest and other landuse categories of Jalpaiguri district in the state of West Bengal. The table shows that the area of the dense *sal* forest has decreased from 10.90% in 1988 to 10.68% in 1994. In regard to dense mixed forest the total coverage of area has increased from 0.69% in 1988 to 1.07% in 1994. Same trend is also found in cases of open *sal* forest and open mixed forest where the area of forest have increased from 4.26% in 1988 to 4.77% in 1994 and 0.77% in 1988 to 1.14% in 1994 respectively. In case of old teak plantations also the area of plantations has increased from 2.39% in 1988 to 4.37% in 1994. It is interesting to note that the old *sal* plantation has gained a momentum in the district as the figure shows, i.e., 0.60% in 1988 to 11.27% in 1994. Regarding plantations the district figures are definitely hopeful for the conservationists and concerned govt. authority.

The table 6.4.4 gives detail about the forest types and other landuse categories of South 24 Parganas district in the state of West Bengal. Regarding dense mangrove forest the figures show increase in the area of forest from 6.05% in 1988 to 8.47% in 1994. But in case of open mangrove forest the table shows the dismal trend, i.e., 8.38% in 1988 to 8.17% in 1994.

The combined figures of total forest coverage in all the three studied districts of West Bengal (Table : 6.4.1) though shows increase in forest coverage but actually the present trend is polar opposite. During 1991 Joint Forest Management (JFM) gained it momentum into the peak. As a result of JFM, with the help of different social forestry programmes and other plantation programmes, forest coverage has increased. Actually, the area of dense *sal*, dense mixed *sal*, open *sal*, open mixed forest is decreasing day by day due to indiscriminate and illegal use of forest resources to meet the immediate need and greed of the fringe people as well as businessman from outside. Our study in the three districts also shows the same trend of degradation of natural biodiversity including forest by human interference. In case of Jalpaiguri we have also observed how businessman from different towns with the help of local people destroying the forest by illegal tree felling. The concerned Forest officials knowingly of unknowingly became silent spectators in this connection and expressed their inability to check the illegal tree felling as lack sufficient manpower. But thanks to Forest Department for timely introduction of plantations of *eucalyptus, acacia*, etc. types of quick growing species through different social forestry programmes that has kept the forest dept functioning and also the statistics on forest alive for future researchers.

Table–6.4.2. Forest Types and Other Land Use Categories of Bankura (South) District (Area in sq. km.)

Category / Class	*1988* Area in sq. km.	*1988* Percentage (%)	*1991* Area in sq. km.	*1991* Percentage (%)	*1994*	*Percentage (%)*
Dense Sal	103.06	3.45	130.22	4.37	114.55	3.84
Dense Mixed Sal	86.55	2.90	75.77	2.54	76.81	2.57
Open Sal	388.32	13.02	493.37	16.54	525.87	17.63
Open Mixed Forest	204.25	6.85	138.87	4.66	112.02	3.76
Eucalyptus	14.46	0.48	49.62	1.66	65.33	2.19
Degraded	334.32	11.21	248.58	8.33	289.57	9.71
Wasteland	445.35	14.93	238.93	8.01	183.92	6.17
Agriculture	1168.70	39.18	1376.01	46.13	1337.21	44.83
Water bodies	165.43	5.55	182.38	6.11	223.33	7.49
Sandy areas	14.01	0.47	30.00	1.01	33.43	1.12
Built – up area	1.25	0.04	5.00	0.17	6.71	0.22
Others (Roads, Rails, etc.)	22.70	0.76	12.91	0.43	12.91	0.43
Unclassified	34.71	1.16	1.45	0.05	1.45	0.05
Total Geographical Area	2983.11	100.00	2983.11	100.00	2983.11	100.00
	1988	**%**	**1991**	**%**	**1994**	**%**
Dense Forest	189.75	6.36	205.90	6.90	191.36	6.41
Open Forest	592.60	1987	632.22	21.19	637.89	21.38
Plantation	14.46	0.48	49.62	1.66	65.33	2.19
Total Vegetation	796.81	26.71	887.74	29.76	894.58	29.99
	1988	**%**	**1991**	**%**	**1994**	**%**
Forest in Bankura (South)	796.81	11.58	887.74	12.90	894.68	13.00

Source : "*Forest Change Detection Studies and Wetland Mapping in West Bengal through Digital Image Processing of Indian Remote Sensing Satellite Data*", collaborative Project of Wildlife Wing, Forest Dept., Govt. of West Bengal and Regional Remote Sensing Service Centre, Kharagpur, I.S.R.O., Dept. of Space, Govt. of India, October, 1997.

Table–6.4.3. Forest Types and Other Land Use Categories of Jalpaiguri District (Area in sq. km.)

Category / Class	*1988*		*1991*			*Percentage*
	Area in Sq. km.	*Percentage (%)*	*Area in sq.km.*	*Percentage (%)*	*1994*	*(%)*
Dense Sal	678.88	10.90	682.44	10.96	665.19	10.68
Dense Mixed Sal	42.66	0.69	65.98	1.06	66.48	1.07
Open Sal	265.22	4.26	295.63	4.75	297.09	4.77
Open Mixed Forest	48.03	0.77	40.32	0.65	70.93	1.14
Village Orchard	177.83	2.86	179.14	2.88	179.25	2.88
Degraded	435.04	6.99	138.54	2.22	139.87	2.25
Riverine	128.70	2.07	112.92	1.81	93.81	1.51
Agriculture	2814.48	45.20	2991.65	48.04	2997.21	48.13
Water bodies	242.94	3.90	247.57	3.98	248.49	3.99
Sandy areas	273.73	4.40	300.21	4.82	301.74	4.85
Young Teak Plantation	20.83	0.33	-	-	-	-
Old Teak Plantation	148.59	2.39	171.48	2.75	272.07	4.37
Young Sal Plantation	50.46	0.81	-	-	-	-
Old Sal Plantation	37.52	0.60	90.54	1.45	701.59	11.27
Tea Gardens	653.33	10.49	698.33	11.21	114.19	1.83

Source : *"Forest Change Detection Studies and Wetland Mapping in West Bengal through Digital Image Processing of Indian Remote Sensing Satellite Data"*, collaborative Project of Wildlife Wing, Forest Dept., Govt. of West Bengal and Regional Remote Sensing Service Centre. Kharagpur. I.S.R.O., Dept. of Space, Govt. of India, October, 1997.

Category / Class	*1988*		*1991*			*Percentage*
	Area in sq. km.	*Percentage (%)*	*Area in sq. km.*	*Percentage (%)*	*1994*	*(%)*
Thatch Grass	132.65	2.13	133.30	2.14	51.61	0.83
Built – up area	60.94	0.98	51.47	0.83	27.39	0.44
Unclassified	15.08	0.24	27.39	0.44	-	-
Total Geographical Area	**6226.91**	**100.00**	**6226.91**	**100.00**	**6226.91**	**100.00**
	1988	**%**	**1991**	**%**	**1994**	**%**
Dense Forest	850.24	13.65	861.34	13.83	825.48	13.26
Open Forest	313.25	5.03	335.95	5.40	368.02	5.91
Plantation	257.40	4.13	262.02	4.21	272.07	4.37
Total Forest in Jalpaiguri	**1420.89**	**22.82**	**1459.31**	**23.44**	**1465.57**	**23.54**

Source : *"Forest Change Detection Studies and Wetland Mapping in West Bengal through Digital Image Processing of Indian Remote Sensing Satellite Data"*, collaborative Project of Wildlife Wing, Forest Dept., Govt. of West Bengal and Regional Remote Sensing Service Centre, Kharagpur, I.S.R.O., Dept. of Space, Govt. of India, October, 1997.

Table–6.4.4. Forest Types and Other Land Use Categories of South 24 Parganas District (Area in sq. km.)

Category / Class	1988 Area in sq. km.	Percentage (%)	1991 Area in sq. km.	Percentage (%)	1994	Percentage (%)
Dense Mangrove	615.15	6.05	799.93	7.87	860.94	8.47
Open Mangrove Forest	851.52	8.38	869.12	8.55	830.13	8.17
Village Orchard	1160.37	11.42	1277.06	12.57	1272.24	12.52
Weeds and Marshy	131.13	1.29	133.36	1.31	130.58	1.29
Degraded Mangrove	551.93	5.43	425.40	4.19	404.86	3.99
Low Sediment Water body	1740.51	17.13	974.32	9.59	1182.12	11.64
High Sediment Water body	1567.85	15.43	2058.69	20.26	1868.19	18.39
Agriculture	3236.31	31.85	3395.05	33.42	3388.86	33.36
Sandy areas	67.01	0.66	58.56	0.58	57.44	0.57
Built – up area	176.80	1.74	134.90	1.33	134.64	1.33
Others (Roads, Rails, etc.)	45.98	0.45	24.91	0.25	22.60	0.22
Unclassified	15.03	0.15	8.29	0.08	6.99	0.07
Total	**10159.59**	**100**	**10159.59**	**100**	**10159.59**	**100**
	1988	**%**	**1991**	**%**	**1994**	**%**
Dense Forest	615.15	6.05	799.93	7.87	860.94	8.47
Open Forest	851.52	8.38	869.12	8.55	830.13	8.17
Weed / Marshy / Degraded	683.06	6.72	558.76	5.50	535.44	5.27
Total Vegetation	**2149.73**	**21.16**	**2227.81**	**21.93**	**2226.51**	**21.92**

Source : "*Forest Change Detection Studies and Wetland Mapping in West Bengal through Digital Image Processing of Indian Remote Sensing Satellite Data*", collaborative Project of Wildlife Wing, Forest Dept., Govt. of West Bengal and Regional Remote Sensing Service Centre, Kharagpur, I.S.R.O., Dept. of Space, Govt. of India, October, 1997.

7

Approaches to Bio-Diversity Conservation : Lessons From The Field

In the earlier chapter detailed discussion has been made regarding facets of Bio-diversity and its utilisation in the studied blocks of selected districts. In this present chapter an attempt has been made to discuss this subject mainly approach to Bio-diversity conservation lessons from the field.

I

Bio-diversity Conservation: Need and Importance

India has a rich and varied heritage of biodiversity, encompassing a wide spectrum of habitats from tropical rainforests to alpine vegetation and from temperate forests to coastal wetlands. Two of the world's 18 hot spots of biodiversity are found in India: the Eastern Himalayas and the Western Ghats. In addition, India has 26 recognised endemic centres that are home to nearly a third of all the flowering plants identified and described to date.

Of the estimated 5–50 million species of the world's biota, only 1.4 million have been described (Wilson, 1988) and the distribution is highly uneven. About seven per cent of the world's total land area is home to half of the world's species, with the tropics alone accounting for five million. The 18 hot spots that have been identified in the world cover 0.746 million square kilometres and house 0.45 million species.

India, with 2.4% of the world's area, has 8.1% of the world's total biodiversity with a species count of about 0.130 million. Some salient features of India's biodiversity have been mentioned below.

India has two major realms called the Palaearctic and the Indo-Malayan, and three biomes, namely the tropical humid forests, the tropical dry/deciduous forests, and the warm desert/semi-deserts.

India has ten bio - geographic regions including the trans-Himalayan, the Himalayan, the Indian desert, the semi-arid zone(s), the Western Ghats, the Deccan Peninsula, the Gangetic Plain, North-East India, and the islands and coasts (Rodgers and Panwar, 1988).

India is one of the 12 centres of origin of cultivated plants. India has five world heritage sites, 14 biosphere reserves, and six Ramsar wetlands. The total protected area is about 3.16 million km2 (4.4% of the geographical area).

The country has extensive aquatic ecosystems with a marine habitat extending over 7500 km of coastline. Of the 49,219 plant species, 5150 are endemic and distributed into 141 genera under 47 families corresponding to about 30% of the world's recorded flora, i.e. 30% of the world's recorded flora is endemic to India. Of these endemic species, 2532 are found in the Himalayas and adjoining regions and 1782 in peninsular India. With 81,251 animal species, India accounts for 6.67% of the world's total. Sixty-two of India's reptiles are endemic.

India's record in agrobiodiversity is equally impressive. There are 166 crop species and 320 wild relatives. India is seventh in terms of contribution to world agriculture.

Keeping the view above in our mind, conservation and sustainable use of bio-diversity to the benefit of both present and future generations has now a global political and legal sanction. Yet, irreversible loss of biological diversity and inequitable distribution of resource base remain the serious problem while deficiencies of state driven conservation approaches have been brought out, proven examples of perfect conservation approaches are lacking. So the conservation of bio-diversity emerges.

II
National Initiatives

India is one of the 12-mega biodiversity centres in the world, representing two of the major realms and three basic biomes of the world. The country is divided into 10 bio geographic regions: Trans-Himalayan, Himalayan, Indian Desert, Semi-Arid, Western Ghats, Deccan Peninsula, Gangetic Plains, North-East India, Islands and Coasts.

India is among the countries, which are in the forefront of environmental protection. India, through its important policies and programmes, has been successful in integrating environmental issues in its agenda for development. India has environmental standards for products and processes, and has environmental impact assessment procedures for identification and adaptation of technologies industries. It has also introduced environmental audit system as a regulation.

India believes that environmentally harmful processes should be averted and that over-exploitation of non-renewable resources should be controlled. Extensive resources have been committed to the conservation of forests and wildlife. A comprehensive approach has been adopted in India for pollution abatement and for promotion of technological inputs to reduce industrial pollutants. In the area of hazardous wastes, the process of prioritising the areas of concern has begun long ago for the sound management of chemicals, wastes and genetically manipulated organism/ cells in order to develop and implement programmes and policies for their effective management. India has been implementing various programmes for enhancement of energy and production efficiency, clean fuels, renewable energy technologies and forestation and wasteland development.

Indicated below are some of the major initiatives undertaken for implementation of various programmes and policies at national level aimed at achieving the goals of sustained economic growth and sustainable development (Nirmal, Andrews, 1998).

River Cleaning Programme

In India, providing potable water to all citizens is a national objective of highest priority. However, the pollution of our rivers, lakes, coastal waters and ground water, caused by disposal of untreated or partially treated domestic sewage, industrial pollution and agricultural run-offs remains a matter of concern. A number of statutory and institutional steps have been taken to protect the water sources from pollution and to improve its water quality. The Government of India took up a major river cleaning initiative in 1985 pertaining to the Ganga Basin. The programme objectives cover pollution from both domestic sewage and trade effluents, and tackling of non-point pollution sources like agriculture and urban run off. It has been reported that the results compare favourably with the programmes taken up for rivers like Rhine, Danube and Thames. Appropriate technologies have been developed to sustain these programmes in a cost-effective manner. Based on the encouraging response, the programme has now been extended to most of the major river systems in the country.

Environmentally Sound Technologies

An important input for sustained economic growth is technology. In order to strengthen the technological capabilities of the various sectors, both for meeting the national needs and for providing global competitiveness, a number of initiatives have been launched in the country. Measures include research on the design of catalytic converters and introduction of battery-operated vehicles in urban areas, use of alternative fuels and quality of fuel to name a few. A Technology Development Board has been set up with the mandate to facilitate the development of new technologies, and the assimilation and adaptation of imported technologies by providing catalytic support to industries and R&D institutions to work in partnership with each other.

India has a large infrastructure of technology support institutions. A National Cleaner Production Centre (NCPC) has been set up with the assistance from UNIDO. Under this Centre, capacity building and awareness rising in the area of cleaner production among small and medium scale industries have been conducted. Under this scheme, training and awareness programmes for personnel were organised through Small Industries Service Institutes. In addition, sector-specific manuals have also been prepared.

The Ministry of Environment and Forests (MoEF) initiated a project on establishment and operation of one hundred waste minimisation circles in clusters of all small-scale industries through the National Productivity Council.

In addition, a number of fiscal incentives are available for pollution control and also for adopting cleaner technologies.

Technology upgrading requires that Indian enterprises of all types have information on relevant technologies available in the international market as well as within the country. The government, through the MoEF, has taken the initiative to set up an Indian Centre for Promotion of Cleaner Technologies (ICPC). This is a network of institutions, which will provide necessary inputs in creating a database on available technologies, their performance, the sources of technologies necessary investment, etc. A long-term perspective called *Technology Vision for India 2020* has been prepared, which could form the basis of Technology development programmes.

Coastal Zone Management

In 1991, for the protection of the coastal areas, the Ministry of Environment and Forests issued a notification, under the Environment (Protection) Act, 1986, declaring coastal stretches at "Coastal Regulation Zones" (CRZs), and regulating activities in the CRZs. As per this notification, all the coastal states/union territories have prepared coastal zone management plans and are now required to regulate development activities in accordance with the provisions of the approved plans.

A National Contingency plan to deal with oil spill disasters has been prepared. India has rectified Marpol 73/78 and adopted the provisions in the Merchant Shipping Act.

The concept of "Integrated Coastal and Marine Area Management" (ICMAM) is being promoted extensively to ensure the sustainable development of the coastal areas, rational utilisation of marine resources, and proper management of the marine environment to prevent its degradations from developmental, commercial, or other activities. To implement ICMAM, a new programme has been formulated.

Management of Hazardous Wastes

Emerging policy directions in the field of hazardous wastes emphasise the need to improve the scientific understanding of the extent and cost of improper disposal, implementation of policies discouraging indiscriminate disposal and of incentives for waste minimisation, adoption of cleaner technologies, and recycling of indigenously generated hazardous waste. Risk reduction, avoidance of generation, and the "Polluter must pay" principle are the major policy principles on hazardous wastes management.

The Hazardous Wastes (Management and Handling) Rules, notified in 1989 under the Environment (Protection) Act, 1986, govern the generation, collection, treatment, storage, disposal, and import of hazardous wastes indicated in the schedule to the rules. The responsibility of enforcing and monitoring these rules is vested in the state pollution boards. In addition, guidelines for management and hazardous waste treatment and disposal facility have been issued.

India is a party to the Basel Convention on the control of Tran boundary movements of hazardous wastes and their disposal. In keeping with the objectives of the Convention, several initiatives have been taken in terms of policy measures, guidelines, and institutional mechanisms for regulating the import, handling, reprocessing, and disposal of hazardous wastes including the wastes, which are generated within the country. The issues concerning regional-co-operation in this regard were brought to the attention of the Environment Ministers of the South Asia Association for the Regional Co-operation (SAARC) countries during a conference held in New Delhi in April 1997.

Rules on Bio-medical Wastes have also been notified on 27th July 1998. They will regulate the disposal of bio-medical wastes, including human anatomical wastes, blood, body fluids, medicines, glassware, and animal wastes. All persons handling such wastes will be required to obtain permission from appropriate authority. Segregation of bio-medical wastes at source has been made mandatory for all institutions and organisations dealing with them. These rules make the generator of bio-medical wastes liable to segregate, pack, store, transport, treat, and dispose the bio-medical wastes in an environmentally sound manner.

Management of Chemicals

The Ministry of Environment and Forests has followed a cradle-to-grave policy towards the management of chemicals. Accordingly, it has brought out regulations covering all aspects of management of hazardous chemicals from manufacturing up to the final disposal.

Regulations brought out by the Ministry in this direction are as follows:

(a) Manufacture, Storage and Import of Hazardous Chemicals Rules, 1989

(b) Chemical Accident (Emergency Planning, Preparedness and Response Rules, 1996

(c) Hazardous Wastes (Management and Handling) Rules, 1989

(d) Public Liability Insurance Act, 1991

(e) National Environment Tribunal Act, 1995

Under Environment (Protection) Act, 1986, Ministry of Environment and Forests has adopted Environment (Protection) Rules, 1986. Rule 13 lays down detailed procedure for banning and restricting on hazardous chemicals. The following chemicals and other substance have been banned under these rules:

(i) Bencidine and benzidine based dyes (47 numbers) banned since 1993.

(ii) Acodyes (70 numbers) banned since 1993.

(iii) Hazardous wastes containing Arsenic, Cyanide, Mercury, Pesticides, PCB, PCT etc., 1997.

(iv) Plastics carry bags (under issued).

Other Ministries of Government of India have also been quite active in this area. Under Insecticides Act, 1968, Ministry of Agriculture has banned and restricted nearly 30 pesticides. Another list of 10 pesticides, which are banned abroad but continue to be used in India are under review. Similarly, Ministry of Health has also banned a number of food additives under Prevention and Food Adulteration Act, 1953.

Management of Industrial Pollution

The Ministry of Environment and Forests is pursuing the policies enunciated in its Policy Statement for Abatement of Pollution, 1992, to deal with the environmental matters, particularly in regard to pollution of water, air and land. The Policy Statement laid the following future directions and objectives for the prevention of environmental pollution.

A comprehensive approach is taken to integrate environmental and economic aspects in development planning; stress is laid on preventive aspects for pollution abatement and promotion of technology inputs to reduce industrial pollutants, and on public cooperation in securing a clean environment to respond to the coming challenges. The objective is to integrate environmental consideration into decision-making process at all levels. To achieve this, steps have to be taken to:

- Prevention pollution at source;
- Encourage, develop and apply the best available practicable technical solutions;
- Ensure that the polluter pays for the pollution and control arrangements;
- Focus protection on heavily polluted areas and river stretches; and
- Involve the public in decision-making.

Action Taken for the Control of Pollution

The meditative measures taken for prevention and control of pollution include the following:

(i) Steps were taken to Control pollution from 17 categories of highly polluting industries. Out of a total of 1551 industries identified in 1991, now only 155 units remain without having adequate facilities to comply with the standards;

(ii) 24 critically polluted areas have been identified and Action Plans prepared for 22 areas are being implemented by Central Pollution Control Board (CPCB)/State Pollution Control Boards;

(iii) Environmental clearance made compulsory for 29 categories of developmental projects involving public hearing/NGO participation as an important component of EIA process;

(iv) Environmental audit in the form of environmental statement has been made mandatory for all the polluting industries;

(v) To promote pollution prevention in small scale industries, 15 waste minimisation circles have been set up in various parts of the country and about 100 more such circles are being established for adoption of clean technology, better work practices and energy conservation techniques;

(vi) Preparation of Zoning Atlas for sitting of industries based on environmental considerations in various districts of the country has been taken up. So far, 19 such districts have been covered;

(vii) A scheme for setting up of Common Effluent Treatment Plants (CETP) projects has been approved which are at various stages of implementation.

III
Eco-Development Approach

India's policies and programmes in the realm of forestry, particularly the developments during the last fifteen years have been largely in consonance with the Forest Principles adopted during the UNCED. India has actively participated in the deliberations of the Intergovernmental Panel on Forests, established by the Commission on Sustainable Development. The Forest (Conservation) Act of 1980 initiated a process by which India's forests were treated as an environmental and social resource rather than as a revenue or commercial resource. The strictest control has been placed on diversion of forestland to other uses and in the rare cases when this is permitted for developmental purposes; compensatory forestation is a prior requirement. Biodiversity conservation has been made an integral part of forest conservation. Various conservation measures have been taken through strengthening of legislation as well as through eco-development efforts.

India's National Forest Policy of 1899 formulated four years before the Earth Summit embodies many of the highlights, which have been repeatedly emphasised in the Rio Principles. The Government's commitment to the management of forests through the participatory process is reflected in the active involvement of tribal and village communities, especially women and persons belonging to the weaker sections of society, and voluntary agencies in strengthening the activities of the State Forest Departments in forest protection and regeneration initiatives.

Review of the social forestry programme launched during the 1980s has resulted in a consolidation of its gains and strengthening of the weaker links. Increasing focus has been given to the conservation of the existing natural forests with emphasis on natural regeneration. The current approach towards a forestation and forest conservation is intended to integrate activities and expertise of different sectors so that various pressures that are responsible for degradation of forests are adequately addressed.

The Wild life (Protection) Act. 1972 and its amendments up to 1991 provide the legal framework for conservation of wildlife in the country. The amendment of 1991 is significant in that it provides protection not only to wild animals and birds but also to plant species and hence addresses forest ecology in its totality.

Introduction of Eco-Development Programme has been one of the recent developments in the field of wildlife management that aim at economic development of the people residing in and around sanctuaries and national parks, in order to reduce their dependence on forest products so that the ecological health of the protected areas can be developed and sustained. The scheme aims at increasing productivity of land and forest resources in the immediate neighbourhood of the people so that alternative avenues of employment and incomes are made available.

For effective implementation and acceleration of the process of eco-development approach the government have formed several sanctuaries and national parks to protect wildlife and marine life. To get success in the project, active involvement of the people in that programme is needed. So the government has decided to form a committee named 'Eco-development Committee', a tool of bio-diversity conservation through eco-development approach.

By virtue of being member of the committee people may get a share of production and development works in a certain condition.

Nature of the committee and its responsibility including method of works are given below:

(A) According to the suggestion and recommendation from standing committee of concerned Panchayat Samity the Beat officer of a concerned beat will nominate the members to form Eco-development Committee.

(B) The committee will be consisted of inhabitants of the forest or ecological area who belong to economically backward class.

(C) A husband and his wife jointly from each family will be the member and present at annual meeting.

(D) The local forest authority ultimately approved the committee.

(E) The concerned Gram Panchayat will assist the committee to carry out the job.

(F) The standing committee for Forest and Land of Zilla Parisad will supervise, monitor, evaluate and justify the works of the Eco-development committee.

(G) There will be a working committee within the Eco-development committee, which supervises all the works.

(H) Formulation of working committee:

  (i) Sabhapati of Panchayat Samity or any member of forest and land reforms standing committee.

  (ii) Concerned Panchayat Pradhan or any member of the Panchayat.

  (iii) Maximum 10% of the ordinary members will be selected into the working committee and among them 30% will be female.

  (iv) Concerned Beat officer will be the secretary.

(I) A secretary will be elected by the members of working committee and the secretary will execute the post of joint secretary.

(J) If it is necessary to make any change in the Eco-development Committee, it requires the permission of Beat officer and recommendation from the standing committee on Forest and Land of the concerned local Panchayat.

(K) Beat officer as well as member convenor and the secretary will jointly convey the general meeting.

(L) In case of meeting of working committee 50% of total members and in case of general meeting at least 30% of total member are required to be present.

1. In each meeting of Eco-development Committee a president will be selected to preside over the meeting.

2. Working Procedure of Eco-development Committee:

   (i) The secretary of the committee keeps a register, which contains the name of the member, age, sex, family member, the name of heir etc. A duplicate copy of the same register will be kept at the office of Range Officer, which is regarded as permanent record.

   (ii) The secretary must have a resolution, which contains the issues discussed in the general meeting. The secretary and president will be signing the resolution.

   (iii) In every year a general meeting will be held to discuss on the benefits to be got by the members and developmental works. The concerned Range officer will be present there as an inspector.

   (iv) Every Eco-development Committee should have its own account at any bank or post office to accumulate the fund. The account will be in favour of Beat officer and secretary jointly.

3. Responsibilities of the Eco-development Committee:

   (i) The members and forest workers should have joint effort so that the forest and wild life can be conserving.

   (ii) The members should convey the massage to the foresters about the persons who are trespassers into the word and deliberately destroy natural wealth in the forest.

(iii) To help the forest guards to restrict trespassing, encroachment, grazing and settling fire on the wood stealing and damaging of forest wealth.

(iv) To help the forest personnel to chase those persons.

(v) To help the forest personnel in the completion of the developmental works so that there are finished in the stipulated time.

(vi) The members should be active to implement the other works and reasonable to protect the wild lives.

(vii) To help the forest officials and local panchayat is employing the required labour to carry out the works in forest.

(viii) The committee should perform developmental works so that the members enjoy the benefits.

(ix) To make sure that the fund and opportunities provided by government are not depreciated.

(x) Anti institutional activities against various laws to protect wild lives must be stopped.

(xi) If the work of a member causes harm to the forest and wild life conservation, the member should be expelled from the committee.

4. Eco-Development Works:

(i) Range officer, Beat officer and the members jointly formulate a micro – plan in view of local needs so that the plan can be implemented within the sanctioned fund and it result in giving the opportunities to the member individually or totally.

(ii) The concerned forest personnel may not give benefits and financial support to the member of a village, if the members of that village have been seen not to co-operate fully in the conservation of bio-diversity.

(iii) The members are supposed to raise a permanent fund for eco-development by giving reciprocal money or labour. The expenditure will be made as per micro-plan.

(iv) After the formulation of micro plan the Range officer and the secretary of the Eco-development committee will sign on it.

Benefits for Consumption

A. In case of Protected Forest.

(i) If any State Government collects any forest produce from any protected forest, the members of eco-development committee may get a share of the forest produce. The share of forest produce in favour of members is as follows:

(a) 25% of collected timber wood,

(b) 100% of collected fuel wood, straw, grass, non-edible fruit, flower, seed and leaf etc. Through the process of thinning.

(ii) The member will get 25% called revenue from that particular forest area provided that they protect the forested carefully for at least one year.

(iii) The forest department deserve the rights to stop above benefits for the members in a special situation.

B. In case of other than Protected Forest:

(i) Following benefits in favour of newly afforested area mention below

(a) The member will get 100% of midterm crops produced by them.

(b) They will get 100% of fuel wood collected through the process of cutting a thinning of forest.

(c) The authorised forest personnel will take initiative to deposit excess earned from selling of above final products and distribute the excess money to the members.

(ii) Any individually procured wealth will go to that member only.

Cancellation of Membership, Society etc.

(i) According to the laws mentioned earlier if a member stands against the rule, the concerned forest officer suspend the membership or even the eco-development committee.

(ii) If any suspended member wants to appeal against the punishment imposed by Range officer, he or she should appeal through concerned Panchayat Samity and Divisional Forest Officer.

(iii) If any one wants to proceed against the punishment imposed by D.F.O., he or she appeals through Zilla Prishad and Chief Conservator of Forest.

IV
Bio-Diversity Conservation and Joint Forest Management Through Eco-development Programme

Being an intelligent animal man has got a dominant position in this planet and only he alone can change the nature into hospitable one to make his own life more comfortable. Whereas the other animals have to take the nature as she provides them. Hence only man has been endangering the environment around him to get immediate and maximum benefits from the nature. He has been associated with different ingredients of the nature particularly forests. From the infancy of human civilization forests sheltered him, protected him and are the greatest means of his survival. Hence, more the progress of civilization has been taken place during the course of time; the exploitation of natural resources has been accelerated more and more. So the advance of civilization carries a new responsibility to protect the biomass of the nature so that the ecological balance of the environment is safe. Here mankind have to play the greatest role to do so. In one word we can say that the conservation is of the people, by the people and for the people.

India is richly endowed with forest wealth. The long history of India, with a chronology of many a dynasties, culminating with the colonial era of the British Raj presents a spectra of contrasting forest administrations. The forest was viewed as resource – base meant for commercial exploitation, with gains accreting to the ruling classes. Legal barricades were erected between the commonness and their natural homeland. So man has excluded from the horizon of forest administration that evolved in the next few decades. The result was a direct confrontation between the aspirations of the young Indian society and the centuries old Indian wilderness.

Various attempts have been made to reconcile the conflict between aspirations of a progressing civilization and natural legacy of past generations. In this regard the state of West Bengal has given a new dimension to the existing structure called 'Joint Forest Management (JFM)'. It's a novel concept of forest resources management. The aspiration and basic needs of forest fringe population have been integrated with sustainable management of forest resources.

Being started in the early nineties the JFM has now set up firmly in West Bengal. A numerous families in Bengal have been directly involved with protection and management of forests. A dynamic relation with continuous dialogue with the people, rather than, a static commercial partnership has been evolved. The culmination of JFM is seen as sharing of revenue from the sale of timber, pole and firewood after clearing felling of the area. This has resulted in the ecological problem of extensive felling over wide area as well as an administrative problem of developing infrastructure of felling process and the quantum of produce.

So a system of management for sustainable harvesting or consumption is the new challenges before JFM. Forests may open up immense scope of viable supply of raw material for a host of industries that obviate the clearing of vegetation from the forestland. Innumerable ways of income generation for local people exist in consonance with forest conservation.

The new concept has to be in coherence with sustainability of forest resources to survive and progress. It has to evolve around the idea that forests do not signify a crop as standing poles and firewood, but rather a multidimensional resource base of land, vegetation and water. It has to aim at a reasonable optimum utilization of these resources in consonance with forest conservation.

The situation demands a new concept and orientation of forest-based industries that are sustained on Non-Timber Forest Produces (NTFP) and inter-phase activities. Forest Department has taken initiative in this regard to make such industries commercially viable through in corporation of new technology so that the people get alternative source of economy. This ensures sustainability of their resource base and also creates awareness.

In this direction the state of West Bengal has done some work. Several activities, known by different technologies, such as, inter-phase activities, support activities and N.T.F.P. scheme, have been started as pilot schemes. This section aims at documentation of such inter-phase activities, analysis of their commercial viability and discusses their relevance to the rural people in coherence with sustainable management of forest resources so that the people get alternative way to earn their livelihood and the ecological balance is kept. It is hope, with renewed optimism, that it shall spawn further improvements and augmentation of the existing schemes, so that the forest resources base is sustained for prosperity. Forest department in the studied district of Bankura and Jalpaiguri mention below is executing a few schemes.

I. Water Harvesting Structure

The area of Chhottanagpur Plato and its surroundings receive the rain mainly in the month of June to August. The remaining period of the year remains dry. The district of Bankura, Purulia and Birbhum suffer not only from low rainfall but also from unequal distribution of the same. Large stretches of land of these districts are devoid of ground vegetation cover due to huge demand for fuel wood and continuous indiscriminate over exploitation. Moreover, high cattle population has made the land barren and the topsoil has been exposed to erosion and soil is getting eroded and soil fertility status is being affected. Moreover the rainwater is being last to the river systems. Here the people fail to harvest water. In summer water becomes such a scarce commodity that it paralyses the entire plateau area from March to May.

So the Forest Department has initiated many steps to mitigate the problem. Most of the plantations works are being done on micro – watershed basis, in corporating soil conservation measures. Earthen embankments are one such measures aiming at soil and water conservation. The earth dam provides multipurpose benefits. It helps in controlling soil erosion by preventing runoff. By impounding water it helps in recharging the ground water. It indirectly benefits the nearby human habitations by raising the ground water table. It caters to the water needs of the villages and provides potable water for various daily purposes. The cattle of the village can also be provided water by it. Excess water can be diverted for irrigation. Not only crop rotations but also the cropping scheme can be improved. Impounded water can sustain pisciculture also.

II. Cattle Improvement Scheme

A huge cattle population always needs the grazing and pastureland. In Bengal this type of land is inadequate to sustain a high population of cattle. So the grazing pressure is almost wholly transferred into the forests, especially on the young plantations. Besides the soaring fuel demand, uncontrolled grazing is the single most important factor of degradation of forests. Cattle grazing have been the bane of young plantations, in fleeting major casualties to the young seeding. The problem, therefore, has to be addressed to affect a lasting solution.

The FPC where the people directly are involved has solved the problem to some extent. The members of FPC have already taken adequate precautions to prevent grazing in plantation areas. This has however, not eliminated the malady, but shifted the problem to the non-FPC areas. An objective approach is essential to solve the problem. The cattle population of various districts suffers from low productivity in terms of milk production. This tends to force the farming community to keep large herd of cattle. Poor breeding stock coupled with consumption of fodder of low nutritional content by cattle, results in poor milk output. So it has been identified that the problem has to be approached from two different angles fodder cultivation leading to stall-feeding and improvement of the genetic stock through "stock improvement programme". The Animal Resource Development Department has also been involved in the implementation to raise the availability of fodder, introduction of fodder cultivation in specified models of forest plantation as an intercrop has been initiated. As a parallel scheme, cattle improvement programme was also started in collaboration with ARD Department. In this scheme same FPC members are selected for Artificial Insemination (A.I.) training. They have been provided with A.I. kits free of cost after successful completion of A.I. training and are being supplied with frozen semen of Halstein breed to be bred with local indigenous species for artificial insemination. It is expected that with continued efforts in this direction an improved genetic stock of live stock population will be created to the benefits of the rural masses in the form of alternative sources of economy.

III. Intercultivation of Forest Based Crops

The essence of Joint Forest Management since its inception has been to generate a system of self-supporting and sustainable interface of man and forests. With this new realisation, the need to involve the communities in forest protection by enlisting their co-operation is realised. We have to constantly create economic incentives to motivate these communities. One such gainful activity is inter-cultivation of suitable forest based and need based crops.

The twin objectives of inter-cultivation is to provide humus and cheap nitrogen to the soil, and providing a ground cover of contour strip cropping to control the soil erosion and water harvesting, thus increasing the productivity of the soil.

Arhar (*Cajanus cajan*) is a legume with high potential for green manuring. It is hardy, suitable to hard soils, adds nitrogen and humus, thus improving soil texture. It is considered as a soil binder also. 10 Kg. of Arhar seed costing Rs. 200 is required for sowing in 1 hectare of plantation. The area needs preparatory cultivation and manuring costing Rs. 500 per hectare. One hectare of legume crop fixes 2 tons of nitrogen, whose market value is around Rs. 16000, calculated as per cost of Urea. Moreover after harvesting the root system will be left to the soil which adds hums and binds materials. The FPC members will also derive direct benefit to the tune of 100 Kg. of Arhar seeds earning Rs. 2000 per hectare. The produce is readily marketable and has a high demand in the local dietary pattern.

Sabai grass is an excellent soil-binding crop. The soil of Bankura is highly susceptible to soil erosion. The topsoil is devoid of vegetative cover due to high degree of grazing. Sabai achieves the twin objectives of binding the soil and forming stubbles which provide resistance to soil erosion. It is unpalatable to cattle and thus is subjected to lesser amount of damage. The hilly slopes, which are not very productive, can also sustain Sabai crop. The cost of raising Sabai as intercrop is around Rs. 500 per hectare. Each hectare gives a yield of 400 Kg. Thus one can earn Rs. 1200 for one cutting. Two cutting can be taken in every year. Value addition can be done by the FPC members by making ropes etc. with Sabai grass. This increases the income and also provides self-employment for the rural families. Introduction of Arhar and Sabai besides improving the productivity of the soil, also gives economic incentives to the rural womenfolk.

IV. Pisciculture

Fish is an integral part of Bengali cuisine. However, to sustain the demands of the market the production of fish is inadequate. There is immense scope of pisciculture in the water bodies in and around the forests. Pisciculture also provides substantial earnings to the FPC Members involved in the activity. Only organisation of FPC members on co-operative basis stands between the present usage pattern and full potential exploitation of this asset. For the development of Pisciculture two type of strategies has been introduced namely transfer of technology to the local people and supply of initial seed stock. New technology of pond maintenance and high yielding stock selection are the two basic criteria for training. Being conversant with the occupation. The new technology is found to be easily adaptable and compatible with the rural environs.

In fishery, capital investment is least but the corresponding outturn is high. It has been estimated that if a person invests Rs. 300 in pisciculture, he stands to get a benefit Rs. 3000 after 8 to 9 months. As such the present set up lacks in proper organisation of people on a co-operative level. A few enterprising individuals have taken up initiative through investment on personal scale. However, as such this investment is confined to a minor scale. In most of the cases, production does not go beyond catering to consumption of the household and only a small fraction goes to the local market for sale. If properly organised, even the scope of a bank loan can be contemplated. If practiced on a larger scale, transport to long distances becomes viable. There exists tremendous scope of value-addition, in this activity. If the marketing network is extended to encompass the town area, pisciculture has a potential to be integrated with the social and economic framework of rural Bengal.

V. Poultry Livestock Improvement Scheme

Backyard poultry for meat and egg production is a common sight in the countryside. Poultry farming is complementary income generation activity, as it does not compete with the main wage earning activity of a family. But the present status of poultry farming lacks from high-tech inputs, scientific management and infrastructure. If the above drawbacks are addressed to in a concerted way the scheme of poultry livestock improvement has got high potential of income generation for keeping in view the needs of this homestead industry, an integrated project has been prepared by Bankura (South) Forest Division. A dialogue has been started with the local ARD Department and members of FPC. A series of meetings have been conducted to create the awareness and prepare the ground of technology transfer from "lab to land".

The objective of the scheme is two-fold (i) to improve the genetic stock of existing population through introduction of improved genetic stock, and (ii) to supplement the income generation of the FPC members. As per the advice of local Animal Husbandry Department "RHODE ISLAND RED" breed has been selected, as it is a dual-purpose breed suited for egg laying and meat production.

The Cost-benefit Analysis of the Scheme is as follows:

Price of a day old bird of "RHODE ISLAND RED" breed is Rs. 3 and for a 15-day-old price is Rs. 9 each. Both are available locally. Vaccination can be done, free of cost from the local veterinary dispensary. The housing shed costs Rs. 20 per Sq. Ft. and feeding cost will be Rs. 150 for six months. From each bird, from sale of eggs itself, Rs. 330 per annuam can be earned, starting from the seventh month. Moreover the "RHODE ISLAND RED" breed scores over the local breeds by its capability of producing double the number of eggs and two-and-half times more meat within the same period. The stock is locally available and is compatible with the local variety. On interbreeding with local variety, the genetic stock of the local breed also will be improved. Even the neighbouring families of the FPC will be improved from the scheme indirectly in this way.

The scheme is highly adaptable to local conditions and does not need very sophisticated high technology. The scheme has been started on a minor scale and on evaluation of its success; it can be taken up in larger areas.

VI. Sericulture

Sericulture commonly known as silkworm rearing is an established industry of Bankura district. It has got a high scope as cottage industry as spinning and weaving skills are available locally. The Baluchari saree of Bishnupur is a culmination of centuries old skills of village artisan.

Larvae of silk moth (*Bombyx mori*) secreted the natural silk, which is cultivated on mulberry leaves. But in Bankura district tassar silkworm (*Antheraea mylitta*) is cultivated on Arjun and Asan trees. It produces inferior quality of silk called tassar silk, which is used in the local silk cottage industry. Arjun plantations for Tassar cultivation are done on a commercial scale. It has high employment potentiality for the rural women and can be grown on poor unproductive soils.

Sericulture involves cultivation of food plants for silk moth larvae, maintenance of proper stock of silk moth, proper rearing of silk moth, precaution against diseases, and extraction of silk and economic management. For Tassar cultivation Arjun and Asan trees are annually pruned in the month of March. Arjun and Asan both are good pollarding species. Profuse branching and new foliage comes in the month of April to May. Trees are inoculated with DEL (Disease Free Layers) after base clearing operation. Around 500 DFL is required per hectare for inoculation. Tassar can be cultivated thrice in a year. The first season of cultivation is July to August of 40 – 45 days duration. Second season is September to October of 40 – 45 days duration. The third season is October to December of 60 days duration. A total of about Rs. 500 per hectare expenditure has to be incurred by the FPC members towards host tree pruning, base clearing and inoculation of DFL. The DFL are locally available. If it is cultivated properly and protected against diseases, fire etc. 9000 – 10000 cocoons per hectare will be produced and annual income from each hectare of Tassar cultivation is around Rs. 9000.

The Tassar silkworms have to be well protected against diseases and pests. The main diseases are Pebrine, Flacherie, Muscardine and Grassarie, Pebrine is a protozoan disease transmitted through eggs. The symptoms of this disease is undernourished larvae atrophy, productions of lesser and defective silk, death of larvae, its control measure is treatment of eggs with warm water (47 degree Centigrade). Flacherie is bacterial disease. Its symptoms are physical disability and softening of the skin. Careful rearing of improved stock in healthy condition is the only control measure. Muscardine is a fungal disease, produces various colour marking along the skin and worm becomes hard. These are the main symptoms. The only control measure is maintenance of stocks, which are resistant to the disease. Grassarie is a viral disease, affects moulting. Skin becomes yellow and blood turns milky in appearance. General cleanliness and separation of affected worms are the control measures.

The harmful insects for Tassar silkworm are fly, mites and beetles. The female fly lays eggs on the body of the larvae. The resulting maggots penetrate the body wall of the caterpillar and feed on the body substance. Beetles eat the cocoon of the silkworms at the time of drying and storing.

VII. Apiculture

Honey is an important NWFP. Apiculture can be a viable complementary industry in forests fringe locations, as it does not require much labour and time. Female members of the family can be gainfully employed in their spare time in apiculture. Honey is basically the glucose with rich calorific value…1 Kg yields 3150 calories. It is rich in minerals and vitamins and is prescribed in many Ayurvedic drugs. Glucose is in readily available from and is easily absorbed by the plants.

Honeybees live in large colonies of beehives. Each hive contains one queen bee, a few drones and many worker bees. *Apis dorsata* lives in wild, making huge beehives on the branches. They are not suitable for Apiculture. *Apis cerena indica* can be domesticated and is used for Apiculture on a commercial basis. Development of Apiculture as interface activity in JFM basically involves transfer of technology and providing initial investment cost. The bee-box is made of wood and can be locally manufactured. Selection of bees for apiary is essential as it forms the "nucles stock" for future expansion. The training should acquire the skill of management of disease free stock, handling of the beehive and honey extraction technique.

Honeybees remain active throughout the year except during winter when they cease to work. During this period they survive on consumption of stored nectare and pollen from flowers. Honey flow period is thus in the period of the year when plants bear nectar in good quantities. Seasonal variation is seen demarcating major honey flow period, minor honey flow period and dearth period. Beekeepers possess good knowledge of bee's pasturage and honey flow period. Faulty extraction during death period can damage the beehives. Natural enemies of honeybees are wax moth (Galleria spp.), wax beetle (Platybolium spp.), black ants and honey bird. Wax moth lays eggs in hives, the larvae that emerge out to consume the honey and wax, thereby destroying it. Honeybee is also susceptible to bacterial, fungal and protozoa diseases. Hygienic maintenance of beehives in well ventilated areas and careful handling can prevent the predators and parasites.

By simple technology, easy adaptability and compatibility with rural environs, Apiculture can be an important NWFP based training programme for FPC members.

VIII. Lae Culture

The lac-producing insects are scientifically known as *Tachardia lacca*. The insect liberates a resinous product, which forms a crust around the female insect. This product is called lac and has a high commercial value. In order to obtain the lac, these insects are cultured by a technique called "lac culture". Lac can be cultured on Kusum, Palash, Khair and Arhar species. It being a slow growing species, occurs naturally only and is not attempted for natural regeneration. Therefore, the Palash vegetation, which can be used for "lac culture", has to be considered a valuable commercial asset, which cannot be replenished with ease.

"Lac culture" involves proper care of host plants and regular pruning of host tree, inoculation and proper harvesting techniques. The branches of medium height Palash trees are pruned in the month of February – March to stimulate growth of new shoots. Older branches containing crust are tied with new branches. This method is called inoculation.

The lac insect nymphs come out of the crust after they hatch. The vacated old crust is called "Phunki" which should be removed within 3 weeks, lest they are susceptible to parasitic infection. The coming out of the nymphs from the old crusts is called "Swarming" and they explore new branches. They settle on suitable spots and liberate a kind of exudates and undergo repeated "Moulting". The exudates with the Moulting forms a crust from lac are extracted.

For extraction of lac, the incrusted twig is cut and washed thoroughly and scrapped to remove the secreted granular lac. It is dried and heated to melt it. Dyes can be added in the molten condition and it is made into sheets. For better production, regular pruning to induce new and soft branches is essential. Prunning of branches, with more than 2.5 cm. Girth is not successful. Timely inoculation is essential and should be completed at least 15 days before the emergence of the nymphs.

IX. Sal Leaf Based Industry

Head and cartloads of sal leaves is a common country sight in forest bearing blocks of Bankura district. The blocks of Taldangra, Simlapal, Raipur (I&II) Ranibandh and Khatra are endowed with rich tracts of sal forest bearing vegetation, which supply unlimited quantities of sal leaves to sustain the sal-leaf based industry. Many families earn their livelihood from the sal-leaf based industry for a substantial period of the year.

Collection of dry fallen leaves to collect material for fuel wood needs is an established practice. It has been found that sal leaves contain a higher component of oven dry weight and less moisture content as compared to any other common species. This also has a high calorific value. Dry leaves can be used as direct fuel wood for household purposes. A bundle of 10 Kg. Fetches Rs. 8 and a person earns, approximately Rs. 20-25 per day. The leaf is transported by carts or by trucks to distant locations, thus mitigating the fuel needs of a large section of the rural population.

The womenfolk also collect green sal leaves, which are used for plate and cup making. They are sold in bundles of 1000 each and a person earns up to Rs. 15 per day. The same is sold in plate or cup form, the income goes up to Rs.22-25 per day. Usually the plate and cup making is a cottage industry, with the involvement of women. Due to complimentary attributes, per individual earning goes up, besides providing employment at home. Each person manually can make about 500 plates per day. Before the commencement of JFM, the industry was unorganised with collection of leaves resulting in direct conflict with forest personal, as it was difficult to distinguish between leaf collectors and those involved in timber theft. But with organisation of people into committees, the theft of pole and timber is stooped. JFM cultivated a spirit of cooperation and organisation of labour force and has made mechanisation a viable commercial proposition.

X. MFP Plantation

So far stress of Joint Forest Management has been on production and sale of wood and pole based products, opening a Pandora –box of problems for marketing and infrastructure. Besides, it requires extensive clear felling of the area. Moreover the income is not recurring, but occurs in a rotational cycle of 10 years. To obviate from need of clear felling of the area, the importance of raising plantations that provide fruits and other products of commercial value on a sustainable basis, has been realised.

Species like Amloki, Haritoki, Bahera, Bamboo and Cashew have been incorporated in the model. Cashew plantations have been raised in several small patches over the year. Cashew is planted 4 mt. Apart it starts yielding from the fourth year onwards and the commercial yield starts from the seventh year. Each cashew tree can produce 2 – 4 Kg. And one hectare of well-maintained plantation can produce up to 200 Kg. of cashew nut, and a large quantum of cashew apples. A cashew plantation is not susceptible to grazing and does not have high calorific content. Therefore, it is not prone to biotic pressure.

Bamboo plantations are also providing good income generation for the FPC members. Some patches of bamboo plantation exist in Taldangra, Indpur and Khatra Ranges. The MFP plantations, which have been raised over the last few years, have not matured so far. But good scope for value-addition is created. One hectare of MFP plantation can provide 250 Bamboos every alternate year, starting from the 5th year and can be recurring source of income to the FPC.

Amloki starts fruiting from the 6th – 7th year. Haritoki and Bahera take about 25 –30 years to come to the fruiting stage. Bahera, Amloki and Haritoki have got local market. As the local people are conversant with collection, processing and marketing of the produce, the scheme does not require high-tech inputs. Centres of successful MFP plantation can generate awareness and incentive for the other FPC members, in sustainable management of forest resources.

XI. Energy Efficient Devices

The requirements of firewood for the local people have been the biggest problem for Forest Department. Over the centuries extensive forest tracts have been exploited and degraded for the requirement of fuel wood.

Forest degradation for energy needs is the single biggest cause of degradation of forest areas, the high density of population around the forest areas, as well as conventional fuel in – efficient devices, used by these people has been resulting in excessive quantum of firewood demand which the forest are not able to support. Of late it has been realised that meeting the fuel wood requirement of fringe areas and forest dwellers has to be incorporated in the scope of forest management.

The biggest success of Joint Forest Management has been the acceptance of leaf litter as fuel in place of conventional spitted firewood. Field studies have shown that the maydays spent by womenfolk on fuel collection takes a major share of the wage-earning component of the family. In spite of several hardships faced by the womenfolk, traversing a long distance for fire wood collection, seasonal scarcity of firewood is a common rural problem.

To obviate the above problems efforts have been made by the Forest Department to transfer the technology of fuel efficient cooking devices to the rural households "Shambhoo Chulla", "Smokeless Chulla" and "Banjyoti Chulla" have been identified as proper suitable technology in the existing rural conditions.

In the district of South 24-Parganas the focus of management activity has been to conserve and consolidate mangrove vegetation and to increase the area under mangrove through restoration of degraded and blank areas, both in the forest as well as in reclaimed areas where the vegetation can thrive. Mangrove plantation is raised in inter-tidal zones and mud flats. Till 1997, an area of 8.80 hector has been covered by mangrove plantation under different schemes.

Following the principles of Joint Forest Management (JFM) voluntary protection to mangrove forest is provided by the Forest Protection Committee (FPC) which has been formed with members from among villagers living in the fringe of the forests and these members enjoy different benefits from the forest provide under Government order. Many areas in and around the reclaimed area of Sundar Ban lying out side the notified forest area, have been restored with mangrove vegetation and are also managed with the help of village mangrove committees or by the beneficiaries selected by different Panchayat Samities through Ban – O – Bhumi Sanaskar Sthayee Samiti.

Each FPC has an Executive Committee to decide on forest and development activities best on the basis on micro plan prepare through participatory Rural Appraisal Exercises. At present, the total number of FPC constituted is 31 involving 12084 families who are involved in protecting 57162 hector of forest. 14 numbers of Eco-development Committee are also constituted with the help of 4283 families who are protecting 20070 hector of forest.

Local Panchayat at district, Block and Village level take active interest in village a forestation and conservation through *Ban-O-Bhumi Sanskar Sthayee Samities*. The conservation efforts are also intensified by encouraging and facilitating alternative employment opportunity in providing livelihood security to the villagers and decreasing their tradition dependents on mangrove forest. New skills are imparted through training in potential areas like (i) Apiary, (ii) Duckry, (iii) Poultry, (iv) Fishery, (v) Tailoring, (vi) Mushroom Cultivation.

Inputs like apiary boxes, poultry animals, sewing machines are provided to convert skill into earning. Livelihood security to the local villagers and FPC members are facilitated through provisions of

1. Water Canals which are dug to collect rainwater and which is used for –

(a) Irrigation of agricultural fields surrounding the canals.

(b) Rearing of fish.

(c) Growing useful trees, both fruit and fuel wood on the banks.

2. Training to improve their traditional knowledge and skill in fishing, agriculture, and animal husbandry to enhance earning.

Following provisions are also made in villages to improve quality of life of the villagers-

(i) Tube-wells are provided for fresh water.

(ii) Slippery and muddy roads are cover with brick soling to make communication with the surrounding areas easers.

(iii) Jetties are constructed to make travel by water boats more convenient.

(iv) Health care is provided through health camps.

(v) Cattle immunisation is organised.

Fuel-efficient smoke less chullahs are supplied to reduced pressure on forest. Encouragement is given to raise plantation on village frame lands to achieve self-sufficiency in fuel wood.

Forest officials with FPC members provide protection to the forest and wild life through regular patrolling vigilance to stop illegal activities like theft of forest produce and poaching of wild animals. But during field visit through informal discussion with elderly village folk members it was under stood that still a certain section of people are involved with many more illegal activities like theft of forest produce and poaching of wild animals.

V

Lessons Drawn from the Field

While discussing with forest officials as well as officials from block development offices along with panchayat officials of the three studied districts namely, Bankura, Jalpaiguri and South 24 Parganas the following field observations were made:

During field visits of two studied districts through informal discussion and group meeting with the local people it has been observed that in both the districts quite a good number of surveyed people are involved with illegal operation of felling the age old valuable trees. It has also been found at the spot such type of felling of big trees in the Dhupguri Block of District Jalpaiguri. The forest officials and Panchayat members remain silent instead of taking any legal action against those persons. According to forest officials they are help less in this regard as they don't have minimum number of forces to protect them. On the contrary they did not get all the time necessary co-operation from district administration. So, question remains to what extent this JFM and Eco-development Committee are in a position to stop those types of activities for sustainability point of view. Regarding biodiversity conservation point of view the officials of both the districts opined that though various income generating as well as infrastructure programme was executed by the Forest Dept. people are not so deceptive to take a maximum return out of those programmes and facilities. According to them this is mainly due to their mere ignorance and availability of forest resources by the side of their homeland. Similar views were expressed by the panchayat personnel when the project staff raised this issues through informal discussion. According to panchayat officials people are quite desperate to exploit the forest resources and this is due to political patronage. In the district of Bankura and Jalpaiguri too, the forest officials are actively involved for regeneration of valuable species locally suited in their respective research demonstration plot. Both the districts developed a good nursery in this regard and from which the forest department used to distribute the saplings to the villagers by charging a minimum cost.

One interesting observation has been made in the studied block of Ranibandh of Bankura district is that the tribal people used to conserve the biodiversity, which is in traditional nature. Sacred groves are one of such finest examples of traditional conservational practices done by the tribal people. In the district of Bankura sacred groves of varying sizes seemed to have existed in the past. The remnant patches of the sacred groves still contain species of trees and endemic to the region, and tribal social and religious festivals are still held in these places. Community worship and gatherings take place in these groves during *Salui* festival, as well as wedding ceremonies. Thus the patches of the grove still continue to function as important islands of biodiversity as well as centres of cultural and religious life of the tribal people over the years.

In the studied block of South 24 Parganas similar observations made with degree of variance due to different ecological set up of the locality. While discussion with the people it has been observed that the programmes and schemes, which are mentioned above, was not received by the people in an uniform way. Same thing when it has been raised while discussing with forest officials and panchayat functionaries the views expressed by them that as the number of schemes are very few in number they have to restricted while distributing the schemes to the members of the eco-development committee. Regarding impact of biodiversity conservation through this programme it is not found to be satisfactory. During visit such type of experiences learnt by us. Still the people are in habit of catching the tiger prawn seeds in an irrational way from the river by disturbing the total river eco-system leads to damage of embankment which results in siltation of river bed. In addition to this during visit it has also been observed too that while surveying a particular village not a single men folk was found for interview. With great hesitation their women folk expressed that all their members entered into the mangrove forest of Sundarban illegally for collection of honey and crabs, and different varieties of fishes, which fetch good amount of money from local markets. And this sort of practices normally this people are accustomed to do at least twice in a month. Normal duration of staying in the forest is at a stretch seven days.. No doubt, it is a very risky job for those persons while carrying out of this sort of activities. Risky in a sense mangrove forest of Sundarban is homeland for the man-eater Royal Bengal Tiger. While interviewing with one woman folk it has been noted that her husband was badly injured by the attack of Royal Bengal Tiger while practising those activities. In this regard the work carried out by the locally based one renowned NGO namely, Tagore Society for Rural Development is praise-worthy. The organisations has taken up many more socio-economic development programmes for the all round development of the poor people residing in small islands of the Sundarban. They organised many more motivation camp for the people who are either regular visitors of mangrove forest of Sundarban or good tiger prawn seed collector. During interview with the officials of concerned NGO to know their perception about biodiversity conservation it has been noted that only possible way to resist those persons from doing such types of illegal operation by providing alternative economy with basic infrastructure facilities.

VI
Sustainable Consumption: A Tool for Bio-diversity Conservation

This section of the chapter deals with sustainable consumption expressed by Honourable Minister Mr. Murli Monohar Joshi, Ministry of Human Resource Development, Govt. of India about the need for a new paradigm of 'sustainable consumptions'. The consumption that makes a rational use of presently available resources to meet the needs of current generation without hampering the scope of consumption of next generation is called 'sustainable consumption'. Hardly a decade ago the researchers were speaking about sustainable consumption. The national and international community was somehow slow to respond to the topic. However, the Ministry also repeated a slogan or 'mantra' of "sustainable consumption". He wanted to put forward his own vision of sustainable consumption and speak about the crucial role that science and technology could play.

Let us look at global trends how the people in the world use the natural resources in an unlimited ways. As a result, the environment around us is being endangered mainly by population explosion, poverty, social and gender inequalities. According to the World Bank, about 3 billion people worldwide lived on an income of less than 2 US dollars per day in 1993. Actually, at the beginning of this millennium nearly 1.5 billion of the world population is predicted to live in severe poverty. Social and economical gap between the rich and the poor is being widened. About 800 million people sleep hungry everyday. At least one billion people around the world suffer from micro nutrient deficiency. Global per capita water supplies are now 30% lower than they were 25 years ago. As much as 42% of the world population is predicted not to have sufficient fresh water stocks to meet their combined needs of agriculture, industry and domestic use.

It is clear from various parameters whatever they may be, that relatively a small fraction of the world's population consumers a disproportionate amount. As for example, 20% of the world's people in the highest income countries account for 86% of total private consumption expenditure where as the poorest 20% live on mere 1.3% consumption expenditure. The consumption of the most affluent past of the population influences the consumption patterns and aspirations of others worldwide.

As an example, the population of Bangladesh is increasing by slightly over 2 million people per year, while that of Britain is 0.1 million per year. Yet, because carbon dioxide emissions per person in Britain are 50 times higher than in Bangladesh, cause more than double the 0.1 million people in Britain carbon dioxide emissions in comparison to about million people in Bangladesh.

It is also a matter of great concern that the developing world is blind imitator of the developed world in case of their consumption pattern. The affluent population of developing countries use of all kinds of gadgets, luxury goods and automobiles. In brief the consumption trends in industrialized nations are assuming unsustainable high levels blindly followed by the developing world in their own time. Rise in world population decline in forest cover and of fresh water availability and a tremendous increase in the demand for primary energy are causes of great concern. If the present consumption patterns go on, the ecosystem that provides us with renewable resources could well collapse long before the world runs out of on-renewable resources. There is thus and urgent need to establish a firm agenda on achieving 'sustainable consumption' in the next few years at a global level.

According to Mr. Joshi, sustainable consumption has to deal with the use of products and services that respond to basic needs and bring a better quality of life. It has to be strongly focussed not only on the present citizens of the globe, but also on the future citizens so that we do not with our greed, tamper with the future generations.

The Minister of Human Resource Development also intended to say that mainly three factors are likely to influence consumption. The first is the continuing improvement is the economic well being of developing nations. The process of globalisation and removal of trade barriers is the second. And the third one is the wiring of the world and the advancement of information technology and emergence of global information and entertainment networks. The monument of increased consumption set up by these three factors is likely to lead to direct conflict with the movement towards sustainable consumption.

In Indian philosophical thought we generally are accustomed with the capital in different forms. Those are human capital, financial capital, physical capital and finally natural capital. Normally what we do is that we use or convert natural capital into the systems such as food, medicine, houses etc. to satisfy our daily needs. For this we use the three forms of capital, namely, the human, the financial and the physical capital. But while we are doing so, we never pay attention to the importance of valuing and balancing the natural capital. We must understand that pure water, clean air, virgin forest are not free goods; they are all an essential part of natural capital that we must pressure at all cost. Respect for natural capital will automatically mean respect for sustainable consumption.

Environmentalists and economists look at sustainable consumption in different ways. The environmentalists interpret sustainable consumption from the viewpoint of the resource use alone. On the other hand the economists use it to describe the total spending in the economy on goods and services. When environmentalists advocate in favour of reduced consumption, they mean a reducing in resource use, while economists interpret this as taking away people's income. We know consumption is to be viewed as an economic activity of purchasing and using goods and services. If it has to be sustainable, it should not only regenerate natural capital but also meet the needs of the poor. But the consumption is treated in different ends. The viewpoint of the individuals, the producers and public sector regarding consumption is somehow different.

According to the individuals consumption is a way of fulfilling materials needs. On the other hand consumption is a necessary step to serve the end-users in the realisation of the producers. For the public sector, consumption is the means to provide collective services, such as education, health and security. But there must be a meeting point for all of these. Sustainable consumption does not only mean to reduce the volumes of goods and services consumed (levels of consumption) but also to improve environmental quality through the substitution of more efficient and less polluting goods and services (pattern of consumption). So Mr. Joshi laid down equal emphasis on both the level and the pattern of consumption, if the people have to save themselves from impending disaster.

The level and distribution of income, demographic trends cultural norms and habits as well as technological innovation producer interests and physical infrastructure are the major determinants of consumption patterns. Many of these patterns are deeply rooted and difficult to change. But consumption simply depends on range of interacting factors:

population, economic activity, technology choices, social values, institutions and policies. The question remains as to whether a global GDP adequate for a life of acceptable quality for the world's rapidly increasing population can be achieved at consumption levels that are sustainable. Then the key question is to define what constitutes an *acceptable quality*, which requires a national as well as global debate. However, we should realise that the current capital stocks of physical infrastructure are such that we have locked our societies into unsustainable patterns of consumption. Therefore, citizens must now be prepared to re-examine their life styles. We must have a community actions rather than focus on an individual to sacrifice and consume less, by setting up collective facilities for consumption; sharing a car while going to office, or investment in public transport etc.

We need to take urgent actions to encourage greater efficiency and equity in the use of energy, land, water and other resources and to minimize and avoid pollution and waste. In particular we need to emphasize on partnership, for sustainable consumption between different sectors of society, and also reinforce those values that support sustainable consumption. We need to establish the policy framework for sustainable consumption, for example, by moving towards environmentally sound pricing.

If consumption of fossil fuels is promoted because of huge subsidy and if they are supported more than the clean and renewable sources of energy such as solar energy and wind power, then we will never be able to reduce the extent of consumption. We need to provide further incentives for sustainable consumption. We also require extending the producer responsibility for the environmental impacts of goods and services. The govt. it self needs to set an example in sustainable consumption through environmentally sound public procurement and administration.

Therefore, sustainable consumption movement has to be finally people's movement. People will force the change in consumption patterns in various ways, be they consumers, households, workers or voters. Women will have also a great role in influencing sustainable consumption decisions. Citizens should be empowered with information on the environmental impact of goods and services in their consumption choices so that they can take effective environmental actions in their homes, communities and work places. Hence information technology can play a big role in this movement.

We will have to develop community-based strategies and change human behaviour to enable citizens to more to sustainable consumption patterns, while maintaining their cultural identity in the face of pressures to adapt to unsustainable life styles. A public awareness campaign should be organised which will high light the relationship between quality of life and consumption patterns. We should also share the lessons learned through consumer campaigns, research and actions of communities, govt. and industry.

The consumption is all about human transformation of materials and energy. It becomes a concern to the extent that it makes the transformed materials of energy less available for future use, or creates a negative impact on the ecosystems in such a way as to threaten human health and welfare of people. The movement for sustainable consumption will require a truly trans disciplinary effort. In deep, several different disciplines, such as economics, physics, chemistry, biology, ecology or sociology will impinge on the issue of consumption. Therefore they must come all together.

Intensive research is needed to asses what consumption rates are sustainable. For example, the rate of regeneration of renewable resources must be understood, alternative sources must be identified and pollutants and their effects must be analysed further. We have to look at research in sustainable energy sources and also at energy efficiency in all its forms. We also require emphasising on the researches on management, protection and regeneration of natural systems as well as reuse of waste streams. We need to launch a programme on accelerated promotion of those technologies for energy efficiency that already exist and also develop and diffuse new 'green' technologies. In this context, the minister wishes to emphasize that the global technology transfer agreements and policies are skewed today. Practically, in all discussions and debates on sustainable development, transfer of technology at fair and most favourable terms to the developing world has been highlighted. The Rio Declaration of 1992 as well as most of the multilateral environment agreements emphasizes the need for such technology transfers. However, the experience of developing countries on 'green' technology is far from satisfactory.

The technologies used by the industries and dependent on petroleum and petrochemicals have caused serious damage to the environment and social systems. If we employ large-scale energy and material intensive manufacturing methods, we cannot achieve sustainable consumption. Particularly in India, we should urge that we do not blindly follow the practices in the western world, but develop our own technologies operating at low temperature and low pressure and are less energy intensive and less polluting.

So we will have to fall back on the mantra, 'Back to nature'. This would mean not only changing our habits and patterns of consumption but also looking into the way nature performs its processes to drive our technology development strategies. Till now many research programmes, driven by the curiosity to mimic nature are not seen. So the minister suggested strongly a major launch of such programmes.

For that purpose the social and natural scientists must work with industry, government and scientists must understand the causes and dynamics of consumptive behaviour. They also can develop indicators that track environmental impacts and link them to computation activities and analyse the effectiveness of different strategies for making and implementing policy choices in the presence of uncertainty.

Now we are well used to the conventional indicators of economic growth measured, in terms of gross national product (GNP) as an indicator does not take into account the issue of sustainability. Many advanced nations have increased their GNP whereas if one looks at the economic output by subtracting the environmental and social costs, then one finds that the real progress is much less. So should we not then think in terms of new indicators such as gross ecological product? To respect sustainable consumption, such indicators will not only themselves measure growth but also be indicative of ecologically sound strategies.

It is an important matter of think that sustainable consumption will require changes of mindsets everywhere, in the government, in industry, among citizens and so on. New and different decisions will have to be made in corporate boardrooms as also in national capital. Such decisions will have to put the needs of the planet ahead of the profits of corporation and their shareholders. We will need to generate a new breed of 'ecopreneurs' who will lead the governance of the globe due to their 'eco-consciousness' on the one hand and their entrepreneurship on the other. We may hope that this movement can certainly be taken a lead in India.

A number of new initiatives have already been launched in the national level. Among them the information of a national innovation foundation, setting up of a bio-resource board, and also recently setting up of a new millennium Indian technology leadership initiative are given priority. We would strongly urge everyone concerned with these initiatives to bring the sustainable consumption agenda on board and support the development and diffusion of those technologies that will sustainable production as well as consumption.

Mr. M. Joshi, the honourable minister wishes to invite our attention briefly to the government's philosophical thought. We basically concentrate on sharing with others. This means that consumption for us becomes secondary. We should start with giving i.e. 'daman'. Consumption or 'Bhoga' for self comes later. In our tradition people share food with animals and birds and even snakes are given importance because of having their role to play in balancing the nature and ecology. We should be 'Karmayagis', non-possessive and entirely devoted to the nation.

It is to think from the law of consumption how we run after unsustainable consumption because desires never get extinct or satisfied by fulfilling them. In other words, consumption is itself does not give satisfaction because by enjoying the desires, the desires grow more and more as fire grows more by the offerings of butter and other objects in it.

So it is ever know that the consumption is severely conditioned by the simplest outlook of life. For that reason the consumption is qualified by 'sustainable'. So we respect nature in all forms and give back to nature what we take from it. Western consumption oriented life style has endangered the marine life, the space, the glaciers, the river system and even the polar ice cap.

In brief our concern and advocacy for sustainable consumption is to preserve and protect the space, the oceans, the water resources like glaciers and river system, the forest cover of our planet, the flora and fauna and above all, the dignity of the majority of human kind, who would not have even the free gift of God, the clean air and water if the present state of un-sustainable consumption is allowed to continue. We are aware that the straggle is long and arduous and the strong and affluent will be hard to convince and change their mindset. Yet there are well meaning people all over the world, who will meaning people all over the world, who will us in creating a consensus on the issue of only sustainable consumption. We all, irrespective of caste, religion and sex, have a responsibility to carry this struggle.

Finally, saying that forest is a treasure – trove of natural resources, can conclude it. The benefits that accrue to mankind cannot be documented in a few pages. Human imagination and skill are the only limiting factors for proper eco-friendly utilization of forest resources. Forests offer many more raw materials industry and final products for human utilization. Proper reconnaissance survey, industry and final products for human utilization can also raise the interface for activities. The interface documentation and quantification of the resources and development and imparting of proper technology.

The forest fringe population extracts various materials, like Kalmegh, Bel fruit and Bahera gum for different purposes and household consumption. The roots of Anantamul and Sitamul, the bulb of Dioscorea, the bark of Kurchi, the flowers of Dhaiphul and Tishiphul, being used in the rural areas and no systematic documentation has been done to analyse the commercial value of these products.

The Mahua tree provides multipurpose products. The flowers, fruits and seeds are sources of good family income. Though collection of sal seeds has not been commercialised in the area, the members get salt in exchange from LAMPS. The Tendu leaves, which are colleted through LAMPS, provide crores of rupees, annually, to the State exchequer. All these products provide a recurring income to the FPC members, without causing ecological disturbance.

Besides, the NWFP, FPC members are being provided various trainings to improve their skills, and increasing their technological capabilities. The FPC members collect mushrooms from the forest. Two particular mushrooms are very popular for their edibility. The "Kurkuri" or "Kurka" mushroom is available in June –July and the "Karang" or "Parab" mushroom is collected in August-September. It has been estimated in Taldangra range that some families exclusively dependent on mushroom collection from forest areas for their livelihood. It has been generally accepted that the protection of sal by FPC's leading to establishment of good sal crop, has increased the quantum of mushroom available in the forest.

The FPC members have also been trying to take up mushroom cultivation as a cottage industry. Besides earning income, it supplements the diet of the rural poor with proteins, carbohydrates, minerals and vitamins. White Button mushroom (*Agaricus bisporus*), Paddy straw mushroom (*Volvariella spp.*) and Oyster mushroom (*Pleurotus spp.*) are suitable for cultivation. White Button mushroom is grown on compost, whereas Paddy straw mushroom is grown on paddy straw, which should be uncrumpled, and hand pressed. The bundles of straw are soaked in water for 18 to 24 hours and excess water is drained off. Mushroom spawn is used for inoculation, and moisture and temperature are controlled.

The future of forest management depends on proper study of the forest resources and development of appropriate technologies for exploitation of these resources on a sustainable basis. Man has to be regarded as an integral part of forest management. Therefore, any management practice that attempts to exclude man from its purview may not be successful. An attempt has been made in this project report to document the scope of man-forest interface that is mutually complementary and efforts to reorient the stress of JFM from revenue – sharing model to resource-optimisation model. An attempt has been made to highlight the commercial scope of NWFP and development of forest fringe areas so that a concept of integrated forest management plan can be evolved.

8
Scope of Sustainable Development

In this chapter an attempt has been made to explore the scope of sustainable development out of existing available resources. To what extent the philosophy of sustainable development put into practice that also has been studied critically.

I
Introduction

To achieve successfully the goal of biodiversity conservation we require to have our best, at least a better alternative economy for the people so that they need not depend directly on the forest produce or the wild lives and the marine lives. From the discussion made in earlier chapters we have noticed that the majority of 95 surveyed households out of 150 households belonging to Scheduled Tribes depend on, to some extent, the forest produce. It has also been noticed from the Table No.4.4.7A that 89% of surveyed households belonging to the Non-scheduled tribes depend on the forest produce in any way for their livelihood. And at least 10% households depend also on the marine lives (in the district of South 24 Parganas) to earn their income. In this way they are endangering various species of plants and animals, which results in the extinction of some marine lives, decrease in plants and wild animals. The people are practicing these harmful doings sometimes knowingly and sometimes unknowingly because they want to get quick earnings in absence of any other suitable source for income. That means if the people were in a position to earn more than what they get directly from environment, they need not depend so much on the biomass of this world. So this chapter makes an attempt to explore the scope of sustainable development through a model for each district separately.

II

Emphasis on Agriculture

Agriculture is a traditional method by which a household may have got his or her livelihood causing minimum damage, if any to the environment. Only two natural resources i.e. land and water are extensively used in agriculture. Through the use of land, a farmer can harm a little to the nature so that s/he uses pesticides and insecticide in a minimum way. On the other hand there is a little scope to cause the environment unhealthy through the use of surface water. According to the consultative group on International Agriculture Research (CGIAR), "Sustainable agriculture is the successful management of resources to satisfy the changing human needs, while maintaining or enhancing the quality of environment and conserving natural resources". The ultimate goal or the ends of sustainable agriculture is to develop farming systems that are productive and profitable, conserve the natural resource base, protect the environment and enhance health and safety and do so over the long term. The means of achieving this is low input methods and skilled management, which seek to optimise the management and the use of internal production inputs (i.e. on farm resources) in ways that provide acceptable levels of sustainable crop yields and livestock production and result in economically profitable returns. This approach emphasises such cultural and management practices as crop rotations, recycling of animal manure and conservation tillage to control soil erosion and nutrient losses and to maintain or enhance soil productivity. Low input farming systems seek to minimise the use of external production inputs such as purchased fertilizer and pesticides, where ever and whenever feasible and practicable; to lower production costs to avoid pollution of surface and group water, to reduce pesticide residues in food, to reduce a farmer's overall risk and to increase both short and long term farm profitability. Hence agriculture may be the best alternative source of income of the people to make them sure to sustain happily.

Before formulating the *'sustainable model'* on agriculture we have to consider a situation in which a cultivator may be induced to cultivate her/his land. Generally it is seen that a small farmer does not have sufficient capital in the cropping season or if s/he has, s/he is not facilitated with minor irrigation facilities to culture her. In such cases the irrigation facilities should be provided or the under utilised irrigation may be strengthened through effective way. In such a situation when a cultivator does not have capital, s/he must be provided with capital through any govt. sponsored development programme.

All the data used here to formulate the model are depicted in table 8.1 to table 8.5. Here the average cost of production and net income per decimal of land has been used. The source of all data is '*Study on Farm Management and Cost of Production of Crops in West Bengal, Vol. XXXVIII (1995-96),* Published by Evaluation Wing, Directorate of Agriculture, Govt. of West Bengal'

Table: 8.1 Average Cost of Production and Net Income per Decimal of Land from the Production of Boro (x_1) (HYV) in the District of Bankura and South 24 Pargans

Name of the item		*Average Cost or Average Income of the Production in each district*	
		Bankura	*24 Parganas (South)*
Yield (quintal)	Main Product	0.24	0.20
	By Product	0.12	0.22
Value (Rs.)	Main Product	95.10	101.99
	By Product	5.31	5.49
Total Value (Rs.)		**100.41**	**107.48**
Human Labour (Rs.)	Family (Imputed)	8.98	18.42
	Hired	15.26	11.51
Bullock Labour (Rs.)	Owned	1.96	0.06
	Hired	0.36	0.35
Machine	Owned	0.00	0.00
Day (Rs.)	Hired	2.33	3.61
Seeds		1.59	3.05
Manures		5.43	1.25
Fertilisers		11.96	7.00
Plant Protection Chemicals		2.67	2.71
Depreciation		1.34	2.13
Irrigation Charges		10.93	8.36
Market Charges		0.00	0.00
Misc. Charges		0.23	0.28
Imputed rent of own land		23.78	25.50
Total Cost per decimal		86.78	84.23
Net Income per decimal		**13.63**	**23.25**

Source :Study on Farm Management & Cost of Production of Crops in West Bengal, Vol. XXXVIII (1995-96), Published by Evaluation Wing, Directorate of Agriculture, Govt. of West Bengal

Table: 8.2 Average Cost of Production and Net Income per Decimal of Land from the Production of Jute (x_2) in the District of Jalpaiguri and South 24-pargans

Name of the item		*Average Cost or Average Income of the Production in each district*	
		Jalpaiguri	*24Parganas (South)*
Yield (quintal)	Main Product	06.86	0.09
	By Product	09.96	0.20
Value (Rs.)	Main Product	72.14	89.04
	By Product	2.99	4.37
Total Value (Rs.)		**75.13**	**94.41**
Human Labour (Rs.)	Family (Imputed)	22.50	25.24
	Hired	4.97	18.39
Bullock Labour (Rs.)	Owned	5.08	-
	Hired	-	0.61
Machine Day (Rs.)	Owned	-	-
	Hired	-	3.08
Seeds		2.06	1.45
Manures		6.05	2.55
Fertilisers		0.81	0.99
Plant Protection Chemicals		-	-
Depreciation		0.58	3.12
Irrigation Charges		-	-
Market Charges		0.69	-
Misc. Charges		-	0.51
Imputed rent of own land		18.04	22.26
Total Cost per decimal		60.78	78.70
Net Income per decimal		**14.35**	**15.71**

Source :Study on Farm Management & Cost of Production of Crops in West Bengal, Vol. XXXVIII (1995-96), Published by Evaluation Wing, Directorate of Agriculture, Govt. of West Bengal

Table: 8.3 Average Cost of Production and Net Income per Decimal of Land from the Production of Potato (x_3) in the District of Bankura, and South 24-pargans

Name of the item		*Average Cost or Average Income of the Production in each district*	
		Bankura	*24 Parganas (South)*
Yield (quintal)	Main Product	0.77	0.94
	By Product	-	0.0
Value (Rs.)	Main Product	163.24	233.82
	By Product	-	0.0
Total Value (Rs.)		**163.24**	**233.82**
Human Labour (Rs.)	Family (Imputed)	13.53	24.89
	Hired	15.53	12.05
Bullock Labour (Rs.)	Owned	0.03	-
	Hired	0.07	0.77
Machine Day (Rs.)	Owned	-	-
	Hired	4.53	5.33
Seeds		36.19	46.52
Manures		04.71	2.80
Fertilisers		32.91	20.07
Plant Protection Chmemicals		2.28	2.42
Depreciation		1.67	3.63
Irrigation Charges		5.19	9.12
Market Charges		-	-
Misc. Charges		0.27	0.59
Imputed rent of own land		38.31	58.46
Total Cost per decimal		155.22	186.65
Net Income per decimal		**9.98**	**47.17**

Source :Study on Farm Management & Cost of Production of Crops in West Bengal, Vol. XXXVIII (1995-96), Published by Evaluation Wing, Directorate of Agriculture, Govt. of West Bengal

Table: 8.4 Average Cost of Production and Net Income per Decimal of Land from the Production of Wheat (x_4) in the District of Jalpaiguri

Name of the item		*Average Cost or Average Income of the Production in each district*
		Jalpaiguri
Yield (quintal)	Main Product	0.07
	By Product	0.00
Value (Rs.)	Main Product	42.86
	By Product	0.00
Total value		**42.86**
Human Labour (Rs.)	Family (Imputed)	10.45
	Hired	2.29
Bullock Labour (Rs.)	Owned	5.53
	Hired	0.00
Machine Day (Rs.)	Owned	0.00
	Hired	0.00
Seeds		3.73
Manures		5.66
Fertilisers		1.92
Plant Protection Chemicals		0.00
Depreciation		0.49
Irrigation Charges		0.21
Market Charges		0.17
Misc. Charges		0.00
Imputed rent of own land		10.72
Total Cost per decimal		42.15
Net Income per decimal		**0.71**

Source : Study on Farm Management & Cost of Production of Crops in West Bengal, Vol. XXXVIII (1995-96), Published by Evaluation Wing, Directorate of Agriculture, Govt. of West Bengal

Table: 8.5 Average Cost of Production and Net Income per Decimal of Land from the Production of Mustard (x_5) in the District of Jalpaiguri

Name of the item		*Average Cost or Average Income of the Production in each district*
		Jalpaiguri
Yield (quintal)	Main Product	3.05
	By Product	0.00
Value (Rs.)	Main Product	30.39
	By Product	0.00
Total Value		**30.39**
Human Labour (Rs.)	Family (Imputed)	8.31
	Hired	0.00
Bullock Labour (Rs.)	Owned	5.53
	Hired	0.00
Machine Day (Rs.)	Owned	0.00
	Hired	0.00
Seeds		0.48
Manures		6.36
Fertilisers		0.83
Plant Protection Chemicals		0.00
Depreciation		0.56
Irrigation Charges		0.00
Market Charges		0.29
Misc. Charges		0.00
Imputed rent of own land		7.60
Total Cost per decimal		29.96
Net Income per decimal		0.40

Source : Study on Farm Management & Cost of Production of Crops in West Bengal, Vol. XXXVIII (1995-96), Published by Evaluation Wing, Directorate of Agriculture, Govt. of West Bengal

III
Linear Programming Model on Agriculture for the District of Bankura

In the District of Bankura major crops are Paddy–Boro (x_1), and Potato (x_3). So the proposed model should deal with the above crops. Before going to propose the agriculture model it is kept in mind that the farmer possesses the land maximum of one acre and s/he is supposed to have Rs. 5,000.00 as capital or s/he is supplied that amount of capital through any govt. sponsored development programme. The use of family labour in one decimal of land for the production of Boro–Paddy is 0.4 mandays, 0.4 mandays for Potato. S/he is also restricted to use his family labour maximum of 50 mandays in a season. Here it is Rabi season. If irrigation facilities are properly utilised through minor irrigation programmes, then the model suits for the farmers in the district of Bankura.

The model is as follows :

Objective Function :

$\text{Max}(Z) = 13.63x_1 + 9.98x_3$

Subject to the budget constraint :

$x_1 + x_3 < 100$ (land)

$86.78x_1 + 155.22x_3 < 5000$ (capital)

$0.3x_1 + 0.4x_3 < 50$ (family labour)

and $x_{1,} x_3 > 0$ (non-negativity restriction)

Introducing slack variables ($s_{1,} s_2$ & s_3) into the given constraints, if we want to get solution by using Simplex Method it is noticed that Max (Z) $= 784.20$ (in Rs.), $x_1 = 57.62$ (in decimal, $x_3 = 0$. This implies that a farmer in the district of Bankura should cultivate only Boro-paddy in maximum 57.62 decimal of land to get maximum benefit Rs. 784.20 out of his possessed land amounting one acre.

IV
Linear Programming Model on Agriculture for the District of Jalpaiguri

In the district of Jalpaiguri major crops are Jute (x_2), Wheat (x_4), Mustard (x_5). So the proposed model should deal with the above crops. Before going to propose the agriculture model it is kept in mind that the farmer possesses the land maximum of one acre and s/he is supposed to have Rs. 5,000.00 as capital or s/he is supplied that amount of capital through any govt. sponsored development programme. The use of family labour in one decimal of land for the production of Jute is 0.6 mandays, 0.4 mandays for Wheat and Mustard each. S/he is also restricted to use his family labour maximum of 50 mandays in a season. Here it is Rabi season. It is noted that in the surveyed areas of the district irrigation facility is fully available from a river called 'Nonai'.

The model is as follows :

Objective Function :

$\text{Max}(Z) = 14.35\,x_2 + 0.71x_4 + 0.4x_5$

Subject to the budget constraint :

$x_2 + x_4 + x_5 < 100$ (land)

$60.78x_2 + 42.15x_4 + 29.96x_5 < 5000$ (capital)

$0.6\,x_2 + 0.4\,x_4 + 0.4\,x_5 < 50$ (family labour)

and $x_2, x_4, x_5 > 0$ (non-negativity restriction)

Introducing slack variables (s_1, s_2 & s_3) into the given constraints, if we want to get solution by using Simplex Method it is noticed that Max (Z) = 1180.43 (in Rs.), $x_2 = 82.26$ (in decimal), $x_4 = 0$, $x_5 = 0$. This implies that a farmer in the district of Jalpaiguri should cultivate Jute in maximum 82.26 decimal of land to get maximum benefit Rs. 1180.43 out of his possessed land amounting one acre.

V

Linear Programming Model on—Agriculture for the District of South 24 Parganas

In the district of South 24 Parganas major crops are Paddy–Boro (x_1), Jute (x_2) and Potato (x_3). So the proposed model should deal with the above crops. Before going to propose the agriculture model it is kept in mind that the farmer possesses the land maximum of one acre and s/he is supposed to have Rs. 5,000.00 as capital or s/he is supplied that amount of capital through any govt. sponsored development programme. The use of family labour in one decimal of land for the production of Boro–Paddy is 0.4 mandays, 0.6 mandays for Jute and Potato each. S/he is also restricted to use his family labour maximum of 50 mandays in a season. Here it is Rabi season. If irrigation facilities are provided through minor irrigation programmes, then the model suits for the farmers in the district of South 24 Parganas.

The model is as follows :

Objective Function :

$Max (Z) = 23.25x_1 + 15.71x_2 + 47.17x_3$

Subject to the budget constraint :

$x_1 + x_2 + x_3 < 100$ (land)

$84.23x_1 + 78.70x_2 + 186.65x_3 < 5000$ (capital)

$0.4x_1 + 0.6x_2 + 0.6x_3 < 50$ (family labour)

and $x_1, x_2, x_3 > 0$ (non-negativity restriction)

Introducing slack variables (s_1, s_2 & s_3) into the given constraints, if we want to get solution by using Simplex Method it is noticed that Max (Z) = 1381.05 (in Rs.), $x_1 = 59.40$ (in decimal), $x_2 = 0$, $x_3 = 0$. This implies that a farmer in the district of South 24 Parganas should cultivate only Boro-paddy in maximum 59.40 decimal of land to get maximum benefit Rs. 1381.05 out of his possessed land amounting one acre.

9

Brief Recommendation and Policy Prescriptions

In view of the above discussions made in earlier chapters the present chapter deals with a set of policy recommendations.

I

Strengthening of Alternative Economy

Forest represents the largest single land-use in the country next to agriculture. It is intimately connected with the national economy and consequently the welfare of the people. Therefore, its development through conservation is linked with the development of the related sectors, such as agriculture, animal resource, rural development poverty alleviation etc. Main objective of biodiversity is not only to rejuvenate the depicted biodiversity, but also to bring about economic development of the forest fringed or ecosystem people, so that a subsidiary income is generated on sustained basis and people can look for alternative employment keeping the forest as the reserve and to draw only such benefit from it which would accrue on sustained basis.

(a) Strengthening of vegetation by using the land use map on water resource, available vegetation in around village, number of oil-seed bearing trees, etc. should be made more meaning;

(b) Mapping of wetland resources by using the remote sensing method may by started for the development of fishery sector. Programmes / Schemes on fishery, Prawn farming, fish business, power boat or boat for fishing, net making etc. may be given to the potential forest fringe people on co-operative basis. In this regard, Gosaba block of the South 24 Parganas district is having such type of potentialities;

(c) The horticulture sector has established its credibility in improving productivity of land, generating employments, improving economic conditions of the farmers and entrepreneurs, enhancing export potential and above all providing nutritional security;

(i) Cultivation of betel nut, banana, guava, papaya and pineapple, orange may extensively be introduced in the district of Jalpaiguri;

(ii) Vegetables like tomato, cabbage, pea, cucumber, cauliflower should be cultivated in all the district;

(iii) Floriculture in Jalpaiguri may have a good return particularly from the culture of gladiolus. The commercial cultivation of orchard may be introduced as early as possible;

(iv) The commercial cultivation of rose, Marigold and Jasmine should be introduced in the study area of Bankura districts;

(v) The Marigold and Nightqueen are appropriate flowers to be cultivated in the studied block of Gosaba of South 24 Parganas distict;

(vi) The commercial cultivation of groundnut and cashew nut may be introduced in Bankura district.

(d) Animal resources / Livestock development should gain a momentoum in all the studied districts under the following heads:

(i) Poultry farming (Layer and Broiler);

(ii) House Dairy;

(iii) Milch cow rearing;

(iv) Duckery;

(v) Goatery;

(vi) Piggery;

Duckery may be potential sources of alternative employment in the Gosaba block of South 24 Parganas;

(e) Sericulture, commonly known as silkworm rearing is an established industry of Bankura district, may be introduced for experimental basis in Dhupguir block of Jalpaiguri Tassar cultivation has high employment potentiality for the rural women and can be grown on poor unproductive soils. It may also be introduced in Jalpaiguri;

(f) Apiculture can be a viable complementary industry in forest fringe locations other than Gosaba block of South 24 Parganas district, as it does not require much labour, time and money. Female members of the family can be gainfully employed in their spare time in apiculture;

(g) Lac culture is an established practice in Bankura (South) including Ranibandh Block. The forest fringe people of Dhupguri block of Jalpaiguri district may be encouraged to undertake lac culture on non-forestlands that exist in their areas;

(h) During survey in the three studied blocks of the three districts of West Bengal it has been observed that those forest areas are richly endowed with wealth of medicinal plants. However, mass collection of medicinal plants from nature has led to critical depreciation level without any plan to regeneration/ plantation. It has been seen that the practice of selling such natural produces by the forest fringe people at an unbelievable no price range. In this regard, the following measures can be taken:

    (i) Prioritise the traditional areas of growth of such medicinal plants in the dry land and upland areas; and

    (ii) Initiate a massive, plant-farming operation for cultivating selected species to meet market demand;

(i) So far stress of Joint Forest Management has been on production and sale of wood and pole based products, opening up a Pandora-box of problems for the marketing an infrastructure. Besides, it requires extensive clear felling of the area. Moreover the income is not recurring, but occurs in a rotational cycle of 10 years. To obviate from need of clear felling of the area, the importance of raising plantations that provide fruits and other products of commercial value on a sustainable basis, has been realised. Species like *Amloki,*

Haritoki, Bahera may be introduced in the studied blocks of Bankura and Jalpaiguri districts respectively;

(j) To supplement the income of the forest fringe people, various forest-based cottage industries have flourished in Bankura. Sal leaf plate making by using machines may be initiated in Jalpaiguri immediately.

   (i) Bead making from the hard fruit coat of Bel (*Aegle mermelos*) and dried stem of Kurchi (*Holare hena antidyseticica*) is another important income generating activity in Bankura and it may also be started in Jalpaiguri;

   (ii) In dry areas Sabai (*Eulalopsis binata*) is collected and used as fodder and for rope making. The sabai grass based handicrafts have attracted the attention of not only the urban people but the foreigners also for its eco-friendly nature. This sabai grass culivation may be experimentally started in the dry and wasteland in Jalpaiguri district.

   (iii) LAMPS should show its interest in the socio-economic development of the forest fringe people from whom it collect *Sal* seed, *Kend* leaves used for '*Bidi*' making, etc and disburse loan on agricultural development.

II
Sustainable Resource Management

Since agricultural development cannot subsist on a deteriorating natural base, it is imperative to develop strategies for conservation and improvement of resources. We have to emphasis on long term truly productive agricultural sustainability by way of sustenance of natural resources, economic viability and social acceptability of production systems and protection of environment. The aim of eco-farming must be to match the crop, soil and climate of a region maintaining the ecology in farming and gaining from the economy and efficiency of inputs. To safeguard the environment from degradation and to maintain the purity of air, water and food, we have to opt for less and less use of chemicals and shift from chemical to ecological agriculture or nature farming, build up strong organic base to fertilise our fields.

III
Environment Protection and Bio-diversity Conservation

Modern civilization, armed with rapidly advancing technology and fast growing economic system is under increasing threat for its own activities causing pollution of air, water and soil. The fast eroding life support system of our biosphere not only endangers the future of human race as such but also is a major threat to life itself. Most people under stand environment to be limited to only one aspects: Pollution. Pollution is only one facet of environmental problem. Environment is not an abstract concern nor it is just a matter of aesthetics or personal tastes. Our physical nature, our mental health, culture and institutions, opportunities for fulfilment, our very survival are directly related to, and affected by, the environment in which we live.

Modern technology for increasing agricultural outputs has also had high environmental costs.

i) Falling water tables due to the indiscriminate sinking of tubewells;

ii) Declining soils fertility with excessive fertiliser use;

iii) Water pollution with pesticides, etc.

At the same time there has been strengthening of official involvement in environmental management, with increase scientific, technical, administrative and legislative back up at central and state levels.

For that purpose following steps should be taken:

(i) **River Cleaning Programme**—A number of statutory and institutional steps should have to strengthen effectively to protect the water resources from pollution and to improve its quality.

(ii) **Environment-sound Technologies**—Research on catalytic converters and introduction of battery –operated vehicles in urban areas should be laid great importance.

(iii) **Costal Zone Management**—Integrated Costal and Marine Area Management have to be promoted extensively to ensure the sustainable development of costal areas, rational utilization of marine resources and proper management of marine environment to prevent its degradation from developmental, commercial or other activities

(iv) **Management of Industrial Pollution**—For preventing industrial pollution following steps have to be taken:

- Prevention pollution at source;
- Encourage, develop and apply the best available practicable technical solutions;
- Ensure that the polluter pays for the pollution and control arrangements;
- Focus protection on heavily polluted areas and river stretches; and
- Involve the public in decision – making.

IV
Training, Awareness and Motivation

The principle for the global consensus management, conservation and sustainable development of all type of forest, urging the governments to promote and provide opportunities for the participation of interested parties including local communities, indigenous people, industries, labourers, non-governmental organisation (NGOs), individuals, forest dwellers and women in the development, implementation and planning of National Forest Policies. The preliminary requirements are, however, micro-level planning with people's involvement as well as broad out look on part of policy makers, planners, organisers, supervisors, managers as well as all field level workers to build up good public relations. Other requirements are:

(a) Technical competence of the personnel working with system has to be augmented by imparting training at various levels, i.e., from grass-root level to top level workers;

(b) Building up awareness and proper motivation of departmental personnel and forest fringe dwellers through dialogue, meeting, conversions, seminars, workshops, conferences and publicity in electronic media for wholehearted participation;

(c) Research for optimum utilisation of resources for maximum production and scientific mobilisation of resources, production of value added produces, improved technology to augment production, improvisation of indigenous methodology of production, extension services like training, demonstrations for the guidance of the forest fringe villages; and

(d) Integrated programmes and co-ordination with various government departments and NGOs in the field of vocational guidance, agricultural productivity animal husbandry, education, health services and cultural upliftment, in particular, are of absolute necessity for all round development of the forest fringe area to have contented population around forests and ensure their wholehearted participation.

V
Scope of Linkages with Other Rural Development Programmes

For Bio-diversity conservation and sustainable development of the forest fringe people the following measures can be taken, as it is not the sole responsibility of Forest Department only.

(i) Functional linkages with different department viz., agriculture, forests, fishery, rural development, bank, Panchayati Raj Institutions, Co-operatives, etc. can be established to have broad support mechanism with reference to proper linkages;

(ii) The forest fringe people can be involved more in JRY, SGSY (specially animal husbandry, goatery, duckery, piggery, poultry, etc.) which will primarily give them sustenance during periods of distress to tide over crisis and to prevent illegal, indiscriminate human interference on forests and other areas of biodiversity;

(iii) Institutional credit with special reference to forest – based industry loan can be provided to the fringe dwellers;

(iv) Provision of minor irrigation to the people living in and around forest in view of going for multiple cropping to improve their economic status;

(v) Various technological inputs for forest-based industry can be provided under the existing rural development programmes;

(vi) Provision of integrated farming approach in the fields of sericulture, lac culture, apiary, goatery, poultry, etc. on cooperative basis.

Bibliography

Agarwal, C. and S. Saigal, 1996, *Joint Forest Management In India : A Brief Review;* New Delhi : Society for Promotion of Wastelands Development (SPWD), Draft.

AKRSP, 1995, *Solia Harvesting – Gender Perspective*, Mimeo. Ahmeabad : Aga Khan Rural Support Programme.

Nirmal, Andrews, 1998, "Sustainable Development - India's Experience", A paper presented at the *Regional Consultative Meeting on Sustainable Development* in Asia and the Pacific, Manila, 10-12 November, 1998.

Appasamy, Paul P., 1993, "Role of Non-timber Forest Products in a Subsistence Economy : The case of a Joint Forestry Project in India", *Econ. Bot.*, 47 : 258 – 267.

Banerjee, N.K., 1996, *Draft Note on history and struggles of Nari Bikas Sangh;* New Delhi : Centre for Women's Development Studies.

Bhat, Seema, 1998, "Conservation through Community Enterprise", in A. Kothari, N. Pathak, R.V. Anuradha and B. Taneja, (Eds.), *Communities and Conservation – Natural Resource Management in South and Central Asia;* New Delhi : Sage Publications, pp. 270 – 286.

Borini-Feyerabend, G., 1996, *Collaborative Management of Protected Areas Tailoring the Approach to the Context, Issues in Social Policy;* Gland (Switzerland) : IUCN.

Brown, M. and B. Wyckoff- Baird, 1992, *Designing Integrated Conservation and Development Projects;* Washington, D.C. : Biodiveristy Support Program.

Cairns, J. Jr., and Pratt, J.R., 1995, "The relationship between ecosystem health and delivery of ecosystem services", in D.J. Rapport, C.L. Gaudet and P. Calow, (Eds.), *Evaluating and Monitoring the Health of large-scale Ecosystems;* Springerverlag, Berlin, Heidelberg : NATO ASI Series, Vol. 128.

Campbell, J., and R.N. Chattopadhyay and C. Das, 1995, "Income Generation through Joint Forest Management in India with a case study of the Participatory Forest Management Project in Nayagram, West Bengal", Paper presented at the Regional Seminar on *Income through Community Forestry*, 18–20 October, 1995, Bangkok, Thailand.

Chandrakanth, M.G. and Romm, J., 1991, "Sacred Forests, Secular Forest Policies and People's Actions", *Journal of Natural Resources,* 31 : 741 – 756.

Chandrasekhara. U.M. and Sankar, S., 1998, "Tribals and Conservation : Chinnar Sanctuary, India", in A. Kothari, N. Pathak, R.V. Anuradha and B. Taneja, (Eds.), *Communities and Conservation – Natural Resource Management in South and Central Asia;* New Delhi : Sage Publications, pp. 467 – 490.

Chatterjee, T.K., 1995, "Participatory Forest Management : The Route to Anti – Poverty and Eco-Conservation Schemes", in *Experiences from Participatory Forest management* ; New Delhi : Iner-India Publications, pp. 165-170.

Chopra, Kanchan, 1993, "The value of Non-timber Forest Products : An estimation for Tropical deciduous forests in India", *Econ. Bot.*, 47 : 251 – 257.

Choudhury, D., 1998, "Conservation by local Communities in North-East India", in A. Kothari, N. Pathak, R.V. Anuradha and B. Taneja, (Eds.), *Communities and Conservation – Natural Resource Management in South and Central Asia;* New Delhi : Sage Publications, pp. 435 – 448.

Colchester, M.., 1994, *Salvaging Nature, Indigenous Peoples, Protected Areas Biodiversity Conservation;* Geneva : UNRISD Discussion Paper No. 55.

Dalton, E.T., 1872, *Descriptive Ethnology of Bengal* ; Calcutta.

Das, A.K and M.K. Raha, 1967, *The Rabhas of West Bengal* (Special Series No. 9); Calcutta : Cultural Research Institute.

Das, Priya and Christopher, K., 1998, "Self – initiated Conservation in India's Protected Areas : The Case of Kailadevei and Dalma Sanctuaries", in A. Kothari, N. Pathak, R.V. Anuradha and B. Taneja, (Eds.), *Communities and Conservation – Natural Resource Management in South and Central Asia;* New Delhi : Sage Publications, pp. 369 – 390.

Data, S.P., 1969, "Rabha Speech : A Preliminary Study" in *District Handbook of West Bengal, Jalpaiguri, 1961 Census*, by B. Roy, Appendix – V.

DeCosse, Phillip J. and Jayawikrama, Sherine S., 1998, "Issues and Opportunities in Co-management : Lesson from Sri Lanka", in A. Kothari, N. Pathak, R.V. Anuradha and B. Taneja, (Eds.), *Communities and Conservation – Natural*

Resource Management in South and Central Asia; New Delhi : Sage Publications, pp. 191 – 218.

Dobriyal, R M, Singh, G.S., Rao, K.S., and Saxena, K.G., "Medicinal Plants Resources in Chhakinal Watershed", *Journal of Herbs, Spices and Medicinal Plants*, 5 : 15 – 27.

Ember, Carol R and Melvin Ember, 1990, *Anthropology* ; New Delhi : Prentice Hall of India Private Limited.

Folke, C. and Berkes, F., 1995, "Mechanisms that link property rights to ecological systems", in S. Hanna and M. Munasinghe, (Eds.), *Property Rights and the Environment : Social and Ecological Issues;* The Beijer International Institute of Ecological Economics & The World Bank, pp. 121 – 137.

Frazer, J.G., 1980, *The golden Bough;* London : MacMillan.

Gadgil, M, 1998, "Grassroots Conservation Practices : Revitalizing the Tradition", in A. Kothari, N. Pathak, R.V. Anuradha and B. Taneja, (Eds.), *Communities and Conservation – Natural Resource Management in South and Central Asia;* New Delhi : Sage Publications, pp. 219 – 238.

Gadgil, M. and Vartak, V.D., 1976, "The Sacred Groves of Western Ghats", *Econ. Bot.*, 30 : 152 – 160.

Gadgil, M., and Berkes, F., 1991, "Traditional Resource Management Systems", *Resource Management and Optimization*, 18 : 127 – 141.

Gadgil, M., Berkes, F. and Folke, C., 1993, "Indigenous Knowledge for Biodiversity Conservation", *Ambio.*, 22 : 151 – 156.

Grierson, G.A., 1903, *Linguistic Survey of India*, Vol. III, No. 2; Calcutta.

Gunatilake, H.M., Senaratne, D.M.A., and Abeygunawardena, P., 1993, "Role of Non-timber Forest Products in the Economy of peripheral Communities of Kunckles National Wilderness Area of Sri Lanka : A Farming Systems Approach", *Econ. Bot.*, 47 : 275 – 281.

Gupta, A., 1997, Getting Creative Individuals and Communities their Due, Paper presented at the South and Central Asian regional Workshop on *Community-based Conservation*, 9-11February, Indian Institute of Public Administration, New Delhi.

Ingles, A.W., 1994, *The influence of Religious and Rituals on Forest Conservation in Nepal*, Discussion Paper; Kathmandu : Nepal Australia Community Forestry Project.

Johnson, N.C., 1995, *Biodiversity in the Balance : Approach to Setting Geographic Conservation Priorities;* Washington, D.C. : Biodiversity Support Programme.

Joshi, Murli Manohar, 2000, "Sustainable Consumption : A New Paradigm", in *Science Reporter*, July, 2000.

Khiewtem, R.S. and Ramkrishnan, P.S., 1989, "Socio-cultural studies of Sacred Groves at Cherapunji and adjoining areas in the North-eastern India", *Man in India*, 69 : 64 – 71.

Kothari, A, R.V. Anuradha and Neema Pathak, 1998, "Commuity-based Conservation : Issues and Prospects", in A. Kothari, N. Pathak, R.V. Anuradha and B. Taneja, (Eds.), *Communities and Conservation – Natural Resource Management in South and Central Asia;* New Delhi : Sage Publications, pp. 25 – 57.

Kothari, A., P. Pande, S. Singh and V. Dilnavaz, 1989, *Management of National Parks and Sanctuaries in India : A Status Report;* New Delhi : Indian Institute of Public Administration.

Lele, S., Murali, K.S., and Bawa, Kamaljit S., 1998, "Community Enterprise for Conservation in India : Biligiri Rangaswamy Temple Sanctuary", in A. Kothari, N. Pathak, R.V. Anuradha and B. Taneja, (Eds.), *Communities and Conservation – Natural Resource Management in South and Central Asia;* New Delhi : Sage Publications, pp. 449 – 466.

Lynch, O.J. and J.B. Alcorn, 1994, "Tenurial Rights and Community–based Conservation", in D. Western and R.M. Wright, (Eds.), *Natural Connections : Perspectives in Community-based Conservation;* Washington, D.C. : Inland Press.

MacIver, R.M and H. Page Charles, 1974, *Society – An Introductory Analysis* ; New Delhi : Macmillan India Limited.

Malhotra, K.C. and Deb, Debal., 1992, "Forest Regeneration and Plantation in Midnapore District : A Status Report", *Wasteland News*, 7, 32 - 33.

Malhotra, K.C., Deb, D., 1997, "Interface Between Biodiversity and Tribal Cultural Heritage : An Explorative Study", *J. Hum. Ecol.*, 8 (3) : 157 – 163.

Malhotra, K.C., Deb, D., Dutta, M., Vasulu, T.S., Yadav, G. and Adhikari, M., 1991, *Role of Non-timber Forest Products in Village Economy*; Mimeo.; Calcutta : IBRAD.

Malhotra, K.C., Deb, D., Vasulu, T.S., 1992, "Restitution of Biodiversity in South-west Bengal Forest", *J. Ind. Anthrop. Soc.*, 27 : 35 – 47.

Malhotra, K.C., N. Satish Chandra, T.S. Vasulu, L. Majumdar, S. Basu, M. Adhikari and G. Yadav, 1992, *Role of Non-timber Forest Produce in a Village Economy : A Household Survey in Jamboni Range, Midnapore District, West Bengal;* Calcutta : IBRAD Working Paper.

McNeely, J.A., 1991, "Common Property Resource Management or Government Ownership Improving the Conservation of Biological Resources", *International Relations*, pp. 211 – 225.

McNeely, N.A, 1988, *Economics and Biological Diversity : Developing and Using Economic Incentives to Conserve Biological Resources;* Switzerland : IUCN-The Conservation Union.

Murmu, E., 1995, *Report of the Meeting dated 19 .04.95 in Village Taldangal, Bihar* : Pragatisheel Mahila Sabha.

Murty, M.N., 1996, "Contractual Arrangements for Sharing Benefits form Preservation : Joint Forest Management of Wildlife", in A. Kothari, N. Singh and S. Suri, (Eds.), *People and Protected Areas : Towards Participatory Conservation in India;* New Delhi : Sage Publications.

Nair, G.H., Gopikumar, K, Krishnan, P.C. and Kumar, K.K.S., 1997, "Sacred Groves of India – Vanishing Greenary", *Current Science*, 27 : 697 – 698.

Narain, Satya, A.K. Mandal and Viji Srinivasan, 1994, *A Case Study of JFM in Santhal Parganas*, Patna : Adithi.

Nipunage, D.S., Kubhojkar, M.S. and Vartak, V.D., 1998, "Studies on Sacred Groves of Maharastra, Part – I : Observations on Sagdara Grove in Pune District", *Indian Journal of Forest*, 11 : 282 – 286.

Panayotou, T. and Ashton, P., 1992, *Not by Timber Alone : The Case for Multiple Use Management of Tropical Forests;* Covelo, C.A. : Island Press.

Plotkin, M. and Famolare, L., 1992, *Sustainable Harvest and Marketing of Rain Forest Products;* Washington, D.C. : Island Press.

Poffenber, M., Josayma, C., Walpole, P. and Lawrence, K., 1995, *Transition in Forest Management : Shifting Community Forestry from Project to Process;* Berkeley : Asia Forest Network.

Poffenberger, M., and C. Singh, 1996, "Communities and the State : Re-establishing the Balance in Indian Forest Policy", in M. Poffenberger and B. McGean, (Eds.), *Village Voices, Forest Choices;* New Delhi : Oxford University Press.

Posey, D.A., 1990, "Intellectual Property Rights and Just Compensation for Indigenous Knowledge", *Anthropology Today*, 6(4) : 13 – 16.

Ramkrishnan, P.S., 1996, "Conserving the Sacred : from species to landscape", *Nature and Resources*, 32 : 11 – 19.

Rathore, B.M.S., 1996, "Joint Management Options for Protected Areas : Challenges and Opportunities", in A. Kothari, N. Singh and S. Suri, (Eds.), *People and Protected Areas : Towards Participatory Conservation in India;* New Delhi : Sage Publications.

Roy Burman, J.J., 1995, "The dynamics of Sacred Groves", *J. Hum. Eco.*, 6 : 245 – 254.

Sarin, M., 1993, *From Conflict to Collaboration : Local Institutions in Joint Forest Management*, JFM Working Paper No. 14, New Delhi : SPWD and The Ford Foundation.

Sarin, M., 1995, "Gender and equity in JFM : Discussion and Emerging Issues", Proceedings of the *Gender & Equity Sub-group Meeting*, 27 – 18 November, 1995, New Delhi : Society for Promotion of Wastelands Development.

Sarin, M., Lipika Ray, Manju S. Raju, Mitali Chatterjee, Narayan Banerjee and Shyamal Hiremath, 1998, "Gender and Equity concerns in Joint Forest Management", in A. Kothari, N. Pathak, R.V. Anuradha and B. Taneja, (Eds.), *Communities and Conservation – Natural Resource Management in South and Central Asia;* New Delhi : Sage Publications, pp. 323 – 348.

Saxena, K.G., Maikhuri, R.K., Nautiyal, Sunil, Rao, K.S., Semwal, R.L., 1998, "Traditional Community Conservation in the Indian Himalayas : Nanda Devi Biosphere Reserve", in A. Kothari, N. Pathak, R.V. Anuradha and B. Taneja, (Eds.), *Communities and Conservation – Natural Resource Management in South and Central Asia;* New Delhi : Sage Publications, pp. 403 – 423.

Shafers, R., 1953, "Classification of the Northernmost Naga Languages" in *J. Bihar Research Soc.*, Vol. II, pp.3.

Shrestha, Bharat, 1998, "Involving Local Communities in Conservation : The Case of Nepal", in A. Kothari, N. Pathak, R.V. Anuradha and B. Taneja, (Eds.), *Communities and Conservation – Natural Resource Management in South and Central Asia;* New Delhi : Sage Publications, pp. 130 – 147.

Singh, G.S., 1997, "Sacred Groves in Western Himalaya : An eco–cultural imperative", *Man in India*, 77 : 247 – 257.

Singh, G.S., Saxena, K.G., Rao, K.S. and Ram, S.C., 1996, "Traditional Knowledge and threats of its extinction in Chhakinal watershed in north-western Himalaya", *Man in India*, 76 : 1 – 17.

Tiwari, B.K., Barik, S.K. and Tripathi, R.S., 1998, "Sacred Groves of Meghalaya", in Ramakrishnan, P.S., Saxena, K.G., and Chandrasekhara, U.M., (Eds.), *Conserving the Sacred : For Biodiversity Management;* New Delhi : Oxford & IBH Publishing Co. Pvt. Ltd., pp. 253 – 262.

Wells, M., K. Brandon and L. Hannah, 1992, *People and Parks : Linking Protected Area Management with Local Communities;* Washington, D.C. : The World Bank, World Wildlife Fund, and U.S. Agency for International Development.

Williams, C.B., 1964, *Pattern in the balance of nature and related problem in Quantitative Ecology;* New York : Academic Press.

WWF-India, 1995, *Community Biodiversity Conservation Movement : A Profile;* New Delhi : World Wide fund for Nature – India.

Index

A

"Green" Technologies, 252
"Mantra" Back to Nature, 253
Adjutant Stork, 190
Aforestation, 16, 189
Age Sex Composition Tab., 155
Age Sex Composition, 154
Agricultural
- Environmental and Macroeconomic Policy, 184
- Labour, 78, 79, 82, 105, 109, 110, 113, 132, 136, 138-140, 159, 161-163, 165
- Practices, 184

Agriculture Loan, 179
Ajodhya, 67
Alpine Vegetation, 219
Alternative Economy, 257, 267
Anantamul and Stamul Roots, 255
Ancestor Cult, 66
Ancestor-Spirits, 66
Animal Husbandry, 78, 79, 82, 86, 98, 105, 109, 127, 132, 136, 138, 139, 159, 161-163, 165, 245, 273
Animal Research Development Dept. (ARD), 235, 237
Annapurna Conservation Area of Nepal, 20
Anti-Poverty and Eco-Conservation Schemes, 16
Apiculture, 239-40, 269
Arhar, 236
Arjun and Asan Trees, 238-39
Artificial Insemination (AI), 235
Artificial Irrigation, 66
Asian Province, 190
Assam and Andaman Islands, 65
Assam Burmese Group, 69
Assam or Duars, 66
Assam, 69
Average Cost of Production,
- Bankura, 259-62
- South 24 Pargana, 259-61
- Jalpaiguri Dist., 262-63

Ayurvedic Drugs, 240

B

Bahera Gum, 255
Baluchari Sarees, 238
Bamboo Plantations, 243
Bangladeshi Communities, 22
Banjyoti Chulla, 243
Bank Rate, 187
Bankura, 65, 72, 188-89, 199, 210, 213, 234, 236, 245-46
- and Jalpaiguri Dist, 270

- District Major Crops, 264
- District, 238, 241, 268-69
- Forest Development, 237
- Jalpaiguri and South 24 Pargana, 26

Bankura Dist. Profile
- Administrative Units, 29
- Agricultural Area, Product and Productivity, 32
- Profile, Area Utilization etc., 32
- Profile, Areas and Production of Crops, 31
- Profile, Commercial Banks, 35
- Consumption of Fertilizers, 32
- Cooperative Societies, 35
- Educational Facilities, 34
- Family Welfare, 35
- Fisheries, 33
- Forest Area, 32
- Geographical Location etc., 29
- Land Utilization Stat., 31
- Literacy by Sex, 34
- Medical Facilities, 35
- Profile, Post and Telegraph, 36
- Rainfall/Temperature etc., 29
- Recording of Bargadars, 37
- Rural and Urban Population by Sex, 30
- Profile, Sale of Electricity-, 36
- SC/ST Population, 30
- Transport and Communication, 36
- Warehousing and Cold Storage Facilities, 33
- Workers/Non Workers by Sex, 31

Banned Chemicals/Substances, 225

Ban-O-Bhumi Sanaskar Sthayee Samiti, 244

Bark Deer, 191

Basel Conventions, 224

Beat Officer, 228, 229

Bel Fruits, 255

Bengal, 234

Bengali (Rajbanshi), 69

Bengali Refugees, 71

Betalnut, Banana, 268

Bhadra Month, 68

Bhui-Kumra—Kurchi, 188

Bhumji (Sarda), Non Aryan Tribe of Jharkhand and WB, 67, 68
- of Bankura, 68
- of Purulia, 67, 69
- Religion, 68

Bidi Making, 270

Biligiri Rangaswamy Temple Sanctuary, 22

Bio-Conservation, 21

Bio-Diversity Fisheries, 22

Bio-Diversity Conservation, 23, 26, 27, 187, 219, 227, 232, 246-48, 257, 271

Bio-diversity, 11, 13, 14, 17, 19
- Biological, 17
- Conservation, 17, 18, 20
- National, 20, 22
- Resources-based, 18

Bio-Geographic Regions, 220

Bio-Medical Wastes Rules, 224

Biomes, 219-20
- Tropical Dry/Desiduous Forests, 219
- Tropical Humid Forests, 219

- Warm Deserts, 219

Bio-Resource Board, 254
Birbhum, 234
Bishnupur, 238
Block Profile, 58
- Dhagpuri, 61
- Gosaba, 63
- Ranibandha, 58

Blocks, 243
- Khatra, 241
- Raipur (I-II), 241
- Ranibandh, 241
- Simlapal, 241
- Taldangra, 243

Bodo Group, 69
Boro Paddy, 264-66
Brahmini Kite, 190
British Raj, 232
Brundt Commission, 183
Brundt Land Report, 180-81
Bulbul, 190
Button Mushroom, 255

C

Cashew Plantations, 242
Cattle Improvement Scheme, 234
Central Pollution Control Board (CPCB), 226
Characteristic Species, 189
Cheetal, 190
Chemical Accident Rules, 1996, 224
Chhatisgarh, 65
Chhotanagpur Plateau, 67
Chhotanagpur, 65, 68, 234
Chinnar Wildlife Sanctuary (South India), 22
Chipco Movement, 23
Christianity, 71
Civilization, 13, 232
- Modern, 271

Coach Behar, 69
Coastal Ecosystem, 190-91
- Marine Environment, 191
- Regulation Zones (CRZs), 223
- Wetland, 219
- Zone Management, 223, 271

Colonial Era, 232
Commission on Sustainability Development, 226
Common Effluent Treatment Plants (CEPT), 226
Community Bio-Diversity Conservation Management (CBCM), 22
Community Conservation Programme, 23
Community Development, 20
Community Forestry (Nepal), 21
Community-based
- Conservation (CBC), 24
- Conservation in Bio-Diversity, 22
- Tenure (System), 21, 22
- Tenurial Rights, 21

Conservation
- Community-based, 17
- Forest, 14
- Practices, 19
- Programme, 22
- Resources, 18
- Strategy, 182
- Traditional, 18, 19

Consumption Rates, 252

Cooperatives Societies, 98
Cottage Industry, 238, 242
Cradle to Grave Policy, 224
Credit Institutions, 125, 127, 152
Crop Rotations, 185
Crow Pheasant, 190
Culture,
- Maternal, 66
- Traditional, 71

Customary Law, 66

D

Deccan Peninsula, 220
Decision Making Processes, 225
Decision Making, 23, 70
DEL (Disease Free Layers), 239
Developing Countries, 14, 25, 181, 184, 249
Development Loans, 98
Dhaiphul and Tshiphul Flowers, 255
Dhalbhum Bhumji, 68
Dhupguri, 120-24, 126
Dhupguri Block (Jalpaiguri), 100, 101, 103, 104, 106, 107, 114, 115, 119, 205, 246, 269
- Age Sex Composition Table, 101
- Age Sex Composition, 100

Diseases, 239
- Flacherie, 239
- Grassaria, 239
- Muscardine, 239
- Pebrine, 239

Distribution Income Pattern, 140 Table, 141
Distribution of Expenditure on Agriculture, 174
Distribution of Household Expenditure, 171
District Administration, 246
Dronga, 190
Dumka (Bihar), 24

D

Earth Summit, 227
Eastern Himalayas, 219
Eco Farming, 270
Eco-Consciousness, 253
Eco-Development Committee, 228-31
- Cancellation of Membership, 231
- Nature, 228
- Responsibility, 229, 230
- Working Procedure, 229
- Works, 230

Eco-Development Program, 227, 232
Ecological
- Agriculture, 270
- Balance, 186, 191, 232, 234
- Change, 182
- Development Committee, 244, 246-47
- Sustainability, 181
- Systems, 183
- Welfare, 182

Economic Development, 19
Economic Growth, 180-82, 222, 253
Economy, 16
- Community, 15

- Monetary, 19
- National, 267
- Sustainable Development of the-, 16
- Sustainable, 19

Eco-Preneur, 253

Eco-System People, 11, 14, 25, 27, 189, 190

Ecosystem, 14, 17, 19, 20, 182, 186, 191, 220, 249, 252

Education Table, 75, 103

- Education, 102

Education, 74, 75, 102, 103, 114, 117, 129, 130, 144, 154, 156, 168, 184, 273

- Formal, 102, 119, 154

Elephants, 189

Endemic Centres, 219

Enterprise-based Conservation, 22

Environmental (Protection) Act, 1986, 223

Environmental

- Audit System, 221
- Improvement Strategies, 16
- Management, 271
- Protection Programmes, 16
- Protection, 16
- Rules, 1986, 224
- Sound Technologies, 271

Existing Fauna

- Moraghat Range, 205
- Sajnekhali Wildlife Sanctuary Range, 209-210
- Table Ranibandh Block, 199

Existing Flora

- Utilization (Sajnekhali Wildlife Sanctuary Range), 206-208
- Utilization Tab. (Morighat Range), 200-205
- Utilization Tab. (Ranibandh Block), 192-199

Expenditure Pattern Tab., 169

Expenditure Pattern, 168

Extraction Technologies, 181

F

Factionalism, 184

Farming Systems, 185, 258

Fauna and Flora, 188-91

Fertility Rates, 181

Fiscal Balance Sheet, 187

Fishery, 113, 140, 165, 273

Fishing and Aquaculture, 163

Flora and Fauna, 182

Floriculture, 268

Food Security, 25

Forest (Conservation) Act, 1980, 226

Forest

- Administration, 232
- Based Cottage Industries, 270
- Based Crops, 235
- Based Industries, 233, 273
- Conservation, 19, 227, 233
- Cover (Nine Dists. of WB), 211-12
- Management Programme, 27
- Management, 14, 16, 243, 256
- Principles, 226
- Produces, 163
- Products, 15
- Protection Committee (FPC) Members, 189

- Protection Committee, (FPC), 21
- Rabhas, 69-71
- Resources Management, 232

Forest Types Table,
- Bankura Dist, 214
- Communities, 15
- Denudation, 15
- Jalpaiguri, 215-16
- South 24 Pargana, 217
- Types, 213

Forests, 189
- Badrinath, 189
- Chandapathar, 189
- Jhilimili, 189
- Joypur, 189
- Ranibandh, 189
- Susunia, 189

Fossil Fuels, 181
FPC (Forest Protection Committee), 24, 235, 237, 243-44
- Members, 236, 238-40, 243-45, 255
- Membership, 24

Fuelwood Saving Technologies, 20

G

Ganga Basin, 221
Gangetic
- Basin, 191
- Dolphin, 190
- Plain, 220

Garo (Jalpaiguri), 69
Garos, 69
GDP, 187
Global GDP, 250
Global Technology Transfer, 252
Globalization Information and Entertainment Network, 249
Globalization, 249
GNP, 253
Gosaba, 137, 139, 141-42, 145-46, 149
Gosaba Block, 206-209, 267-69
Gosaba Block (South 24 Pargana), 127-28, 130-31, 133-34
Age Sex Composition, 127-28
Gram Panchayat, 228
Gramin Banks, 98
Green Turtle, 190
Groundnut and Cashew, 268
Guava, Pappaya, Pineapple, 268
Gujarat, 23

H

Halstern Breed, 235
Handicrafts, 16
Harda Forest of Central India, 21
Hare, 189-90
Hawk's Turtle, 190
Hazardous Wastes, 223
Hazardous Wastes (Management and Handling) Rules, 223-24
Hazaribagh, 67
Health Services, 20
Himalayas, 220
Hindu Customs, 67
Hindu Immigrants, 67
Hinduism, 71
Hinduism and Animism, 71
Hindus, 67
Ho, 68
Ho and Santal, 66

Household Expenditure
- Distribution Pattern, 145
- on Agriculture, 93-95
- Pattern on Agriculture, 170, 173
- Pattern, 89, 91, 92, 114, 118
- Expenditure Tab., 140, 142

Husuks, 70
Hyena, Fox, 189-90

I

Illegal Tree Felling, 218
Imported Technology, 222
Income Distribution Pattern, 165
- Table, 167

Income Pattern, 87, 88, 114
Income Pattern Distribution, 88
- Table, 115

Income Sources, 165
- Table, 166

India's
- Bio-Diversity, 219
- Forests, 227
- National Forest Policy, 227
- Policy for Forestry, 226
- Reptiles, 220

Indian Centre for Promotion of Cleaner Technology (ICPC), 222
Indian Deserts, 220
Indian Institute of Technology, Kharagpur, 23
Indian Society, 232
Indian Technology, 254
Indo-Malayan, 219
Indpur and Khatra Region, 243
Industrial
- Nations, 249
- Pollutants, 221, 225
- Pollution Management, 225
- Pollution, 221
- Wood Products, 14

Industries (try), 221-22, 233, 239, 242, 252-53, 255, 269, 272
Industry, 16
- Sal Leaf Based, 241

Inflation Rate, 187
Information Technology, 249
Infrastructure Facilities—West Bengal, 53-56
Infrastructure of Technology, 222
Insecticides Act, 1968, 225
Integral Farming, 273
Integral Panel on Forests, 226
Integrated Coastal and Marine Area Management (IAMAM), 223
Integrated Conservation Development Project (ICDP), 20
International Agriculture Research (CGIAR), 185, 258
International Community, 181, 248
Intra-Community Disputes, 21
Irrigation Facilities, 173, 258, 266

J

Jackal, 189-90
Jalpaiguri Dist. Major Crops, 264
Jalpaiguri, 65, 69, 71, 72, 189-90, 205, 210, 213, 217, 234, 245, 265, 269-70, 268
Jalpaiguri Dist. Profile,
- Administrative Units, 37

- Agricultural Area, Production etc., 39
- Area Irrigation etc., 41
- Commercial Banks, 43
- Consumption of Fertilizers, 39
- Cooperatives Societies, 44
- Distribution—Landless and Small Cultivators, 44
- Educational Facilities, 42
- Fisheries, 41
- Forest Area, 40
- Fuelwood, 43
- Geographical Locations, Area—Rainfall etc., 37
- Land Utilization Stat., 39
- Literacy by Sex, 42
- Medical Facilities, 42
- Post and Telegraph, 44
- Recording of Bargadars, 45
- Roads, 44
- Rural and Urban Population by Sex, 38
- Sale of Electricity, 43
- SC/ST Population, 38
- Sericulture Industries, 45
- Tea Industry, 45
- Warehousing and Cold Storage Facilities, 41
- Workers/Non Workers by Sex, 39

Javan Rhino, 191
Jawahar Rozgar Yojna (JRY), 273
JFM, 240, 242, 269
Jharkhand, 65
Joint Community Forestry Programme (South India), 22
Joint Forest Management (JFM), 23, 189, 213, 232-33, 235, 242-44, 246, 256
Joshi, M, 254 see Joshi, Murli Manohar also
Joshi, Murli Manohar, Min. HRD, 248-50, 254
JUNGLE MAHAL, 188
Jurassic, 190
Jute, 265

K

Kachari Race, 69
Kailadevi Sanctuary (Raj.), 23
Kali or Mahamaya, 68
Kalmegh, 255
Karang/Parab Mushroom, 255
Karmayogis, 254
Kend Leaves, 270
Keoladeo (Bharatpur) National Park (Raj.), 21
Kheria

- Families, 66
- Religion, 66
- Social Organization, 66

Kheria/Kharias (Tribe), 65

- Dhelki Kheria, 65, 66
- Dudh Kheria, 65, 66
- Pahari/Hill Kheria, 65, 66

Koch Sub Group, 69
Koch-Rabha and Pati Rabha Group, 69
Kolarian Races, 69
Kolerian, 67
Kolkatta, 191

Kurchi Bark, 255
Kurchi, 270
Kurkuri/Kurka Mushroom, 255

L

Lac Culture, 240-41, 269, 273
Lagoons, 190
LAMPS, 255, 270
Langoor, 189, 190
Law and Custom, 66
Law of Consumption, 254
Legislation and Regulations, 180
Leopard, 189-90
Life Cycle Ceremonies, 98, 151-52, 177
Loan, 125-27, 147, 151-52, 179
  Table, 99, 153, 178
  Types-, 153
Local Panchayat, 244
Local Silk Cottage Industry, 238
Local Traders, 98, 125, 147, 151-52
Lohardanga, 67

M

Mahua Trees, 255
Male Illiteracy, 157
Management
- Forest, 244, 247
- of Industrial Pollution, 272
- Plantation, 244

Mangrove Forests, 213
Mangrove Tiger Land, 190
Manufacture, Storage and Import of Hazardous Chemicals Rules, 224
Marab Sen, 71
Marital Status, 76, 102, 129, 157
Marital Status Table, 77, 104, 106, 130, 158,
Marpol, 223
Matrilineal Tribe, 71
Mayurbhanj Hills, 65
Mech Family, 69
Medicinal Plants, 23, 25, 188-90, 269
Merchant Shipping Act, 223
MFM Plantation, 242-43
Midnapore (WB), 23
Midnapore, 65, 69
Midnapore West Forest Division, 24
Migration, 65, 67
Migratory Birds, 189
Mill, JS, 182
Ministry of
- Agriculture, 225
- Environment and Forest (MoEF), 223-25
- Health, 225
- Human Resource Development, 248
- Tribal Affairs, 11

Minor Forest Produces (MFP), 189
Modern Science Management, 18
Mongloid Traits, 69
Monsoon Rains, 66
Moraghat Range, (Jalpaiguri Dist), 188-89
Mother Goddess, 66
Multilateral Environmental Agreements, 252
Multiple Shoot (MS), 24
Munda Group, 65

Munda, 66
Mundari Language, 67
Mundari Speaking Tribe (India), 66
Mundas, 67, 68

N

National
- Bio-diversity Conservation Fund, 20
- Cleaner Production Centre (NCPC), 222
- Economies, 187
- Environmental Tribunal Act, 224
- Forest Policies, 272
- Parks, 227-28
- Productivity Council, 222

Nationalized Banks, 98
Natural Resource Management, 184
Nature of Indebtedness, 173
Nature of Indebtedness Table, 96, 97, 121, 124, 147, 149-50, 175-76
Nepal, 20
NGO, 24, 226, 247, 272, 273
Non Scheduled Tribe Community, 74, 78, 80, 82, 86, 87, 89, 92, 94, 98, 99-101, 102, 104-106, 110-15, 117, 119-22, 125-35, 136-49, 152-57, 178
Non Scheduled Tribe, 74, 257
Non-Agricultural Labour, 16, 63, 78, 79, 82, 83, 86, 105, 109, 113, 159, 161, 165, 132, 136, 138-39, 140
Non-FPC Area, 235
Non-Timber Forest Produces (NFTP), 15, 188-90
North Bengal, 65
North East India, 21
North East Region, 220
Notified Forest Area, 244
NTFP, 23, 233
- Prices, 22

NWFP, 188, 239-40, 255-56

O

Occupational Distribution Table, 133, 160
Occupational Distribution, 105, 132, 159
Occupational Mobility, 105, 132, 159
Occupational Mobility Table, 107-108, 134, 161-62
Oil Seeds, 188
Olive Ridley Turtle, 190
Organic Farming, 185
Orissa, 65

P

Pady Straw Mushroom, 255
Palaearctic, 219
Panchayat, 246-47
Panchayat Samities, 244
Panchayat Samity, 228, 231
Panchayat System, 71
Panchayati Raj Institutions, (PRIs), 273
Pangolin, 189-90
Participating Forest Management (PFM), 16, 23

W

Waste Treatment, 186
Water Conservation, 234
Water System Management, 186
West Bengal, 24, 26, 65, 154, 157, 159-60, 163, 165-68, 170-71, 173, 178-79, 188-89, 192, 199, 200, 206, 210, 215, 232-33, 269
Western Ghats, 219-20
Wetland Management, 21
Wetland Waterways, 22
Widow Marriage, 68
Wild Boar, 189-90
Wild Buffalo, 191
Wildlife (Protection), Act, 1992, 227
Wildlife and Marine Life, 228
Wildlife Management, 189, 227
Wildlife Management Schemes, 25
Wildlife, 182, 187, 221, 245
Wolf, 189-90
Women in Development, 272
Women's Organizations, 24
World Bank, 248
World Commission on Environmental Development, 184
WWF India, 22

Z

Zila Parishad, 228, 232
Zoning Atlas, 226